™

W9-BKB-593

References for the Rest of Us!®

BESTSELLING BOOK SERIES FROM IDG

Are you intimidated and confused by computers? Do you find that traditional manuals are overloaded with technical details you'll never use? Do your friends and family always call you to fix simple problems on their PCs? Then the *...For Dummies*® computer book series from IDG Books Worldwide is for you.

...For Dummies books are written for those frustrated computer users who know they aren't really dumb but find that PC hardware, software, and indeed the unique vocabulary of computing make them feel helpless. *...For Dummies* books use a lighthearted approach, a down-to-earth style, and even cartoons and humorous icons to diffuse computer novices' fears and build their confidence. Lighthearted but not lightweight, these books are a perfect survival guide for anyone forced to use a computer.

> *"I like my copy so much I told friends; now they bought copies."*
>
> — Irene C., Orwell, Ohio

> *"Quick, concise, nontechnical, and humorous."*
>
> — Jay A., Elburn, Illinois

> *"Thanks, I needed this book. Now I can sleep at night."*
>
> — Robin F., British Columbia, Canada

Already, millions of satisfied readers agree. They have made *...For Dummies* books the #1 introductory level computer book series and have written asking for more. So, if you're looking for the most fun and easy way to learn about computers, look to *...For Dummies* books to give you a helping hand.

™

IDG BOOKS

WORLDWIDE

8/98

Networking For Dummies,® 3rd Edition

For those times when you're too lazy to read this book, here is a quick reference of a few essential items.

Cheat Sheet

My Network And Welcome To It

Write down important stuff about your own network in the spaces provided below.

Network server type: (check one)
- ___ NetWare
- ___ Windows NT Server
- ___ Windows 95 or Windows 98

My user id: _____

Name of NetWare Server or Windows NT Domain: _____

Mapped network drives

Drive letter	Description
_____	_____
_____	_____
_____	_____
_____	_____
_____	_____

Network printers

Printer name	Description
_____	_____
_____	_____
_____	_____

Network Administrator

Name: _____

Phone number: _____

E-mail name: _____

Favorite snack food: _____

Ethernet Cable Stuff

Thick Coax (10base5)

- ✔ Segment limited to 500 meters (1,640 feet).
- ✔ Transceivers required to connect to network card via 15-pin AUI port.
- ✔ Terminators required at both ends of segment.

Thin Coax (10base2)

- ✔ Segment limited to 185 meters (600 feet).
- ✔ Uses BNC connectors.
- ✔ T-connectors used to connect cable to computers.
- ✔ Terminators required at both ends of segment.

Twisted Pair (10baseT)

- ✔ Maximum cable length: 100 meters (330 feet).
- ✔ All computers cabled to central wiring hub.
- ✔ Terminators not required.
- ✔ RJ-45 connector wired as follows:

Pin 1	White/green
Pin 2	Green/white
Pin 3	White/orange
Pin 4	Orange/white

- ✔ Up to 3 hubs may be daisy chained together.
- ✔ Some hubs may also be linked using thin or thick coax.

...For Dummies: #1 Computer Book Series for Beginners

Secrets to Network Happiness

- Back up religiously.
- Document your network layout and keep your documentation up to date.
- Keep an adequate supply of spare parts and tools on hand.
- Never turn off or restart the server while users are logged in.
- Don't be afraid, Luke.

Top NetWare Commands

CAPTURE	Sets up network printing.
LOGIN	Logs in to the network.
LOGOUT	Logs out of the network.
MAP	Assigns drive letters to network drives.
PCONSOLE	Controls network printing.
SEND	Sends a message to another user.

Top Windows NET Commands

NET LOGON	Logs in to the network.
NET LOGOFF	Logs out of the network.
NET USE	Enables you to access network disk drives and printers.
NET PRINT	Controls network printing.
NET VIEW	Displays the list of computers that are on the network.

Help, Mr. Wizard!

Before calling the network guru, try this:

- Make sure that everything is plugged in.
- Make sure that the network cable is properly attached. For 10baseT networks, the little light on the back of your computer where the cable plugs in should be glowing.
- If your computer is frozen solid, try restarting it by pressing Ctrl+Alt+Del.
- Press Ctrl+S if error messages fly by so fast you can't read them. Press it again to resume.
- If all else fails, try restarting the entire network.

E-Mail Shorthand

BTW	By The Way
FWIW	For What It's Worth
IMO	In My Opinion
IMHO	In My Humble Opinion
IOW	In Other Words
PMJI	Pardon Me for Jumping In
ROFL	Rolling On the Floor Laughing
ROFL,PP	Rolling On the Floor Laughing, Peeing my Pants
TIA	Thanks In Advance
TTFN	Ta Ta For Now
TTYL	Talk To You Later
<g>	Grin
<bg>	Big Grin
<vbg>	Very Big Grin

NETWORKING FOR DUMMIES®

3RD EDITION

by Doug Lowe

IDG
BOOKS
WORLDWIDE

IDG Books Worldwide, Inc.
An International Data Group Company

Foster City, CA ♦ Chicago, IL ♦ Indianapolis, IN ♦ New York, NY

Networking For Dummies® 3rd Edition

Published by
IDG Books Worldwide, Inc.
An International Data Group Company
919 E. Hillsdale Blvd.
Suite 400
Foster City, CA 94404
www.idgbooks.com (IDG Books Worldwide Web site)
www.dummies.com (Dummies Press Web site)

Library of Congress Catalog Card No.: 98-70108

ISBN: 0-7645-0346-4

Printed in the United States of America

10 9 8 7 6 5 4 3

3O/QT/RR/ZY/IN

Distributed in the United States by IDG Books Worldwide, Inc.

Distributed by Macmillan Canada for Canada; by Transworld Publishers Limited in the United Kingdom; by IDG Norge Books for Norway; by IDG Sweden Books for Sweden; by Woodslane Pty. Ltd. for Australia; by Woodslane (NZ) Ltd. for New Zealand; by Addison Wesley Longman Singapore Pte Ltd. for Singapore, Malaysia, Thailand, Indonesia and Korea; by Norma Comunicaciones S.A. for Colombia; by Intersoft for South Africa; by International Thomson Publishing for Germany, Austria and Switzerland; by Toppan Company Ltd. for Japan; by Distribuidora Cuspide for Argentina; by Livraria Cultura for Brazil; by Ediciencia S.A. for Ecuador; by Ediciones ZETA S.C.R. Ltda. for Peru; by WS Computer Publishing Corporation, Inc., for the Philippines; by Unalis Corporation for Taiwan; by Contemporanea de Ediciones for Venezuela; by Computer Book & Magazine Store for Puerto Rico; by Express Computer Distributors for the Caribbean and West Indies. Authorized Sales Agent: Anthony Rudkin Associates for the Middle East and North Africa.

For general information on IDG Books Worldwide's books in the U.S., please call our Consumer Customer Service department at 800-762-2974. For reseller information, including discounts and premium sales, please call our Reseller Customer Service department at 800-434-3422.

For information on where to purchase IDG Books Worldwide's books outside the U.S., please contact our International Sales department at 650-655-3200 or fax 650-655-3295.

For information on foreign language translations, please contact our Foreign & Subsidiary Rights department at 650-655-3021 or fax 650-655-3281.

For sales inquiries and special prices for bulk quantities, please contact our Sales department at 650-655-3200 or write to the address above.

For information on using IDG Books Worldwide's books in the classroom or for ordering examination copies, please contact our Educational Sales department at 800-434-2086 or fax 317-596-5499.

For press review copies, author interviews, or other publicity information, please contact our Public Relations department at 650-655-3000 or fax 650-655-3299.

For authorization to photocopy items for corporate, personal, or educational use, please contact Copyright Clearance Center, 222 Rosewood Drive, Danvers, MA 01923, or fax 978-750-4470.

About the Author

Doug Lowe has written more than 20 computer books, including *PowerPoint For Windows 95 For Dummies* and *Word for Windows 95 SECRETS*. Doug enjoys presenting boring technostuff in a style that is both entertaining and enlightening. He is a contributing editor for the magazine *DOS Resource Guide*.

ABOUT IDG BOOKS WORLDWIDE

Welcome to the world of IDG Books Worldwide.

IDG Books Worldwide, Inc., is a subsidiary of International Data Group, the world's largest publisher of computer-related information and the leading global provider of information services on information technology. IDG was founded more than 25 years ago and now employs more than 8,500 people worldwide. IDG publishes more than 275 computer publications in over 75 countries (see listing below). More than 90 million people read one or more IDG publications each month.

Launched in 1990, IDG Books Worldwide is today the #1 publisher of best-selling computer books in the United States. We are proud to have received eight awards from the Computer Press Association in recognition of editorial excellence and three from *Computer Currents'* First Annual Readers' Choice Awards. Our best-selling *...For Dummies®* series has more than 50 million copies in print with translations in 38 languages. IDG Books Worldwide, through a joint venture with IDG's Hi-Tech Beijing, became the first U.S. publisher to publish a computer book in the People's Republic of China. In record time, IDG Books Worldwide has become the first choice for millions of readers around the world who want to learn how to better manage their businesses.

Our mission is simple: Every one of our books is designed to bring extra value and skill-building instructions to the reader. Our books are written by experts who understand and care about our readers. The knowledge base of our editorial staff comes from years of experience in publishing, education, and journalism — experience we use to produce books for the '90s. In short, we care about books, so we attract the best people. We devote special attention to details such as audience, interior design, use of icons, and illustrations. And because we use an efficient process of authoring, editing, and desktop publishing our books electronically, we can spend more time ensuring superior content and spend less time on the technicalities of making books.

You can count on our commitment to deliver high-quality books at competitive prices on topics you want to read about. At IDG Books Worldwide, we continue in the IDG tradition of delivering quality for more than 25 years. You'll find no better book on a subject than one from IDG Books Worldwide.

John Kilcullen
CEO
IDG Books Worldwide, Inc.

Steven Berkowitz
President and Publisher
IDG Books Worldwide, Inc.

Eighth Annual Computer Press Awards ≥1992

Ninth Annual Computer Press Awards ≥1993

Tenth Annual Computer Press Awards ≥1994

Eleventh Annual Computer Press Awards ≥1995

IDG Books Worldwide, Inc., is a subsidiary of International Data Group, the world's largest publisher of computer-related information and the leading global provider of information services on information technology. International Data Group publishes over 275 computer publications in over 75 countries. More than 90 million people read one or more International Data Group publications each month. International Data Group's publications include: ARGENTINA: Buyer's Guide, Computerworld Argentina, PC World Argentina; AUSTRALIA: Australian Macworld, Australian PC World, Australian Reseller News, Computerworld, IT Casebook, Network World, Publish, Webmaster; AUSTRIA: Computerwelt Österreich, Networks Austria, PC Tip Austria; BANGLADESH: PC World Bangladesh; BELARUS: PC World Belarus; BELGIUM: Data News; BRAZIL: Annuário de Informática, Computerworld, Connections, Macworld, PC Player, PC World, Publish, Reseller News, Supergamepower; BULGARIA: Computerworld Bulgaria, Network World Bulgaria, PC & MacWorld Bulgaria; CANADA: CIO Canada, Client/Server World, ComputerWorld Canada, InfoWorld Canada, NetworkWorld Canada, WebWorld; CHILE: Computerworld Chile, PC World Chile; COLOMBIA: Computerworld Colombia, PC World Colombia; COSTA RICA: PC World Centro America; THE CZECH AND SLOVAK REPUBLICS: Computerworld Czechoslovakia, Macworld Czech Republic, PC World Czechoslovakia; DENMARK: Communications World Danmark, Computerworld Danmark, Macworld Danmark, PC World Danmark, Techworld Denmark; DOMINICAN REPUBLIC: PC World Republica Dominicana; ECUADOR: PC World Ecuador; EGYPT: Computerworld Middle East, PC World Middle East; EL SALVADOR: PC World Centro America; FINLAND: MikroPC, Tietoverkko, Tietoviikko; FRANCE: Distributique, Hebdo, Info PC, Le Monde Informatique, Macworld, Reseaux & Telecoms, WebMaster France; GERMANY: Computer Partner, Computerwoche, Computerwoche Extra, Computerwoche FOCUS, Global Online, Macwelt, PC Welt; GREECE: Amiga Computing, GamePro Greece, Multimedia World; GUATEMALA: PC World Centro America; HONDURAS: PC World Centro America; HONG KONG: Computerworld Hong Kong, PC World Hong Kong, Publish in Asia; HUNGARY: ABCD CD-ROM, Computerworld Szamitastechnika, Internetto online Magazine, PC World Hungary, PC-X Magazin Hungary; ICELAND: Tolvuheimur PC World Island; INDIA: Information Communications World, Information Systems Computerworld, PC World India, Publish in Asia; INDONESIA: InfoKomputer PC World, Komputek Computerworld, Publish in Asia; IRELAND: ComputerScope, PC Live!; ISRAEL: Macworld Israel, People & Computers/Computerworld; ITALY: Computerworld Italia, Macworld Italia, Networking Italia, PC World Italia; JAPAN: DTP World, Macworld Japan, Nikkei Personal Computing, OS/2 World Japan, SunWorld Japan, Windows NT World, Windows World Japan; KENYA: PC World East African; KOREA: Hi-Tech Information, Macworld Korea, PC World Korea; MACEDONIA: PC World Macedonia; MALAYSIA: Computerworld Malaysia, PC World Malaysia, Publish in Asia; MALTA: PC World Malta; MEXICO: Computerworld Mexico, PC World Mexico; MYANMAR: PC World Myanmar; NETHERLANDS: Computer! Totaal, LAN Internetworking Magazine, LAN World Buyers Guide, Macworld Netherlands, Net, WebWereld; NEW ZEALAND: Absolute Beginners Guide and Plain & Simple Series, Computer Buyer, Computer Industry Directory, Computerworld New Zealand, MTB, Network World, PC World New Zealand; NICARAGUA: PC World Centro America; NORWAY: Computerworld Norge, CW Rapport, Datamagasinet, Financial Rapport, Kursguide Norge, Macworld Norge, Multimediaworld Norge, PC World Ekspress Norge, PC World Nettverk, PC World Norge, PC World ProduktGuide Norge; PAKISTAN: Computerworld Pakistan; PANAMA: PC World Panama; PEOPLE'S REPUBLIC OF CHINA: China Computer Users, China Computerworld, China InfoWorld, China Telecom World Weekly, Computer & Communication, Electronic Design China, Electronics Today, Electronics Weekly, Game Software, PC World China, Popular Computer Week, Software Weekly, Software World, Telecom World; PERU: Computerworld Peru, PC World Profesional Peru, PC World SoHo Peru; PHILIPPINES: Click!, Computerworld Philippines, PC World Philippines, Publish in Asia; POLAND: Computerworld Poland, Computerworld Special Report Poland, Cyber, Macworld Poland, Networld Poland, PC World Komputer; PORTUGAL: Cerebro/PC World, Computerworld/Correio Informático, Dealer World Portugal, Mac*In/PC*In Portugal, Multimedia World; PUERTO RICO: PC World Puerto Rico; ROMANIA: Computerworld Romania, PC World Romania, Telecom Romania; RUSSIA: Computerworld Russia, Mir PK, Publish, Seti; SINGAPORE: Computerworld Singapore, PC World Singapore, Publish in Asia; SLOVENIA: Monitor; SOUTH AFRICA: Computing SA, Network World SA, Software World SA; SPAIN: Communicaciones World España, Computerworld España, Dealer World España, Macworld España, PC World España; SRI LANKA: Infolink PC World; SWEDEN: CAP&Design, Computer Sweden, Corporate Computing Sweden, Internetworld Sweden, it.branschen, Macworld Sweden, MaxiData Sweden, MikroDatorn, Nätverk & Kommunikation, PC World Sweden, PCaktiv, Windows World Sweden; SWITZERLAND: Computerworld Schweiz, Macworld Schweiz, PCtip; TAIWAN: Computerworld Taiwan, Macworld Taiwan, NEW ViSiON/Publish, PC World Taiwan, Windows World Taiwan; THAILAND: Publish in Asia, Thai Computerworld; TURKEY: Computerworld Turkiye, Macworld Turkiye, Network World Turkiye, PC World Turkiye; UKRAINE: Computerworld Kiev, Multimedia World Ukraine, PC World Ukraine; UNITED KINGDOM: Acorn User UK, Amiga Action UK, Amiga Computing UK, Apple Talk UK, Computing, Macworld, Parents and Computers UK, PC Advisor, PC Home, PSX Pro, The WEB; UNITED STATES: Cable in the Classroom, CIO Magazine, Computerworld, DOS World, Federal Computer Week, GamePro Magazine, InfoWorld, I-Way, Macworld, Network World, PC Games, PC World, Publish, Video Event, THE WEB Magazine, and WebMaster; online webzines: JavaWorld, NetscapeWorld, and SunWorld Online; URUGUAY: InfoWorld Uruguay; VENEZUELA: Computerworld Venezuela, PC World Venezuela; and VIETNAM: PC World Vietnam.   5/7/98

Dedication

To Debbie, Rebecca, Sarah, and Bethany.

Author's Acknowledgments

The list of thank-yous for this book is long and goes back several years. I'd like to first thank John Kilcullen, David Solomon, Janna Custer, Erik Dafforn, Greg Robertson, and Ray Marshall for all their help with the first edition. Then came the second edition, for which I would like to thank Tim Gallan, Mary Goodwin, and Joe Salmeri.

For this third edition, I'd like to thank project editor Jennifer Ehrlich who did a great job putting this book together in spite of missed deadlines, copy editor Constance Carlisle who made sure the i's were dotted and the t's were crossed, and technical editor Jamey Marcum who made many pertinent suggestions throughout. And, as always, thanks to all the behind-the-scenes people who chipped in with help I'm not even aware of.

Publisher's Acknowledgments

We're proud of this book; please register your comments through our IDG Books Worldwide Online Registration Form located at http://my2cents.dummies.com.

Some of the people who helped bring this book to market include the following:

Acquisitions, Development, and Editorial

Senior Project Editor: Jennifer Ehrlich

Acquisitions Editor: Michael Kelly

Copy Editor: Constance Carlisle

Technical Editor: Jamey Marcum

Editorial Manager: Mary C. Corder

Editorial Assistant: Michael D. Sullivan

Production

Project Coordinator: Karen York

Layout and Graphics: Lou Boudreau, Maridee V. Ennis, Angela F. Hunckler, Todd Klemme, Jane E. Martin, Heather N. Pearson, Brent Savage, Deirdre Smith

Proofreaders: Christine Berman, Vickie Broyles, Nancy L. Reinhardt, Rebecca Senninger, Carrie Voorhis, Janet M. Withers

Indexer: David Heiret

General and Administrative

IDG Books Worldwide, Inc.: John Kilcullen, CEO; Steven Berkowitz, President and Publisher

IDG Books Technology Publishing: Brenda McLaughlin, Senior Vice President and Group Publisher

Dummies Technology Press and Dummies Editorial: Diane Graves Steele, Vice President and Associate Publisher; Mary Bednarek, Director of Acquisitions and Product Development; Kristin A. Cocks, Editorial Director

Dummies Trade Press: Kathleen A. Welton, Vice President and Publisher; Kevin Thornton, Acquisitions Manager

IDG Books Production for Dummies Press: Michael R. Britton, Vice President of Production and Creative Services; Cindy L. Phipps, Manager of Project Coordination, Production Proofreading, and Indexing; Kathie S. Schutte, Supervisor of Page Layout; Shelley Lea, Supervisor of Graphics and Design; Debbie J. Gates, Production Systems Specialist; Robert Springer, Supervisor of Proofreading; Debbie Stailey, Special Projects Coordinator; Tony Augsburger, Supervisor of Reprints and Bluelines

Dummies Packaging and Book Design: Robin Seaman, Creative Director; Kavish + Kavish, Cover Design

◆

The publisher would like to give special thanks to Patrick J. McGovern, without whom this book would not have been possible.

◆

Contents at a Glance

Cartoons at a Glance

By Rich Tennant

page 71

page 141

page 7

page 195

page 223

page 259

page 297

Fax: 978-546-7747 • E-mail: the5wave@tiac.net

Table of Contents

Introduction

· ·

Welcome to the Third Edition of *Networking For Dummies,* the book that's written especially for people who have this nagging feeling in the back of their minds that they should network their computers but haven't a clue as to how to start or where to begin.

Do you often copy a spreadsheet file to a floppy disk and give it to the fellow in the next office so that he can look at it? Are you frustrated because you can't use the fancy laser printer that's on the financial secretary's computer? Do you wait in line to use the computer that has the customer database? You need a network!

Or maybe you already have a network, but there's just one problem: They promised that the network would make your life easier, and instead, it's turned your computing life upside down. Just when you had this computer thing figured out, someone popped into your office, hooked up a cable, and said, "Happy networking!" Makes you want to scream.

Either way, you've found the right book. Help is here, within these humble pages.

This book talks about networks in everyday   and often irreverent — terms. The language is friendly; you don't need a graduate education to get through it. And the occasional potshot will help unseat the hallowed and sacred traditions of networkdom, bringing just a bit of fun to an otherwise dry subject. The goal is to bring the lofty precepts of networking down to earth where you can touch them and squeeze them and say, "What's the big deal? I can do this!"

About This Book

This isn't the kind of book you pick up and read from start to finish, as if it were a cheap novel. If I ever see you reading it at the beach, I'll kick sand in your face. This book is more like a reference, the kind of book you can pick up, turn to just about any page, and start reading. You have 31 chapters, and each one covers a specific aspect of networking — such as printing on the network, hooking up network cables, or setting up security so that bad guys can't break in. Just turn to the chapter you're interested in and start reading.

Each chapter is divided into self-contained chunks, all related to the major theme of the chapter. For example, the chapter on hooking up the network cable contains nuggets like these:

- What Ethernet is
- The different types of network cable
- Using coax cable
- Using twisted pair cable
- Mixing coax and twisted pair on the same network
- Professional touches for your cabling

You don't have to memorize anything in this book. It's a "need-to-know" book: You pick it up when you need to know something. Need to know what 10baseT is? Pick up the book. Need to know how to create good passwords? Pick up the book. Otherwise, put it down and get on with your life.

How to Use This Book

This book works like a reference. Start with the topic you want to find out about. Look for it in the table of contents or in the index to get going. The table of contents is detailed enough that you should be able to find most of the topics you're looking for. If not, turn to the index, where you can find even more detail.

After you've found your topic in the table of contents or the index, turn to the area of interest and read as much as you need or want. Then close the book and get on with it.

Of course, the book is loaded with information, so if you want to take a brief excursion into your topic, you're more than welcome. If you want to know the big security picture, read the whole chapter on security. If you just want to know how to make a decent password, read just the section on passwords. You get the idea.

If you need to type something, you'll see the text you need to type like this:

TYPE THIS STUFF

In this example, you type **TYPE THIS STUFF** at the keyboard and press Enter. An explanation usually follows, just in case you're scratching your head and grunting "Huh?"

Whenever I describe a message or information that you'll see on the screen, I present it as follows:

```
A message from your friendly network
```

This book rarely directs you elsewhere for information — just about everything you need to know about networks is right here. For more information about DOS, try *DOS For Dummies,* 2nd Edition (IDG Books Worldwide, Inc.). For more NetWare information, you can get a copy of *NetWare For Dummies,* 2nd Edition. And there's a ...*For Dummies* book that covers just about every program known to humanity (or there will be soon).

What You Don't Need to Read

Much of this book is skippable. I've carefully placed extra-technical information in self-contained sidebars and clearly marked them so that you can steer clear of them. Don't read this stuff unless you're really into technical explanations and want to know a little of what's going on behind the scenes. Don't worry; my feelings won't be hurt if you don't read every word.

Foolish Assumptions

I'm going to make only two assumptions about who you are: (1) You're someone who works with a PC, and (2) you either have a network or you're thinking about getting one. I hope that you know and are on speaking terms with someone who knows more about computers than you do. My goal is to decrease your reliance on that person, but don't throw away his or her phone number quite yet.

Is this book useful for Macintosh users? Absolutely. Although the bulk of this book is devoted to showing you how to link Windows-based computers to form a network, you can find information about how to network Macintosh computers, as well.

How This Book Is Organized

Inside this book, you'll find chapters arranged into seven parts. Each chapter is broken down into sections that cover various aspects of the chapter's main subject. There is a logical sequence to the chapters, so it makes sense to read them in order (if you want to read the whole thing). But the book is modular enough that you can pick it up and start reading at any point.

Here's the lowdown on what's in each of the seven parts:

Part I: The Absolute Basics (A Network User's Guide)

The chapters in this part present a layperson's introduction to what networking is all about. This is a good place to start if you're clueless about what a network is. It's also a great place to start if you're a hapless network user who doesn't give a whit about optimizing network performance, but you want to know what the network is and how to get the most out of it.

Part II: Building Your Own Network

Oh, oh. The boss just gave you an ultimatum: Get a network up and running by Friday or pack your things. The chapters in this section cover everything you need to know to build a network, from picking the network operating system to understanding a mail-order advertisement to installing the cable.

Part III: The Dummies Guide to Network Management

I hope that the job of managing the network doesn't fall on your shoulders, but in case it does, the chapters in this part can help you out. You'll find out all about backup, security, performance, dusting, mopping, and all the other stuff network managers have to do.

Part IV: Webifying Your Network

After you get your network up and running, the first thing your users will do is bang on your door and demand Internet access. The chapters in this part show you how to grant their request. Not only that, but you'll find out how to set up your own Web server so that you can create a Web site of your own. And you'll discover how to turn your network into an Intranet so that your LAN users can access information on a local Web server.

Part V: More Cool Things You Can Do with Your Network

The chapters in this part describe some interesting things you can do with your network after you get the basic network up and running — things like sharing a CD-ROM drive or fax modem; dialing in to your network from your computer at home or from a laptop computer while you're on the road; setting up a network at home; and welcoming Macintosh computers into your network fold.

Part VI: The Part of Tens

It wouldn't be a ...*For Dummies* book without a collection of lists of interesting snippets: ten network commandments, ten network gizmos only big networks need, ten tricks to networking Windows 3.1, and more!

Part VII: References for Real People

The two chapters in this section give an overview of the commands available with the two most popular networking systems: NetWare and Windows networks, which include Windows NT Server, Windows for Workgroups, Windows 95, and Windows 98. After that, a handy glossary helps you to decipher even the ugliest of networking terms.

Icons Used in This Book

Hold it — technical stuff is just around the corner. Read on only if you have your pocket protector.

Pay special attention to this icon — it lets you know that some particularly useful tidbit is at hand — perhaps a shortcut or a little-used command that pays off big.

Did I tell you about the memory course I took?

Stop the presses! This icon highlights information that may help you avert disaster.

Information specific to NetWare. Skip this stuff if you don't use or plan not to use NetWare.

Information specific to Windows 95-based networks is in the vicinity.

Keep your eye out for this icon. It alerts you to information that's specific to Windows 98, the soon-to-be-released successor to Windows 95. Remember that in many cases, what applies to Windows 98 also applies to Windows 95 (and vice versa).

Windows NT Server info ought to be within visual range.

Where to Go from Here

Yes, you can get there from here. With this book in hand, you're ready to plow right through the rugged networking terrain. Browse through the table of contents and decide where you want to start. Be bold! Be courageous! Be adventurous! And above all, have fun!

Part I
The Absolute Basics (A Network User's Guide)

The 5th Wave   By Rich Tennant

"THE PRINTER AND DISK DRIVE ARE CONTAINED IN THE HAT. IT'S GREAT FOR KEEPING AN UNCLUTTERED DESK, BUT IT'S HARD GETTING MORE THAN THREE OF US ON AN ELEVATOR AT THE SAME TIME."

In this part . . .

One day the Network Thugs barge into your office and shove a gun in your face. "Don't move until we've hooked you up to the network!" one of them says while the other one rips open your PC, installs a sinister-looking electronic circuit card, closes the PC back up, and plugs a cable into its back. "It's done," they say as they start to leave. "Now . . . don't call the cops. We know who you are!"

If this has happened to you, you'll appreciate the chapters in this part. They provide a gentle introduction to computer networks written especially for the reluctant network user.

What if you don't have a network yet, and you're the one who's supposed to do the installing? Then the chapters in this part will clue you in to what a network is all about. That way, you'll be prepared for the unfortunately more-technical chapters contained in Part II.

Chapter 1

Networks Will Not Take Over the World, and Other Network Basics

• •

• •

Computer networks get a bad rap in the movies. In *War Games,* a kid with zits nearly starts World War III by playing games on a computer network. In *Sneakers,* the mob tries to take over the country by stealing a fancy black box that can access any computer network in existence. And in the *Terminator* movies, a computer network of the future called Skynet takes over the planet, builds deadly terminator robots, and sends them back through time to kill everyone unfortunate enough to have the name Sarah Connor.

Fear not. These bad networks exist only in the dreams of science fiction writers. Real-world networks are much more calm and predictable. They don't think for themselves, they can't evolve into something you don't want them to be, and they won't hurt you — even if your name is Sarah Connor.

Now that you're over your fear of networks, you're ready to breeze through this chapter. It's a gentle introduction to computer networks, superficial even, with a slant toward the concepts that can help you use a computer that's attached to a network. This chapter isn't very detailed; the really detailed and boring stuff comes later.

What Is a Network?

A *network* is nothing more than two or more computers connected together by a cable so that they can exchange information.

Of course, other ways to exchange information between computers exist besides networks. Most of us have used what computer nerds call the *sneakernet.* That's where you copy a file to a diskette and walk the diskette to someone else's computer. The term sneakernet is typical of computer nerds' attempts at humor.

The whole problem with sneakernet is that it's slow, plus it wears a trail in your carpet. One day, some penny-pinching computer geeks discovered that connecting computers together with cables was actually cheaper than replacing the carpet every six months. Thus, the modern computer network was born.

With a computer network, you hook all the computers in your office to-gether with cables, install a special network adapter card (an electronic circuit card that goes inside your computer — ouch!) in each computer so that you have a place to plug in the cable, set up and configure special network software to make the network work, and voilá, you have a working network. That's all there is to it. Figure 1-1 shows a typical network with four computers. You can see here that all four computers are connected with a network cable. You can also see that Ward's computer has a fancy laser printer attached to it. Because of the network, June, Wally, and the Beaver can also use this laser printer. (Also, you can see that the Beaver has stuck yesterday's bubble gum to the back of his computer. Although not recom-mended, the bubble gum shouldn't affect the network adversely.)

- Networks are often called LANs. *LAN* is an acronym that stands for local-area network. It's the first *TLA,* or three-letter acronym that you see in this book. You don't need to remember it, or any of the many TLAs that follow. In fact, the only three-letter acronym you need to remember is TLA.

- You may guess that a four-letter acronym is called an FLA, but you'd be dead wrong. A four letter acronym is called an *ETLA,* which stands for *extended three-letter acronym.*

- Every computer connected to the network is said to be *on the network.* The technical term (which you can forget) for a computer that's on the network is a *node.*

- When a computer is turned on and is able to access the network, the computer is said to be *on-line.* When the computer is unable to access the network, it is *off-line.* A computer can be off-line for several reasons. It can be turned off, it can be broken, the cable that connects it to the network can be unplugged, or a wad of gum can be jammed into the disk drive.

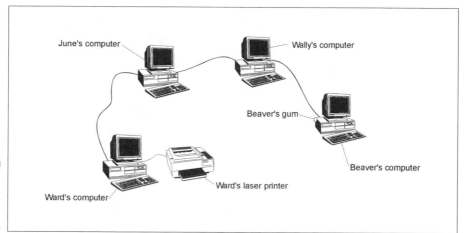

Figure 1-1:
A typical
network.

✔ When a computer is turned on and working properly, it's said to be *up*. When a computer is turned off or when it's broken, it's said to be *down*. Turning off a computer is sometimes called *taking it down*. Turning it back on is sometimes called *bringing it up*.

✔ Don't confuse local-area networks with the Internet. The Internet is a huge amalgamation of computer networks strewn about the entire planet. Networking the computers in your home or office so that they can share information with one another and connecting your computer to the worldwide Internet are two entirely separate things. If you want to use your local-area network to connect your computers to the Internet, you can consult Chapter 16 for instructions.

Why Bother?

Frankly, computer networks are a bit of a pain to set up. So why bother? Because the benefits of having a network make the pain of setting one up bearable. You don't have to be a Ph.D. to understand the benefits of networking. In fact, you learned everything you need to know in kindergarten: Networks are all about sharing. Specifically, networks are about sharing three things: files, resources, and programs.

✔ **Sharing files.** Networks enable you to share information with other computers on the network. Depending on how you set your network up, you can share files in one of three ways. The most direct way is to send the file from your computer directly to your friend's computer. The second way is to send your file to an intermediate resting place, where your friend can pick it up later, kind of like dropping a bag full of ransom money at a phone booth. A third way is to permanently store the file at that intermediate place, where both of you can get at the file whenever you want. One way or the other, the data travels to your friend's computer over the network cable, not on a floppy disk like it does in a sneakernet.

✔ **Sharing resources.** You can set up certain computer resources — like a disk drive or a printer — so that all the computers on the network can access them. For example, the laser printer attached to Ward's computer in Figure 1-1 is a shared resource, which means that anyone on the network can use it. Without the network, June, Wally, and the Beaver would have to buy their own laser printers.

Disk drives can be shared resources, too. In fact, a disk drive must be set up as a shared resource in order to share files with other users. Suppose Wally wants to share a file with the Beaver, and a shared disk drive has been set up on June's computer. All Wally has to do is copy his file to the shared disk drive in June's computer and tell the Beaver where he put it. Then, when the Beaver gets around to it, he can copy the file from June's computer to his own. (Unless, of course, Eddie Haskel deletes the file first.)

You can share other resources, too, such as CD-ROM drives (those devices that store megabytes of data and are most useful for large clip art libraries and encyclopedias and for playing tunes while you're supposed to be working) or modems (which enable you to access other computers that aren't on your network).

✔ **Sharing programs.** Rather than keeping separate copies of the programs on each person's computer, sometimes putting programs on a shared disk that everyone uses is best. For example, if you have ten computer users who all use a particular program, you can purchase and install ten copies of the program — one on each computer — or you can purchase a ten-user license for the program and then install just one copy of the program on a shared disk. Each of the ten users can then access the program from the shared disk.

In most cases, however, running a shared copy of a program over the network is unacceptably slow. A more common way of using a network to share programs is to use a copy of a program installed onto a shared network disk to then install separate copies of the program onto each user's local disk. For example, Microsoft Office enables you to do this, provided that you purchase a license from Microsoft for each computer on which you'll install Office. The advantage of installing Office from a shared network drive is that you don't have to lug around the installation disks or CDs to each user's computer. And the system administrator can customize the network installation so that the software is installed the same way on each user's computer.

Remember that purchasing a single-user copy of a program and putting it on a shared disk, so that everyone on the network can access it, is illegal. If you have five people who use the program, you need to either purchase five copies of the program or purchase a network license that specifically allows five or more users.

Servers and Clients

The network computer that contains the disk drives, printer, or other resources that are shared with other network computers is called a *server*. That's a term that will come up over and over again, so you have to remember it. Write it on the back of your left hand.

Any computer that's not a server is called a *client*. You have to remember this term, too. Write it on the back of your right hand.

Only two kinds of computers are on a network: servers and clients. Look at your left hand and then look at your right hand. Don't wash your hands until you have these terms memorized.

The distinction between servers and clients in a network would be kind of fun to study in a sociology class. It's kind of like the distinction between the haves and the have-nots in society.

- ✓ Usually, the most powerful and expensive computers in a network are the servers. That makes sense because their resources are shared by every user on the network.

- ✓ The cheaper and less-powerful computers are the clients. They're the computers used by individual users for everyday work. Because clients' resources don't have to be shared, they don't have to be as fancy.

- ✓ In most networks, more clients exist than servers. For example, a network with ten clients can probably get by with one server.

- ✓ In many networks, a clean line of segregation exists between servers and clients. In other words, a computer is either a server or a client, not both. A server can't become a client, nor can a client become a server.

- ✓ Other networks are more progressive, allowing any computer in the network to be a server, and allowing computers to be both server and client at the same time. The network illustrated in Figure 1-1 is this type of network.

Dedicated Servers and Peers

In some networks, a server computer is a server computer and nothing else. It's dedicated solely to the task of providing shared resources such as disk drives and printers to be accessed by the network client computers. Such a server is referred to as a *dedicated server* because it can perform no other task besides network services.

The more modern approach to networking enables any computer on the network to function both as a client and as a server. Thus, any computer can share its printers and disk drives with other computers on the network. And while that computer is working as a server, you can still use that same computer for other functions such as word processing. This type of network is called a *peer-to-peer network,* because all the computers are thought of as peers, or equals.

Here are some points to ponder concerning the difference between dedicated server networks and peer-to-peer networks while you're walking the dog tomorrow morning:

- Dedicated servers don't run the standard DOS or Windows operating systems. Instead, they run a special operating system called a *Network Operating System,* which is specially designed to handle networking functions. I describe the two most common network operating systems, NetWare and Windows NT Server, in the next section, "The NOS Choice."

- A peer-to-peer network doesn't require a separate Network Operating System. Peer-to-peer network functions are built in to Microsoft's newest incarnation of Windows, Windows 95. And the soon-to-be-released Windows 98 will have even better networking capabilities. For older computers which can't run Windows, you can purchase peer-to-peer networking software such as LANtastic (by Artisoft) to add networking capabilities to DOS.

- Even though you don't have to, you can still use a dedicated server with a peer-to-peer network. In many cases, setting aside a computer to function just as a server in a peer-to-peer network is a good idea. That's because when you use a server computer for word processing or some other application, network access to the server slows to a snail's pace.

- Besides being dedicated, it's helpful if your servers are also sincere.

Historical stuff that's not worth reading

Networks are nothing new. In the dinosaur era of computing, known as the Mainframerassic, the computing world was dominated by big, overgrown systems called *time-sharing systems.*

Time-sharing systems enable you to use a mainframe computer via a dumb terminal, which consisted only of a monitor and a keyboard. A dumb terminal looked superficially like a PC, but it didn't have its own processor. With dumb terminals, hundreds or even thousands of users could access a single mainframe computer all at the same time.

How did this work? By the magic of time-sharing, which divided the mainframe computer's time into slices, allocating time slices to the users one at a time. The slices were short, but long enough to maintain the illusion that the terminal user had the mainframe computer all to himself or herself.

In the 1970s, big time-sharing systems were replaced by smaller minicomputer systems, which used the time-sharing concept on a smaller scale. It wasn't until the invention of the PC in the late 1970s that networks as we think of them today developed.

The NOS Choice

All computers require an operating system to function. In addition, the network itself requires its own software operating system to coordinate the sharing of information among the networked computers. This special network software is called a *Network Operating System* or *NOS.*

Basically, two Network Operating Systems exist to choose from for dedicated server networks: NetWare and Windows NT Server.

✔ The most popular NOS is NetWare, from a company called Novell. NetWare is very advanced but also very complicated. So complicated, in fact, that it has an intensive certification program that rivals the Bar. The lucky ones who pass the test are awarded the coveted title Certified NetWare Engineer, or CNE, and a lifetime supply of pocket protectors. Fortunately, a CNE is really required only for large networks with dozens or even hundreds of computers attached. Building a NetWare network with just a few computers isn't too difficult.

✔ Windows NT Server is a special network server version of the Windows NT operating system, which is itself a more advanced version of the popular Windows operating system from Microsoft. Windows NT Server is a bit easier to set up and use than NetWare due to its familiar Windows interface.

What Makes It Tick? (You Should Probably Skip This)

To use a network, you don't really have to know much about how it works. Still, you may feel a little better about using the network if you realize that it doesn't work by voodoo. A network may seem like magic, but it isn't. Following is a list of the inner workings of a typical network:

- **Network interface cards.** Inside any networked computer is a special electronic circuit card called a network interface card. The TLA (Come on! Three-letter acronym!) for network interface card is *NIC*. **Important note:** Using your network late into the evening is not the same as watching NIC at night.

- **Network cable.** The network cable is what actually connects the computers together. It plugs into the network interface card at the back of your computer. One common type of cable, coaxial (sometimes called *coax*), is similar to the cable used to bring Nick at Night to your TV. The cable used for cable TV is not the same as the cable used for computer networks, though. So don't try to replace a length of broken network cable with TV cable. It won't work.

  Another common type of network cable looks like phone cable. In fact, in some offices the computer network and the phone system can share the same cable. Beware, though, that ordinary phone cable won't work for a computer network. For a computer network, each pair of wires in the cable must be twisted in just a certain way. That's why this type of cable is called *twisted-pair cable*. Standard phone cable doesn't have the right twists.

  For the complete low-down on networking cables, refer to Chapter 9.

- **Network hub.** If your network is set up using twisted-pair cable, your network probably also has a network hub. The hub is a small box with a bunch of cable connectors. Each computer on the network is connected by cable to the hub. The hub, in turn, connects all the computers to each other. If your network uses coax cable, the cable goes directly from computer to computer, so a network hub isn't used.

- **Network software.** Of course, the software really makes the network work. To make any network work, a whole bunch of software has to be set up just right. Although the Setup programs that come with the various Network Operating Systems can configure the network software automatically, you'll probably have to tweak the software a bit to get it to work just right. For more information about choosing which network software to use for your network, refer to Chapter 7. To find out what you need to know to configure the software so that your network runs smoothly, refer to Chapters 11 through 15.

Bogus buzzword drivel you should skip

An introductory chapter on networking concepts wouldn't be complete if it didn't include a definition for one of the computer industry's most popular networking buzzwords — *client/server.* Unfortunately, nobody really knows what client/server means, not even the experts who made up the term. The lowest-common-denominator definition is: "A computer network in which a PC (the client) can request information from a computer that can share resources (the server)." In other words, a network.

A more technically precise definition is "A computer application in which a significant portion of the application's processing is performed on the server computer rather than on the client computer." This definition is a bit much to swallow at this stage of your network education, so don't worry too much about it.

Very few networks fit this last technical definition of client/server, but client/server is such a trendy buzzword that most computer vendors want to be able to claim they do client/server. Hence the third definition, one more suitable for the real world: "Any computer product, hardware or software, that the manufacturer's marketing department feels will sell more if this trendy buzzword appears in its advertising."

It's Not a Personal Computer Anymore!

If there's one thing I want you to remember from this chapter more than anything else, it's that once your personal computer (PC) is hooked up to a network, it's not a personal computer anymore. You are now a part of a network of computers, and in a way, you've given up one of the key things that made PCs so successful in the first place: independence.

I got my start in computers back in the days when mainframe computers ruled the roost. Mainframe computers are big, complex machines that used to fill whole rooms and had to be cooled with chilled water. My first computer was a water-cooled Binford Power-Proc Model 2000. Argh argh argh. (I'm not making up the part about the water. A plumber was frequently required to install a mainframe computer. In fact, the really big ones were cooled by liquid nitrogen. I am making up the part about the Binford 2000.)

Mainframe computers required staffs of programmers and operators just to keep them going. They had to be carefully managed. A whole bureaucracy grew up around managing mainframes.

Mainframe computers used to be the dominant computer in the workplace. Personal computers changed all that. Personal computers took the computing power out of the big computer room and put it on the user's desktop, where it belongs. PCs severed the tie to the centralized control of the mainframe computer. With a PC, a user could look at his or her computer and say, "This is mine . . . all mine!" Mainframes still exist, but they're not nearly as popular as they once were.

Networks change everything all over again. In a way, it's a change back to the mainframe computer way of thinking. True, the network isn't housed in the basement and doesn't have to be installed by a plumber. But you can no longer think of your PC as your own. You're part of a network, and like the mainframe, the network has to be carefully managed.

Here are but a few of the ways in which a network robs you of your independence:

- ✔ You can't just indiscriminately delete files from the network. They may not be yours.

- ✔ Just because Wally sends something to Ward's printer doesn't mean it will immediately start printing. The Beave may have sent a two-hour print job before that. Wally will just have to wait.

- ✔ You may try to retrieve a Lotus 1-2-3 spreadsheet file from a network disk, only to discover that someone else is using it. Like Wally, you'll just have to wait.

- ✔ If you copy that 150MB database file to a server's disk, you may get a call later from an angry coworker complaining that no room is left on the server's disk for his or her important file.

- ✔ If you want to access a file on Ward's computer but Ward hasn't come in and turned his computer on yet, you'll have to go into his office and turn it on yourself. To add insult to injury, you have to know Ward's password if Ward decided to password-protect his computer.

- ✔ If your computer is a server, you can't just turn it off when you're finished using it. Someone else may be accessing a file on your hard disk or printing on your printer.

- ✔ Why does Ward always get the best printer? If *Leave It to Beaver* were made today, I bet the good printer would be on June's computer.

The Network Manager

Because so much can go wrong, even with a simple network, designating one person as the *network manager* (sometimes also called the *network administrator* or *supervisor*) is important. That way, someone is responsible for making sure that the network doesn't fall apart or get out of control.

The network manager doesn't have to be a technical genius. In fact, some of the best network managers are complete idiots when it comes to technical stuff. What's important is that the manager be organized. The manager's job is to make sure that plenty of space is available on the file server, the file server is backed up regularly, new employees are able to access the network, and so on.

Also the network manager's job includes solving basic problems that the users themselves can't solve and knowing when to call in an expert when something really bad happens.

- Part III of this book is devoted entirely to the hapless network manager. So if you're nominated, read that section. If you're lucky enough that someone else is nominated, celebrate by buying him or her a copy of this book.

- In small companies, picking the network manager by drawing straws is common. The person who draws the shortest straw loses and becomes manager.

- Of course, the network manager can't really be a complete technical idiot. I was using a bit of exaggeration (for those of you in Congress, that means I was "appropriating necessary hyperbole") to make the point that organizational skills are more important than technical skills. The network manager needs to know how to do various maintenance tasks. This knowledge requires at least a little technical know-how, but the organizational skills are more important.

What Have They Got That You Don't Got?

With all this stuff to worry about, you may begin to wonder if you're smart enough to use your computer after it's attached to the network. Let me assure you that you are. If you're smart enough to buy this book because you know you need a network, you're more than smart enough to use the network after it's put in. You're also smart enough to install and manage a network yourself. This isn't rocket science.

I know people who use networks all the time. And they're no smarter than you are. But they do have one thing that you don't have: a Certificate. And so, by the powers vested in me by the International Society for the Computer Impaired, I present you with the certificate in Figure 1-2, confirming that you've earned the coveted title, Certified Network Dummy, better known as *CND*. This title is considered much more prestigious in certain circles than the more stodgy CNE badge worn by real network experts.

Congratulations, and go in peace.

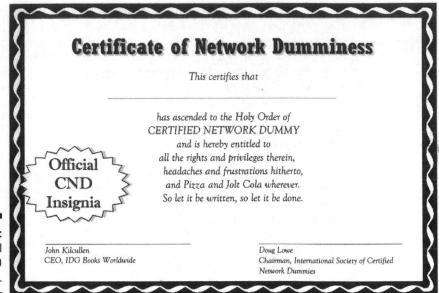

Figure 1-2:
Your official
CND
certificate.

Chapter 2

Life on the Network

. . . .

In This Chapter

▶ Using local resources and network resources

▶ Playing the name game

▶ Logging in to the network

▶ Mapping network drives

▶ Using shared folders

▶ Using a network printer

▶ Logging off the network

. . . .

After your PC is hooked up to a network, it's not an island anymore, separated from the rest of the world like some kind of isolationist fanatic waving a "Don't tread on me" flag. The network connection changes your PC forever. Now your computer is a part of a "system," connected to "other computers" on the "network." You have to worry about annoying network details like local and shared resources and logging in and accessing network drives and using network printers and logging off and who knows what else.

Bother.

This chapter brings you up to speed on what living with a computer network is like. Unfortunately, the chapter gets a little technical at times, so you may need your pocket protector.

Local Resources and Network Resources

In case you didn't catch this in the Chapter 1, one of the most important differences between using an isolated computer and using a network computer is the distinction between *local resources* and *network resources*. Local resources are things such as disk drives, printers, modems, and CD-ROM drives that are connected directly to your computer. You can use local resources whether you're connected to the network or not. Network resources are the disk drives, printers, modems, and CD-ROM drives that are connected to the network's server computers. You can use network resources only after your computer is connected to the network.

The whole trick to using a computer network is knowing which resources are local resources (they belong to you) and which are network resources (they belong to the network). In most networks, your C: drive is a local drive. And if a printer is sitting next to your PC, it's probably a local printer. You can do anything you want with these resources without affecting the network or other users on the network (as long as the local resources aren't shared on the network).

✔ You can't tell whether a resource is a local resource or a network resource just by looking at it. The printer that sits right next to your computer is probably your local printer, but then again, it may be a network printer. The same holds for disk drives: The hard disk in your PC is probably your own, but it may be a network disk, which can be used by others on the network as long as the local resources aren't shared on the network.

✔ Because dedicated network servers are full of resources, you may say they aren't only dedicated (and sincere) but also resourceful. (Groan. Sorry, this is but another in a tireless series of bad computer-nerd puns.)

What's in a Name?

Just about everything on a computer network has a name: The computers themselves have names, the people that use the computers have names, and the disk drives and printers that can be shared on the network have names. Knowing all the names that are used on your network isn't essential, but you do need to know some of them.

✔ Every person who can use the network has a user identification (user ID for short). You need to know your user ID in order to log in to the network. You also need to know the user IDs of your buddies, especially if you want to steal their files or send them nasty notes. More about user IDs and logging in later.

✔ Letting the folks on the network use their first names as their user IDs is tempting, but not a good idea. Even in a small office, you eventually run into a conflict. (And what about that Mrs. McCave, made famous by Dr. Seuss when she had 23 children and named them all Dave?) I suggest that you come up with some kind of consistent way of creating User IDs. For example, you may use your first name plus the first two letters of your last name. Then Wally's user ID would be wallycl and Beaver's would be beavercl. Or, you may use the first letter of your first name followed by your complete last name. Then Wally's user ID would be wcleaver and Beaver's would be bcleaver. (Note that in most networks, capitalization does matter in the user name. Thus, bcleaver is different than BCleaver.)

✔ Every computer on the network must have a unique computer name. You don't have to know the names of all the computers on the network, but it helps if you know your own computer's name and the names of any server computers you need to access. The computer name is often the same as the user ID of the person who uses the computer most often. Sometimes the names indicate the physical location of the computer, such as OFFICE-12 or BACK-ROOM. Server computers often have names that reflect the group that uses the server most, like ACCTNG-SERVER or CAD-SERVER.

✔ Then again, some network nerds like to assign techie-sounding names like BL3K5-87A.

✔ Or you may want to use names from science fiction movies. HAL, Collosus, M5, and Data come to mind. Cute names such as Herbie are not allowed. (However, Tigger and Pooh are entirely acceptable. Recommended, in fact.)

✔ Network resources such as disk drives and printers have names too. For example, a network server may have two printers, named LASER and INKJET (to indicate the type of printer), and two disk drives, named C-DRIVE and D-DRIVE.

✔ When NetWare is used, disk drives' names are called volume names. Often, names such as SYS1, SYS2, and so on are used. NetWare administrators often lack sufficient creativity to come up with more interesting volume names

✔ Most people think Juliet said, "A rose by any other name would smell as sweet." Hah! The actual quote, in full, is "What's in a name? That which we call a rose by any other word would smell as sweet." (*Romeo and Juliet,* act II, scene ii, 43-44.)

✔ Every network has a user ID for the network supervisor. If you log in using the supervisor's ID, you can do anything you want: Add new users, define new network resources, change Wally's password, anything. The supervisor's user ID is usually something very clever, such as SUPERVISOR.

Logging In to the Network

To use network resources, your computer must be connected to the network, and you must go through a super-secret process called *logging in*. The purpose of logging in is to let the network know who you are so that it can decide if you're one of the good guys.

Logging in is the computer network equivalent of the exchange from The *Andromeda Strain* in which Leavitt completed a ritual exchange of code words, and was allowed to enter the top-secret underground laboratory. Gaining access to a computer network usually requires a similar exchange:

> "User ID," the computer said.
>
> The human replied tersely, "Beave."
>
> The computer nodded. "Password?"
>
> "Gumwad," the human replied.
>
> "Verified."

Logging in is also a little like cashing a check: The process requires two forms of identification. The first is your user ID, the name by which the network knows you. Your *user ID* is usually some variation of your real name, like "Beave" for "The Beaver." Everyone who uses the network must have a user ID.

Your *password* is a secret word that only you and the network know. If you type the right password, the network believes you are who you say you are. Every user has a different password, and the password should remain a secret.

In the early days of computer networking, you had to type a LOGIN command at a stark MS-DOS prompt and then supply your User ID and password. In the days of Windows 95 and Windows 98, however, you log in to the network through a special network logon dialog box. If you wish, you can instruct the logon dialog box to remember the User ID and password you used the last time you logged in to the network, so you don't have to type your User ID and password every time you log in. However, you may choose *not* to have Win95 remember your password; otherwise, anyone who turns on your PC can log on as you.

If you're not using Windows 95 or Windows 98, you may still have to type a LOGIN command to access your network. Your network administrator can cheerfully show you how to do this. (If he or she grumbles, offer a jelly doughnut.)

- ✔ The terms *user name* and *login name* are sometimes used instead of user ID. They mean the same thing.

- ✔ As long as we're talking about words that mean the same thing, *log in* and *log on* mean the same thing.

- ✔ As far as the network is concerned, you and your computer are not the same thing. Your user ID refers to you, not to your computer. That's why you have a user ID and your computer has a computer name. You can log in to the network using your user ID from any computer that's attached to the network. And other users can log in at your computer using their own user IDs.

When someone logs in at your computer using their own User ID, that person cannot access any of your network files that are protected by your password. However, that person *will* be able to access any local files which you have not protected. So be careful who you let use your computer.

✔ Your computer may be set up so that it logs you in automatically whenever you turn it on. In that case, you don't have to type your user ID and password. This set up is convenient, but takes the sport out of it. And it's a terrible idea if you're the least bit worried about bad guys getting into your network or personal files.

✔ Guard your password with your life. I'd tell you mine, but then I'd have to shoot you.

Shared Network Drives and Folders

Before Network (B.N.), your computer probably had just one disk drive, known as drive C:. Maybe two, C: and D:. Either way, these drives are physically located inside your PC. They are local drives.

Now that you're on a network, you probably have access to disk drives that aren't located inside your PC but are located instead in one of the other computers on the network. These network drives can be located on a dedicated server computer or, in the case of a peer-to-peer network, on another client computer.

In some cases, you can access an entire network drive over the network. But in most cases, you can't access the entire drive. Instead, you can access only certain folders (*directories* in old MS-DOS lingo) on the network drives. These folders are known as *shared folders* because they're available for sharing on the network.

If you're using Windows 95, you can easily access network drives and shared folders by double-clicking the Network Neighborhood icon on your desktop. All the resources that are available to you on the network are listed in exactly the same format as your local resources appear when you click the My Computer icon. Windows 95 enables you to access network drives and folders in the same way that you access your local disk drives.

You can also retrieve files stored on a network drive from any Windows 95 application program by using the standard File⇨Open command. Just choose Network Neighborhood in the Look In list box to access your network drives and then select the file you want to open.

You can also access shared folders from any Windows 95 application program. For example, suppose that you're working with Microsoft Word and would like to open a document file which has been stored on a shared folder in your network. All you have to do is choose the File⇨Open command to bring up an Open dialog box. Near the top of the Open dialog box is a list box labeled Look In. Choose the Network Neighborhood icon from this list and then locate the document file you want to open on the network.

Network drives and shared folders can be set up with restrictions on how you may use them. For example, you may be granted full access to some shared network folders, so that you can copy files to or from them, delete files on them, create or remove directories on them, and so on. On other shared folders, your access may be limited in certain ways. For example, you may be able to copy files to or from the drive, but not delete files, edit files, or create new directories. You may also be asked to enter a password before you can access a protected folder. For information about setting up file-sharing restrictions, refer to Chapter 12.

Mapping Network Drives

If you haven't yet upgraded to Windows 95, you must use a special trick called *mapping* to access shared network drives and folders (if you're using Windows 95, feel free to skip this section entirely). Mapping assigns a drive letter to a shared network drive or folder. Then you can use the drive letter to access the shared network drive or folder as if it were a local drive. In this way, you can access files from a network drive from any MS-DOS or Windows program.

For example, a shared folder named \Data on a network server may be mapped to drive G on your computer. Then to access files stored in the shared \Data folder, you would look on drive G.

You can map drives letters to shared folders in Windows 95 too, but you have little reason to. Using the Network Neighborhood icon to access the network is easier than fussing with mapped drive letters.

Every network is set up differently, so I can't tell you how your network drives and folders are set up or what restrictions are in place for accessing network drives. But your network guru can tell you, and you can write it down here so that you won't have to ask him or her again when you forget:

Drive letter for first network drive:

What I'm supposed to use it for:

What I can or can't do with it:

Drive letter for second network drive:

What I'm supposed to use it for:

What I can or can't do with it:

Drive letter for third network drive:

What I'm supposed to use it for:

What I can or can't do with it:

(If you have more than three network drives, you have to make your own chart. Sorry. We had to cut costs somewhere. Write your senator.)

✔ Assigning a drive letter to a network drive is called *mapping the drive* or *linking the drive* by network nerds. "Drive H is mapped to a network drive," they'll say.

✔ The drive letter you use to map a drive on a network server doesn't have to be the same drive letter that the server uses to access the file. For example, suppose that you use drive H to link to the server's C drive. This is confusing, so have another cup of coffee. In this scenario, drive H on your computer is the same drive as drive C on the server computer. This shell game is necessary for one simple reason: You can't access the server's C drive as drive C because your computer has its own drive C! You have to pick an unused drive letter and map or link it to the server's C drive.

✔ Network drive letters don't have to be assigned the same way for every computer on the network. For example, a network drive that is assigned drive letter H on your computer may be assigned drive letter Q on someone else's computer. In that case, your drive H and the other computer's drive Q are really the same drive. This can be very confusing. If your network is set up this way, put pepper in your network administrator's coffee. Or insist that everyone be upgraded to Windows 95 (or Windows 98, if it's available when you read this) so that you can use the Network Neighborhood and kiss network drive mapping goodbye forever.

Four Good Uses for Shared Folders

After you know which shared network folders are available, you may be wondering what you're supposed to do with them. Here are four good uses for a network folder.

Use it to store files everybody needs

A shared network folder is a good place to store files that more than one user needs to access. Without a network, you have to store a copy of the file on everyone's computer, and you have to worry about keeping the copies synchronized (which can't be done, no matter how hard you try). Or you can keep the file on a diskette and pass it around. Or you can keep the file on one computer and play musical chairs — whenever someone needs to use the file, he or she goes to the computer that contains it.

With a network, you can keep one copy of the file in a shared folder on the network and everyone can access it.

 If you're trying to share a file that's accessed by an older program — for example, an ancient DOS version of a spreadsheet program like Lotus 1-2-3 — you may have a problem. You have to make sure that two people don't try to update the file at the same time. For example, suppose that you retrieve a spreadsheet file and start to work on it and then another user retrieves the same file a few minutes later. That user won't see the changes you've made so far because you haven't saved the file back to disk yet. Now, suppose you finish making your changes and you save the file while the other user is still staring at the screen. Guess what happens when the other user saves his or her changes a few minutes later? All the changes you made are gone, lost forever in the Black Hole of Unprotected Concurrent Access.

The root cause of this problem is that older programs don't *reserve* the file while they are working on it. As a result, other programs aren't prevented from working on the file at the same time. The result is a jumbled mess. Fortunately, most newer application programs tend to be more tolerant of networks, so they do reserve files when you open them. These programs are much safer for network use.

Use it to store your own files

You can also use a shared network folder as an extension of your own disk storage. For example, if you have a puny 500MB drive with almost no free space, but billions and billions of gigabytes of free space exist on a shared network drive, you have plenty of disk space. Just store your files on the network drive!

✔ Using the network drive for your own files works best if the network drive is set up for private storage that other users can't access. That way, you don't have to worry about the nosy guy down in Accounting who likes to poke around in other people's files.

✔ Don't overuse the network drive. Remember that other users probably want to use the space on the network drive, too.

✔ Before you store personal files on a network drive, make sure that you have permission. A note from your mom will do.

Use it as a pit stop for files on their way to other users

"Hey, Wally, could you send me a copy of last month's baseball stats?"

"Sure, Beave." But how? If the baseball stats file resides on Wally's local drive, how does Wally send a copy of the file to Beaver's computer? One way is for Wally to copy the file to a network folder. Then Beaver can copy the file to his local drive.

✔ Don't forget to delete files that you've saved to the network folder after they've been picked up! Otherwise, the network folder quickly fills up with unnecessary files.

✔ Creating a directory on the network drive just for holding files enroute to other users is a good idea. Call this directory PITSTOP or something similar to suggest its function.

✔ Most electronic mail packages also enable you to deliver files to other users. This is called "sending a file attachment." The advantage of sending a file via e-mail is that you don't have to worry about details like where to leave the file on the server and who's responsibility it is to delete the file.

Use it to back up your local disk

If enough disk space is on the file server, you can use it to store backup copies of the files on your hard disk. Just copy the files you want to back up to a shared network folder.

Obviously, copying all your data files to the network drive can quickly fill up the network drive. You'd better check with the network manager before you do it. He or she may request that you use a special program such as PKZip to compress your files before you copy them to the network drive, or may ask that you copy your backup files to a particular network drive on which all files are automatically compressed to save space.

Using a Network Printer

Using a network printer is much like using a network disk drive. If you're using Windows 95, you can print to a network printer by choosing File⇨Print to call up a Print dialog box from any Windows 95 program and choosing a network printer from the list of printers which are available.

If you're using MS-DOS or an earlier version of Windows (such as Windows 3.11), the network uses smoke and mirrors to trick your MS-DOS and Windows into believing that the network printer is actually attached to your own computer as a local printer. After the smoke and mirrors are in place, use your program's regular printing functions to print to the network printer.

With or without Windows 95, however, printing on a network printer isn't exactly the same as printing on a local printer. When you print on a local printer, you're the only one who is using that printer. But when you print to a network printer, you're sharing that printer with other network users. This complicates things in several ways:

- ✔ If several users print to the network printer at the same time, the network has to keep the print jobs separate from one another. If it didn't, the result would be a jumbled mess, with your 35-page report being mixed up with the payroll checks. That would be bad. Fortunately, the network takes care of this situation using a fancy feature called print spooling.

- ✔ It never fails that when I get in line at the hardware store, the person in front of me is trying to buy something that doesn't have a product code on it. I end up standing there for hours waiting for someone in Plumbing to pick up the phone for a price check. Network printing can be like that. If someone sends a two-hour print job to the printer before you send your half-page memo, you have to wait. Network printing works on a first-come, first-served basis, unless you know some of the tricks I discuss in Chapter 3.

- ✔ Before you were forced to use the network, your computer probably had just one printer attached to it. Now, you may have access to a local printer and several network printers. You may want to print some documents on your cheap (oops, I mean local) dot-matrix printer but use the network laser printer for really important stuff. To do that, you have to find out how to use your application programs' functions for switching printers.

- ✔ Network printing is really too important a subject to squeeze into this chapter. So Chapter 3 goes into it in more detail.

Logging Off of the Network

After you're finished using the network, you should log off. Logging off the network makes the network drives and printers unavailable. Your computer is still physically connected to the network (unless you cut the network cable with pruning sheers — bad idea! Don't do it!), but the network and its resources are unavailable to you.

✔ After you turn off your computer, you're automatically logged off of the network. After you start your computer, you have to log in again. Logging off the network is a good idea if you're going to leave your computer unattended for a while. As long as your computer is logged in to the network, anyone can use it to access the network. And because unauthorized users can access it under your user ID, you get the blame for any damage they do.

✔ In Windows 95 (and Windows 98), you can log off the network by clicking the Start button and choosing the Log Off command. This process logs you off the network without restarting Windows. (In some versions of Windows 95, you must use the choose the Start⇨Shut Down command to log off the network.)

✔ If you use Novell NetWare with an MS-DOS computer, log off by typing the command **LOGOUT**.

✔ If you use Windows for Workgroups, you can log off by double-clicking the Network icon in the Control Panel, selecting the Network Settings dialog box, clicking the Logon button to pop up the Logon Settings dialog box, and then clicking the Log Off button. Click. Click. Click. Click. Isn't Windows great?

Chapter 3
Using a Network Printer

*I*f there's one thing you'll come to hate about using a network, it's using a network printer. Oh, for the good ol' days when your slow but simple dot-matrix printer sat on your desk right next to your computer for you and nobody else but you to use. Now you have to share the printer down the hall. It may be a neat printer, but now you can't watch it all the time to make sure that it's working.

Now you send an 80-page report to the printer, and when you go check on it 20 minutes later, you discover that it hasn't printed yet because someone else sent an 800-page report before you. Or the printer's been sitting there for 20 minutes because it ran out of paper. Or your report just disappeared into Network-Network Land.

What a pain. This chapter can help you out. It clues you in to the secrets of network printing and gives you some Network Pixie Dust (NPD) to help you find those lost print jobs. (It may also convince you to spend $300 of your own money to buy your own printer so that you won't have to mess around with the network printer!)

What's So Special about Network Printing?

Why is network printing such a big deal? In Chapter 2, I talk about sharing network disk drives and folders and show that sharing is really pretty simple. After everything is set up right, using a network drive doesn't require much more than clicking the Network Neighborhood icon.

It would be great if sharing a printer were just as easy. But it isn't. The problem with network printing is that printers are slow and finicky devices. They run out of paper. They eat paper. They run out of toner or ink. And sometimes they just croak. Dealing with all these problems is hard enough when the printer is right next to the computer on your desk, but using the printer that's accessed remotely via a network is even harder.

Ports and printer configuration

Start with some printing basics. A *port* is a connection on the back of your computer. You use ports to connect devices to the computer. You plug one end of a cable into the port and plug the other end of the cable into a connector on the back of the device you want to connect. Most computers have two devices connected to ports: a printer and a mouse. Some computers have other devices, such as a modem or a scanner.

Ports come in two varieties: *parallel* and *serial*. Parallel ports are the type most often used for printers. Certain types of older printers used serial port connections, but most of these printers have long since been used to make beehives. The serial port is used nowadays mostly to connect a mouse or a modem to the computer.

Another type of port that your computer may or may not have is a SCSI port. *SCSI,* which stands for *Small Computer System Interface,* is a special type of high-speed parallel port which is used mostly to connect disk drives, tape drives, CD-ROM drives, and other devices such as scanners to your computer. Since the SCSI port isn't used to connect a printer, you can ignore it for now.

- Most computers have one parallel port and two serial ports. The maximum limit is three parallel ports and four serial ports.

- After the introduction of the first IBM Personal Computer way back in 1492, the names LPT1, LPT2, and LPT3 have been assigned to the parallel ports (LPT stands for "Line Printer"). The first parallel port (and the only parallel port on most computers) is LPT1. LPT2 and LPT3 are the second and third parallel ports. Even today, Windows 95 uses these same names.

Please skip this explanation of parallel and serial ports

Parallel and serial ports use different methods to send individual bytes of data from one end of the cable to the other. A parallel port sends its data to the printer over eight wires, one for each of the bits that make up a byte (well, the parallel port requires more than eight wires, but we'll be good citizens and not ask too many questions). Parallel ports use all eight wires to send data one byte at a time.

A serial port is like a funnel that's only wide enough to let one bit through at a time. Instead of sending all eight bits through at once, a serial port forces the bits to go through just one wire, single file.

✔ LPT1 has a pseudonym: PRN. The names LPT1 and PRN both refer to the first parallel port and can be used interchangeably.

✔ COM1, COM2, COM3, and COM4 are the names used for the four serial ports. (COM stands for "communications," a subject the people who came up with names like LPT1 and COM1 should have studied more closely.)

✔ Hopefully, the name assigned to each port on your computer is printed next to the port's connector on the back of your computer. If not, you have to check your computer's manual to find out which port is which.

✔ Your computer's software must be configured properly for your printer. Basically, that means the software has to know what type of printer you're using and what port the printer is connected to. For example, a configuration like "Binford LaserBlaster 450P on LPT1" means that you have a Binford LaserBlaster model 450P printer attached to your computer via the first parallel port (LPT1).

✔ In the old days of pre-Windows computing, every program had to be configured separately for your printer. You had to follow one set of procedures to get WordPerfect to work with your printer and then you had to follow an entirely different set of procedures to get Lotus 1-2-3 to work with the very same printer.

✔ With Windows, the printer must be configured only one time. To make a printer work with Windows, you must install a special piece of software called a *printer driver* which tells Windows how to print to your printer. Each different type of printer has its own printer driver. Drivers for the most common printers come with Windows. For more exotic printers or for printers that weren't available at the time you purchased Windows, the printer manufacturer supplies the driver on a disk along with the printer. After the printer driver is installed in Windows, you can print to the printer from any program you run under Windows.

What is the Universal Serial Bus?

In 1997, a new type of serial bus called the *Universal Serial Bus*, or *USB*, became available on new computers. The USB is designed to eventually replace *all* the external connections required by your computer. Windows 98 provides full support for USB.

Think about all the external devices that have to be connected to a typical computer: keyboard, monitor, mouse, printer, and perhaps a modem, scanner, or a tape drive. Each of these devices needs its own type of cable, and each must be plugged into the correct receptacle at the back of the computer.

If USB catches on, only one type of receptacle will be on the back of your computer: USB. You can plug any USB-compatible device into a receptacle. And many USB devices enable you to daisy-chain other USB devices so that you can (at least in theory) connect all your computer's external devices to your computer through a single USB receptacle.

Besides saving you the hassle of untangling a multitude of cables and connectors, USB devices are also designed to automatically configure themselves after you attach them to your computer. You'll no longer have to fuss with IRQ settings or other configuration details. You can even add or remove USB devices without turning off your computer or restarting Windows. Windows 98 automatically recognizes USB devices after you connect them.

It remains to be seen whether USB catches on. But if it does, you may find that your next computer and printer utilize the USB rather than the parallel port which has been the norm for printer connections since the first IBM PC rolled off the assembly line back in 1984.

✔ If your computer has more than one printer, each is attached to a separate port. Then you have to configure Windows or, if you're not using Windows, your application programs for each printer. Then you must select the printer that you want to use whenever you print something.

Redirecting printer output

When you use an application program's Print command to send output to a network printer, the application program assumes that it's sending output to a local printer connected to one of the computer's printer ports. Ha! Sucker! Without your program even realizing it, the network software jumps in, intercepts the print output, and redirects it to a network printer.

Figure 3-1 shows how John Madden might explain network printer redirection by using his famous electronic chalkboard. The application program (Word, Lotus 1-2-3, or whatever) sends output to a printer port. Before the output gets to the port, the network software comes out of nowhere and — bam! — intercepts the output and hands it off to the network print queue.

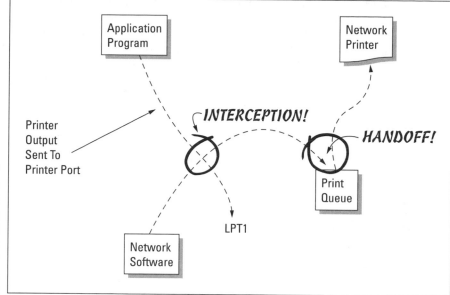

Figure 3-1:
How John
Madden
might
explain
printer
redirection.

✔ Because DOS supports three printer ports (LPT1, LPT2, and LPT3), you can create up to two or three printer redirections at once when you're working with DOS programs. For example, you can redirect LPT1 to a network laser printer and LPT2 to a network dot-matrix printer. To switch between these printers, you must use your application program's printer configuration commands. For example, to print a Lotus 1-2-3 spreadsheet on the network dot-matrix printer, you configure Lotus 1-2-3 so that it prints to LPT2.

✔ If your computer has a local printer attached to it, the local printer is probably set up as LPT1. The network printers are set up as LPT2 and LPT3.

✔ Printer redirection is handled automatically in Windows for Workgroups and Windows 95. If you're using Windows for Workgroups or Windows 95, you don't have to worry about which port the network printer is redirected to. In addition, Windows for Workgroups and Windows 95 aren't subject to the three-printer maximum that plain DOS is.

✔ If you're not using Windows, you have to use special commands to activate printer redirection. You can find these commands in your AUTOEXEC.BAT file. That way, your primary network printer is set up for you automatically. I show you how to use those commands later in this chapter.

✔ If you're not using Windows, switching from one network printer to another or switching between a local printer and a network printer is a tedious process best handled by batch files. For example, if you have a local printer and access to two network printers — one a laser printer and the other an ink-jet printer, you may create batch files named LOCAL.BAT, LASER.BAT, and INKY.BAT. Then you run one of these batch files to select the printer you want to use. You see examples of these batch files for Novell NetWare and Windows NT networks later in this chapter. (Keep in mind that you don't need batch files such as these if you're using Windows.)

✔ *Alien Resurrection* is an example of a movie that should have been redirected.

Spooling and the print queue

Printers are far and away the slowest part of any computer. As far as your computer's central processing unit (CPU) is concerned, the printer takes an eternity to print a single line of information. To keep the CPU from twiddling its microscopic thumbs, computer geeks invented *spooling*.

Spooling is really pretty simple. Suppose that you use Microsoft Word to print a 20-page report. Without spooling, Word would send the report directly to the printer. You'd have to play Solitaire until the printer finished printing.

With spooling, Word doesn't send the report directly to the printer. Instead, Word sends it to a disk file that lives on a network server computer. Because the network server's disk drive is so much faster than the printer, you have to wait only a few seconds for the print job to finish.

Well, that's not the whole story. After the report has been sent to the network server, you can continue to use Word for other work. But your print job hasn't actually printed yet. The print job isn't really finished until the network server has copied it from the temporary disk file to an actual printer. The network server does that automatically. That's what spooling is all about.

Don't forget that you have to share the network printer with other users. If someone else sends a print job to the printer before you send yours, your print job has to wait in line before the server can print it. That's where the *print queue* comes in. Print queue is the network nerd term for the line your print job has to wait in while other print jobs that got in line before it are printed. Your print job isn't actually printed until it gets to the front of the line; that is, until it gets to the front of the queue.

What *spool* stands for, as if you care

Believe it or not, the word *spool* is actually an acronym — a five-letter acronym, or EETLA ("Expanded Extended Three-Letter Acronym") to be precise. Brace yourself, because this acronym is really nerdy: Spool stands for "Simultaneous Peripheral Output On-Line."

Remember, you read it here first.

✔ The people who invented network printing way back in the '60s thought it would be uncool to call the line that print jobs wait in a "line." The Beatles and anything British were popular back then, so they picked the British-sounding word "queue" instead.

✔ Although it's rude, cutting to the front of the queue is possible. You find out how later in this chapter. This trick is good to know, especially if you're the only one who knows.

✔ Brits always use too many letters. They like to throw extra ones into words like "colour." The word *queue* is pronounced like "cue," not "cue-you." "Cue-you" is spelled queueue and is often used by Certified Network Dummies as an insult.

What is a print job?

I've used the term *print job* several times without explaining what it means, so you're probably already mad at me. I'd better explain before it's too late. A print job is a collection of printed pages that are kept together, treated as a set. If you print a 20-page document from Word, the entire 20-page printout is a single print job. Every time you use Word's Print command (or any other program's Print command), you create a print job.

How does the network know when one print job ends and the next one begins? Because application programs that know about networks send a special code at the end of each Print command that says, "This is the end of the print job. Everything up to this point belongs together, and anything I print after this point belongs to my next print job."

Metaphor alert! You can think of this code as kind of like the little stick you use at the grocery-store checkout stand to separate your groceries from the groceries that belong to the person in line behind you. The stick tells the clerk that all the groceries in front of the stick belong together, and the groceries behind the stick belong to the next customer.

✔ All Windows (3.*x* or 95) programs know about network printing, as do most recent versions of DOS-based programs. However, some older DOS programs don't know enough about network printing to put the stick down behind their print jobs. These programs just stop after they finish printing without sending the special code. When you print to the network with one of these programs, the network waits for a certain amount of time — usually ten seconds — before deciding that a print job has been completed. This solution isn't perfect, but it works most of the time.

✔ When you print to a network, you can do lots of neat stuff with print jobs. You can tell the print server to print more than one copy of your job, to print a full page banner at the beginning of the job to make finding it in a stack of print jobs easy, or to stop printing when your job gets to the front of the line so that you can change from plain paper to preprinted invoices or checks. These tricks are handled from the standard Windows Print dialog boxes.

Network Printing with Windows 95

Windows 95 is the easiest of all operating systems to use a network printer with. To print a document to a network printer, you must first install a driver for that printer on your computer. To do that, double-click My Computer and then double-click Printers. Finally, double-click the Add Printer icon. You're asked several questions about the printer, such as whether it's a local printer (that is, attached directly to your computer) or a network printer, where the printer is located, and the type of printer. All you have to do is follow the bouncing ball, answer the questions, and presto, you have access to the network printer. (You may be asked to insert your Windows 95 CD-ROM so that Windows can copy the driver for the printer to your hard drive. Or, you may have to insert the driver disk that comes with the printer.)

After the network printer is installed in Windows 95, printing to the network printer is a snap. From any Windows 95 program, call up the Print dialog box by choosing the File⇨Print command. Choose the network printer from the list of available printers that appears at the top of the Print dialog box and then click OK to print your document. That's all there is to it!

Because Windows 95 has peer-to-peer networking built in, you can set up your local printer to act as a network printer if you want to. To share your printer with other network users, follow these steps:

1. **Double-click on the My Computer icon.**

2. **Double-click on the Printers icon.**

   This opens a window that lists all the printers that are attached to your computer.

3. **Select the printer you want to make available to other network users.**

4. **Choose File⇨Sharing.**

   A dialog box such as the one in Figure 3-2 appears.

5. **Mark the file as a shared printer, type in a name for the printer, and click OK.**

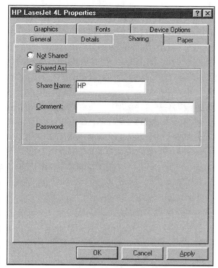

Figure 3-2:
Marking a
shared
printer in
Windows 95.

Other users on the network are now able to use your printer as a network printer.

Network Printing with Windows for Workgroups

Network printing for Windows for Workgroups is similar to network printing in Windows 95, but a few additional steps are required to access a network printer from Windows for Workgroups.

Before you can use a network printer in Windows for Workgroups, you must first install a driver for the printer. You do that from Print Manager by choosing the Options⇨Printer Setup command and clicking the Add button. You can either use a driver supplied with Windows for Workgroups or a driver supplied on disk by the manufacturer of your printer.

After the driver for a network printer is installed in Windows for Workgroups, the next step is connecting to the printer. To do that, fire up Print Manager again and click the Connect Network Printer button located in the toolbar. Select the port (LPT1, LPT2, COM1, or COM2) you want to use for the printer redirection and then select the name of the network printer you want to be assigned to that port.

After a printer is installed and connected, you can print to it from any Windows program by first going into Print Manager, choosing the Options⇨Printer Setup command, and designating the network printer as your default printer. Many Windows programs also enable you to choose from among your installed printers when you print a document. With these programs, you don't have to use Print Manager to designate the network printer as your default printer.

You can speed up network printing by bypassing the Print Manager on your workstation. That way, your programs send output directly to the Print Manager spooler on the computer to which the network printer is attached. If you don't bypass Print Manager on your computer, your print output is spooled twice: first by Print Manager on your computer and then by Print Manager on the printer's computer.

To bypass Print Manager, choose Background Printing from the Print Manager's Options menu and check the Send Documents Directly to Network box.

Windows for Workgroups has peer-to-peer networking services built in, which means that you can share your local printer with other network users. To designate your printer as a shared network printer, fire up Print Manager, select the printer you want to share, and click the Share Printer As button. A dialog box appears in which you can assign a network name to your printer.

Network Printing with DOS Programs

If you're unlucky enough to be using a computer that doesn't run Windows, you have to use DOS commands to enable network printing. The following two sections explain how to use network printing commands for NetWare and for Windows NT with DOS computers. After that, I show you how to direct a document to a network printer using three popular DOS-based application programs: WordPerfect, Lotus 1-2-3, and dBase IV.

If you're working with a modern Windows computer, you can skip these sections entirely.

Redirecting printer output with Novell NetWare

If your network is Novell NetWare and you're using NetWare's DOS client software, you set up redirection for a network printer by using the CAPTURE command. This command tells the NetWare software to capture everything sent to a particular printer port and redirect it to a network print queue.

Here's a typical CAPTURE command:

```
CAPTURE Q=LJET TI=10
```

This command redirects any printer output you send to LPT1 to a print queue named LJET. TI=10 sets the time-out value to ten seconds. If your program stops sending output to the printer for ten seconds, NetWare assumes the print job is finished.

If you have a local printer attached to your LPT1 port, you set up LPT2 as a network printer. Here's a CAPTURE command that does that:

```
CAPTURE L=2 Q=LJET TI=10
```

The L=2 tells CAPTURE to redirect LPT2.

- A CAPTURE command is set up in your AUTOEXEC.BAT file, after the LOGIN command. That way, your network printer is set up for you automatically when you start your computer.

- Sometimes ten seconds isn't long enough for the time-out value. If your reports are being broken apart into several print jobs, try a higher time-out value. If you omit TI altogether, time-out checking is turned off. Then your programs can take as long as they want to create the output.

- To cancel printer redirection, use the ENDCAP command. Good news! ENDCAP doesn't have any parameters, switches, or other adornments! Just say ENDCAP.

- CAPTURE has an AUTOENDCAP option that automatically releases output to the network printer whenever you exit an application. Don't confuse this option with the ENDCAP command, which not only re-leases any pending printer output to the network, but cancels printer redirection as well.

- Suppose that you have a local printer and two network printers: A laser printer named LASER and an ink-jet printer named INKY. To easily switch between these printers, create three batch files named

LOCAL.BAT, LASER.BAT, and INKY.BAT. The LOCAL.BAT file should contain this command:

```
ENDCAP
```

LASER.BAT should contain this command:

```
CAPTURE Q=LASER TI=10
```

And INKY.BAT should contain this command:

```
CAPTURE Q=INKY TI=10
```

To switch to the local printer, just type LOCAL at the DOS prompt. To switch to a network printer, type LASER or INKY.

Redirecting printer output with Windows NT

If your network is Windows NT and you're using Microsoft's MS-DOS client software, you set up printer redirection by using the NET USE command. This command tells the MS-DOS client software to use a particular network printer whenever you send output to a printer.

Here's a typical NET USE command to set up a network printer:

```
NET USE LPT1: \\WARD\LASER
```

This command redirects any printer output you send to LPT1 to a printer named LASER on the server named WARD.

- ✔ A NET USE command should be set up in your AUTOEXEC.BAT file. That way, your network printer is set up for you automatically after you start your computer.
- ✔ To cancel printer redirection, use the NET USE /DELETE command, like this:

```
NET USE LPT1: /DELETE
```

- ✔ Suppose that you have a local printer and two network printers: a laser printer named LASER and an ink-jet printer named INKY. To easily switch between these printers, create three batch files named LOCAL.BAT, LASER.BAT, and INKY.BAT. The LOCAL.BAT file should contain this command:

```
NET USE LPT1: /DELETE
```

This command disables any network connection for LPT1, so LPT1 reverts to your local printer. LASER.BAT should contain this command:

```
NET USE LPT1: \\WARD\LASER
```

And INKY.BAT contain this command:

```
NET USE LPT1: \\WARD\INKY
```

To switch to the local printer, just type LOCAL at the DOS prompt. To switch to a network printer, type LASER or INKY.

Network printing with WordPerfect

The DOS versions of WordPerfect enable you to manage printers from the Print menu. To switch to a network printer, follow these steps:

1. **Start WordPerfect and open the document you want to print.**
2. **Press Shift+F7.**
3. **Press S to select the printer to use.**

   WordPerfect displays a list of the printers that have been configured previously. If you're lucky, the network printer you want to use is already on this list.

4. **Move the cursor to the printer that you want to use and press S to select it.**
5. **Press F7 to return to the document.**

If you're down on your luck, you have to add the network printer to the WordPerfect printer list. Press A for Additional Printers and then press L to list the available printer drivers. If the correct printer driver for the network printer appears in the list, select it and then set its Port option to the printer port you redirected to the network. If the printer driver for the network printer isn't displayed, you have to find the WordPerfect installation disks (they're probably tossed in the back of a drawer somewhere; good luck finding them) to install the driver.

✔ As a lowly network user, configuring WordPerfect for a network printer isn't really your job. If your network guru hasn't done it already, offer him or her a large bag of Cheetos. But make sure that the person washes his or her hands before touching your keyboard.

✔ If you're crazy enough to have found out how to create and use WordPerfect macros, switching to the network printer and back is a good candidate for macro-ization. For example, you can make a macro named NETPRT, which selects the network printer, and another macro named LOCALPRT, which selects the local printer. Then assign these macros to key combinations you think you'll remember (like Shift+F12 for the NETPRT and Ctrl+F12 for LOCALPRT).

If you don't already know how to create macros, this isn't the place to find out. Sorry.

✔ The term for that orange gunk that gets on your fingers when you eat Cheetos is *Cheetum.*

Network printing with Lotus 1-2-3

With Lotus 1-2-3, switching from a local printer to a network printer can get you all tied up in knots. Assuming that 1-2-3 has been configured with the printer drivers required for your local printer and your network printer, you must change both the printer name and the printer port to switch from the local printer to the network printer and back again. Both settings are changed from the /Worksheet Global Default Printers menu. Type **/WGDP** to get there.

To change the printer name, press N. A list of defined printers appears; pick the one that represents the network printer you want to use.

To change the port, press I (for Interface) and then pick option 5, 6, or 7 for DOS Device LPT1, LPT2, or LPT3, depending on which device you've redirected to the network printer.

To switch from the network printer back to your local printer, you again must access the /Worksheet Global Default Printer menu. Use the Name command to select the printer name and the Interface command to select the local printer port (usually option 1, Parallel 1).

✔ Lotus 1-2-3 provides two ways to access the printer ports. Options 1 and 3 access Parallel 1 and Parallel 2, and options 5 through 8 access DOS Device LPT1 through DOS Device LPT2. Options 1 and 5 both send output to LPT1, and 3 and 6 both send output to LPT2. A significant technical difference exists between how options 1 and 3 versus options 5 through 8 work. You don't want to know what the difference is, but you do want to know that options 5 through 8 are best for network printers, and 1 and 3 are best for local printers.

✔ If the network printer you want to use doesn't show up on the list when you pick the Names command from the /Worksheet Global Default Printer menu, get help. Unless you're a Lotus wiz, you don't want to contend with installing a printer device driver for 1-2-3 if you can possibly avoid it.

Network printing with dBASE IV

With dBASE IV, you use the SET PRINTER command to change the destination for printed output. You issue this command from the infamous dot prompt.

Suppose that a local printer is attached to LPT1 and that LPT2 is redirected to a network printer. dBASE IV print output is sent to LPT1 by default, so no action is required to print to the local printer. To send output to the network printer, you use a SET PRINTER command, like this:

```
SET PRINTER TO LPT2
```

If you later want to revert to the local printer, you use this command:

```
SET PRINTER TO LPT1
```

Then output is sent to LPT1.

Database reports can take forever and a day to prepare, especially if more than one file is accessed. You may have to increase the time-out value or disable the time-out feature altogether.

Playing with the Print Queue

After you've sent your output to a network printer, you usually don't have to worry about it. You just go to the network printer and voilà! Your output is there waiting for you.

That's what happens in the ideal world. In the real world where you and I live, all sorts of things can happen to your print job between the time you send it to the network printer and the time it actually is printed:

✔ You discover that someone else already sent a 50-trillion page report ahead of you that isn't expected to finish printing until the national debt is completely paid off.

✔ The price of framis valves goes up $2 each, rendering foolish the recommendations you made in the report.

✔ Your boss calls and tells you that his brother-in-law will be attending the meeting, and won't you please print an extra copy of the proposal for him. Oh, and a photocopy won't do. Originals only, please.

✔ You decide to take lunch, so you don't want the output to be printed until you get back.

Fortunately, your print job isn't totally beyond your control just because you've already sent it to the network printer. By using your network software's features for managing the print queue, you can change the status of jobs you've already sent. You can change the number of copies to be printed, hold a job so that it won't be printed until you say so, or cancel a job altogether.

You can probably make your network print jobs do other tricks, too — like shake hands, roll over, and play dead. But the basic tricks — hold, cancel, and print multiple copies — are enough to get you started.

Windows 95 printer tricks

Windows 95 manages to do away with one of the most hated of all Windows programs: Print Manager. Three cheers for Microsoft! Well, almost. As it turns out, getting rid of Print Manager doesn't eliminate the headaches associated with Windows printing. It just replaces old headaches with new ones.

To manage a Windows 95 printer, double-click My Computer, double-click the Printers icon, and then double-click the icon for the printer you want to use. A window, which looks suspiciously like the old Print Manager window, appears listing any print jobs the printer is handling. You can then use the following tricks to manipulate the print queue:

✔ To temporarily stop a job from printing, select the job and use the Document⇨Pause Printing command. Choose the same command again to release the job.

✔ To stop the printer, choose the Printer⇨Pause Printing command. To resume, choose the command again.

✔ To delete all print jobs, choose the Printer⇨Purge Print Jobs command.

✔ To cut to the front of the line, drag the print job you want to print to the top of the list.

The best thing about Windows 95 printer management is that it shelters you from the details of working with different network operating systems. Whether you print on a NetWare printer, a Windows NT printer, or a Windows 95 shared printer, the Printers icon manages all print jobs the same.

Printer tricks with Windows for Workgroups

With Windows for Workgroups, you control network printing by using a beefed-up version of the familiar Print Manager. Controlling a print job in the Print Manager queue is easy. You can find the commands for manipulating print jobs in the Print Manager's Document menu.

As expected, Windows Print Manager uses slightly different terminology to describe network printing functions. A print job isn't a "print job," it's a document. You don't "hold" a print job, you pause it. Get used to it. It's the Windows Way.

- ✔ To hold a print job so that it won't be printed until it's released, high-light the job and use the Document menu's Pause Printing command.

- ✔ To release a held print job, use the Document menu's Resume Printing command.

- ✔ To cut to the front of the line, use the Document menu's Move Document Up command. Use the Move Document Down command to move toward the end of the queue.

- ✔ In keeping with the Windows Way, you also can activate these commands by clicking buttons that have pictures, which resemble the intended functions about as much as a Picasso represents real life.

NetWare print queue tricks: The PCONSOLE command

If your network is Novell NetWare and you're not using Windows 95 or Windows for Workgroups on your computer (in other words, if you're stuck using DOS), you can use the PCONSOLE command to perform print queue tricks. You don't have to go to the file server to use the PCONSOLE command; just type PCONSOLE at the DOS prompt on your own computer and press Enter. PCONSOLE displays the menu shown in Figure 3-3.

Figure 3-3:
The
NetWare
Available
Options
menu.

```
        Available Options
┌────────────────────────────────┐
│ Change Current File Server      │
│ Print Queue Information          │
│ Print Server Information         │
└────────────────────────────────┘
```

Choose Print Queue Information, and the menu shown in Figure 3-4 appears.

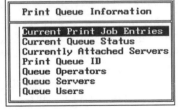

```
 Print Queue Information
┌─────────────────────────────┐
│ Current Print Job Entries   │
│ Current Queue Status        │
│ Currently Attached Servers  │
│ Print Queue ID              │
│ Queue Operators             │
│ Queue Servers               │
│ Queue Users                 │
└─────────────────────────────┘
```

Choose Current Print Job Entries, and PCONSOLE displays a list of print queues. Choose the one you redirected print output to, and you see a list of all the jobs waiting in the queue.

To change the status of a print job, highlight the job you want to change and press Enter. PCONSOLE displays a screen like the one in Figure 3-5.

From this display, you can:

- ✔ Place a User Hold on the job, which holds the job in the queue until you or someone with operator or supervisor rights releases it.

- ✔ Place an Operator Hold on the job, which holds the job in the queue until an operator releases it.

- ✔ Change the number of copies to be printed.

```
NetWare Print Console  V1.51                Monday  September 20, 1993  12:07 pm
                 User SUPERVISOR On File Server HERBIE Connection 5

        Available Options

Print job:          452              File size:         4198
Client:             WALLY
Description:        LPT1 Catch
Status:             Ready To Be Serviced, Waiting For Print Server

User Hold:          No               Job Entry Date:    September 21, 1993
Operator Hold:      No               Job Entry Time:    1:04:30 pm
Service Sequence:   1

Number of copies:   1                Form:              0
File contents:      Byte stream      Print banner:      No
Tab size:                            Name:
Suppress form feed: No               Banner name:
Notify when done:   No
                                     Defer printing:    No
Target server:      (Any Server)     Target date:
                                     Target time:
```

Figure 3-5:
PCONSOLE
displays the
status of a
print job.

- ✔ Change the job's position in the queue by typing a new value for the Service Sequence field.

- ✔ Specify a special form for the print job, like invoices or checks. If you do that, NetWare prompts the operator to mount the correct forms in the printer before it prints the job.

- ✔ Tell NetWare to print a banner page at the start of the print job. This command makes separating print jobs from one another easier.

- ✔ Do lots of other stuff, which you probably won't ever worry about.

What to Do When the Printer Jams

The only three sure bets in life are (1) *Rocky* will always be Sylvester Stallone's best movie, (2) the 49ers will never be the same without Joe Montana, and (3) the printer will always jam shortly after your job reaches the front of the queue.

What do you do when you walk in on your network printer while it's printing all 133 pages of your report on the same line?

1. **Start by yelling "Fire!"**

   No one will save you if you yell "Printer!"

2. **Find the printer's on-line button and press it.**

   This step takes the printer off-line so that the server stops sending information to it and the printer stops. This doesn't cure anything, but it stops the noise. If you must, turn the printer off.

3. **Pull out the jammed paper and reinsert the good paper into the printer. Nicely.**

4. **If necessary, restart the job that was printing, from the beginning.**

   Depending on your printer, this may not be necessary. Some printers resume printing automatically after you clear the jam.

   With NetWare, you can run the PCONSOLE command to rewind the printer. Select Print Server Information and then Print Server Status/ Control. Then select Printer Control and Rewind Printer. Rewind the printer to the beginning of the file by specifying "Rewind to byte 0." This resets the print job so that it's reprinted.

5. **Press the on-line button so that the printer resumes printing.**

Chapter 4

Mr. McFeeley's Guide to E-Mail

• •

In This Chapter

▶ What e-mail is, and why it's so cool

▶ How to use Microsoft Exchange

▶ Other e-mail goodies

▶ Smileys and e-mail etiquette

• •

*D*o you often return to your office after a long lunch to find your desk covered with those little pink "While You Were Out" notes and your computer screen plastered with stick-on notes?

If so, maybe it's time you bite the bullet and find out how to use your computer network's electronic mail, or e-mail, program. Most computer networks have one. If yours doesn't, bug the network manager until he or she gets one.

This chapter introduces you to what's possible with a good e-mail program. So many e-mail programs are available that I can't possibly show you how to use all of them, so I'm focusing on Exchange, the e-mail program that comes with Windows 95 and Windows NT. Other e-mail programs are similar.

What E-Mail Is and Why It's So Cool

E-mail is nothing more than the computer-age equivalent of Mr. McFeeley, the postman from *Mr. Rogers' Neighborhood*. E-mail enables you to send messages to and receive messages from other users on the network. Instead of writing the messages on paper, sealing them in an envelope, and giving them to Mr. McFeeley to deliver, e-mail messages are stored on disk and electronically delivered to the appropriate user.

Sending and receiving mail

To send an e-mail message to another network user, you must activate the e-mail program, compose the message by using a text editor, and provide an address — the user ID of the user you want the message sent to. Most e-mail programs also require that you create a short comment that identifies the subject of the message.

After you receive a message from another user, the e-mail program copies the message to your computer and displays it on-screen so that you can read it. You then can delete the message, print it, save it to a disk file, or forward it to another user. You can also reply to the message by composing a new message to be sent back to the user who sent the original message.

- ✔ When someone sends a message to you, most e-mail programs immediately display a message on your computer screen or make a sound to tell you to check your mail. If your computer isn't on the network when the message is sent, you're notified the next time you log in to the network.

- ✔ Most e-mail packages can be set up so that they check for new mail automatically when you log in to the network.

- ✔ Besides sending text messages, most e-mail packages enable you to attach a file to your message. You can use this feature to send a word processing document, a spreadsheet, or a program file to another network user.

- ✔ Most e-mail programs enable you to keep a list of users you commonly send mail to in an address book. That way you don't have to retype the user ID every time.

- ✔ Most programs also enable you to address a message to more than one user — the electronic equivalent of a carbon copy. Some programs also enable you to create a list of users and assign a name to the list. Then you can send a message to each user in the list by addressing the message to the list name. For example, June may create a list including WARD, WALLY, and BEAVER, and call the list BOYS. To send e-mail to all the boys on her family network, she simply addresses the message to BOYS.

The post office

Most e-mail programs use a network server as an electronic post office where messages are stored until they can be delivered to the recipient. This post office is sometimes called a *mail server*. A network server used as a mail server doesn't have to be dedicated to that purpose, although in larger networks it sometimes is. In smaller networks, the network file server doubles as the mail server.

✔ Depending on the e-mail program, setting up more than one mail server on a network is possible. In that case, you must check mail on all the servers. If you check just one of the mail servers, you won't be notified of any mail that's waiting for you on the other mail servers.

✔ Disk space on a mail server is often at a premium. Be sure to delete unneeded messages as you read them.

Using Microsoft Exchange or Microsoft Outlook

Microsoft Exchange is the electronic mail program that comes built-in with Windows 95 and Windows NT 4.0, both the Server and Workstation editions. If you're using Windows 95 or Windows NT to build your network, Exchange is your e-mail program.

If you've installed Microsoft Office 97 on your computer, the Exchange program that came with Windows 95 or Windows NT is replaced by a newer e-mail program called Microsoft Outlook. Outlook is compatible with Exchange so that you can use either one to handle your e-mail.

Windows 98 comes with a scaled-back version of Outlook called Outlook Express. Outlook Express enables you to access mail from all your e-mail accounts (for example, you can access both LAN e-mail and Internet e-mail), and you can also use Outlook Express to access Internet newsgroups.

The procedures for working with Outlook and Outlook Express are similar to the procedures for using Exchange as described in the following sections.

Sending mail

To send an e-mail message to another network user, start the Exchange program by double-clicking on the Inbox desktop icon. Exchange appears in its own window, as shown in Figure 4-1.

To create a message to send to another user, click the New Message button. A window appears in which you may type the network user ID of the recipient, the subject of the message, and the message itself.

Figure 4-2 shows a message composed and ready to be delivered.

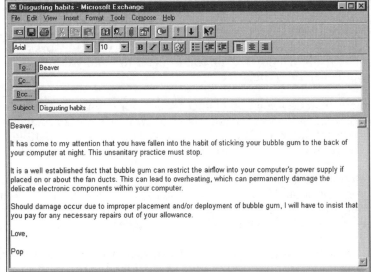

Figure 4-1:
Microsoft
Exchange's
main
display.

Figure 4-2:
Creating an
e-mail
message.

 After you've finished typing the message, click the Send button. The message is delivered to the user listed in the To field.

✔ The recipient must run Exchange (or another e-mail program on his or her computer to check for incoming mail). When the recipient runs his or her e-mail program, your message is delivered.

✔ You can keep a personalized address list using the Address Book, which is available from the Tools menu in Exchange.

✔ Exchange can be used to send mail to other users of your local network and to send and receive mail to users of other computer networks, such as CompuServe, the Microsoft Network, America Online, or the Internet. However, a modem is necessary to send e-mail to an address that's not in the network.

✔ Exchange enables you to include files as attachments to your e-mail messages. When the recipient opens the message, the file appears as an icon. The recipient can then drag and drop the icon to his or her desktop in order to access the attachment. Or, he or she can double-click the icon to open it directly.

Reading your mail

To read mail sent to you by other users, simply start Microsoft Exchange by double-clicking on the Inbox desktop icon. After you start Exchange, the program automatically checks to see if you have any new mail. If you have received new mail, a simple dialog box appears, which tells you that you have new mail and offers to let you read it immediately.

After you've read an electronic mail message, you have several options on dealing with the message.

 If the message is worthy of a reply, click the Reply to Sender button. A new message window appears, enabling you to compose a reply. The new message is automatically addressed to the sender of the original message, and the text of the original message is inserted at the bottom of the new message.

 If the message was intended for someone else, or if you think that someone else should see it (maybe it contains a juicy bit of gossip), click the Forward button. A new message window appears, enabling you to type the name of the user you want the message forwarded to.

 If you want a hard copy of the message, click the Print button.

 If the message is unworthy of even filing, click the Delete button. Poof! The message is deleted.

 If you have more than one message waiting, you can read the next message in line by clicking the Next button.

Other E-Mail Goodies

Most e-mail packages include features beyond simply reading and writing messages.

Chatting on-line

Some e-mail systems enable you to chat with another network user. This feature is similar to vanilla e-mail, but it's not the same thing. With e-mail, you compose a message that's delivered to another user, who may read the message immediately, a few minutes later, or a few days later. Chatting on-line is more similar to using the phone: You *call* a network user; if the user is available, he or she answers and you talk electronically.

✔ Chatting is a two-way form of communication. You type something, the other party types something, you type again, she types again. You can even both type at the same time.

✔ When you call someone to chat, you may not get an answer. The other user may not be there. Or he may be chatting with another user. Or he may know it's you and just not answer — especially if you reminded him about the $20 he owes you from the last time you chatted.

✔ Avoid the chat feature if you're embarrassed about your typing skills. Chat sends characters across the network one at a time as you type them, so the other person sees all your typing mistakes as you make them!

✔ Network chat is a great feature, especially for offices that don't have phones yet. If you've already arrived in the twentieth century and your office has a phone system, you should probably use it instead.

Electronic scheduling

Scheduling software takes advantage of the communication features of e-mail to enable you to schedule meetings with other network users. You tell the scheduling program the people you want at the meeting as well as when and where you'd like the meeting to occur, and the program checks the people's schedule to see whether they can make the meeting. If so, the scheduling program notifies everyone of the meeting by sending an e-mail note. If not, the scheduling program suggests an alternate meeting time.

Microsoft Exchange doesn't include scheduling features, but Outlook does. That's one of the reasons you may want to switch to Outlook if you've installed Office 97 on your computer.

✔ Most scheduling programs keep track of room usage so that they don't schedule two meetings at the same place and time.

✔ For scheduling software to work, everyone must use it religiously. If Bob forgets to tell the scheduling program about his Friday golf match, the program may well schedule a meeting for him for Friday morning.

> ✔ Scheduling software is most appropriate for large offices. Purchasing and maintaining the software for an office of three isn't worth the money.

E-Mail Etiquette

Communicating with someone via e-mail is different from talking with that person face-to-face or over the phone. You need to be aware of these differences, or you end up insulting someone without meaning to. Of course, if you do mean to insult someone, pay no attention to this section.

> ✔ Always remember that e-mail isn't as private as you'd like it to be. It's not that difficult for someone to electronically steam open your e-mail and read it. Be careful what you say, to whom you say it, and about whom you say it.

> ✔ Don't forget that all the rules of social etiquette and office decorum apply to e-mail, too. If you wouldn't pick up the phone and call the CEO of the company, don't send her e-mail, either.

> ✔ When you reply to someone else's e-mail, keep in mind that the person you're replying to may not remember the details of the message he or she sent to you. Providing some context for your reply is polite. Some e-mail systems (such as Exchange) do this for you by automatically tacking on the original message at the end of the reply. If yours doesn't, be sure to provide some context — such as including a relevant snippet of the original message in quotation marks — so that the recipient knows what you're talking about.

> ✔ E-mail doesn't have the advantage of voice inflections. This limitation can lead to all kinds of misunderstandings. You have to be careful that people know when you're joking and when you mean it. E-mail nerds have developed a peculiar way to convey tone of voice: they string together symbols on the computer keyboard to create smileys. Table 4-1 shows some of the more commonly used (or abused) smileys.

Table 4-1	Commonly Used and Abused Smileys
Smiley	*What It Means*
:-)	Just kidding
;-)	Wink
:-(	Bummer
:-0	Well, I Never!
:-x	My lips are sealed

✔ If you don't get it, tilt your head to the left and look at the smiley sideways.

✔ E-mail nerds also like to use shorthand abbreviations for common words and phrases, like FYI for "For Your Information" and ASAP for "As Soon As Possible." Table 4-2 lists the more common ones.

Table 4-2	Common E-Mail Abbreviations
Abbreviation	*What It Stands For*
BTW	By The Way
FWIW	For What It's Worth
IMO	In My Opinion
IMHO	In My Humble Opinion
IOW	In Other Words
PMJI	Pardon Me for Jumping In
ROFL	Rolling On the Floor, Laughing
ROFL,PP	Rolling On the Floor Laughing, Peeing my Pants
TIA	Thanks In Advance
TTFN	Ta Ta For Now (quoting Tigger)
TTYL	Talk To You Later
<g>	Grin
<bg>	Big Grin
<vbg>	Very Big Grin

✔ Note that the abbreviations referring to gestures or facial expressions are typed between a less-than sign and a greater-than sign: <g>. Other gestures are spelled out, like <sniff>, <groan>, or <sigh>.

✔ You're not able to italicize or underline text on many e-mail programs (although you can in Exchange, Outlook, or Outlook Express). Type an asterisk before and after a word you *wish* you could italicize. Type an underscore _ before _ and _ after _ a word you'd like to underline.

✔ Capital letters are the electronic equivalent of SHOUTING. TYPING AN ENTIRE MESSAGE IN CAPITAL LETTERS CAN BE VERY ANNOYING AND CAN CAUSE YOU TO GET THE ELECTRONIC EQUIVALENT OF LARYNGITIS.

Chapter 5
Help! The Network's Down!

*F*ace it: Networks are prone to break.

They have too many "C" parts. Cables. Connectors. Concentrators. Cards. All these parts must be held together in a delicate balance; the network equilibrium is all too easy to disturb. Even the best-designed computer networks sometimes act as if they were held together with baling wire and chewing gum.

To make matters worse, networks breed suspicion. After your computer is attached to a network, you're tempted to blame the network every time something goes wrong, regardless of whether the problem has anything to do with the network. Can't get columns to line up in a Word document? Must be the network. Your spreadsheet doesn't add up? The @#$% network's acting up again.

This chapter doesn't begin to cover everything that can go wrong with a computer network. If it did, you'd take this book back and demand a refund after you got about 40 pages into "Things that can go wrong with IPX.COM."

Instead, this chapter focuses on the most common things that go wrong with a network that an ordinary network user (that's you) can fix. And best of all, you're pointed in the right direction when you come up against a problem that you can't fix yourself.

When Bad Things Happen to Good Computers

What do you do when your computer goes on the blink? Here are some general ideas for finding out what the problem really is and deciding whether you can fix it yourself. I explain each of these suggestions in detail later in the chapter:

1. **Make sure that your computer and everything attached to it is plugged in.**

    Computer geeks love it when a user calls for help and they get to tell the user that the computer isn't plugged in. They write it down in their geek logs so they can tell their geek friends about it later. They may even want to take your picture so that they can show it to their geek friends. (Most "accidents" involving computer geeks are a direct result of this kind of behavior.)

2. **Make sure that your computer is properly connected to the network.**

3. **Note any error messages that appear on the screen.**

4. **Do a little experimenting to find out whether the problem is indeed a network problem or a problem with just your computer.**

5. **Try restarting your computer.**

6. **Try restarting the entire network.**

7. **If none of these steps corrects the problem, scream for help.**

    Have a suitable bribe prepared to encourage your network guru to work quickly. (You can find a handy list of suitable bribes at the end of this chapter.)

My Computer's Dead!

If your computer seems totally dead, here are some things to check:

- Is it plugged in?

- If your computer is plugged into a surge protector or a power strip, make sure that the surge protector or power strip is plugged in and turned on. If the surge protector or power strip has a light, it should be glowing.

- Make sure that the computer's On/Off switch is turned on. This sounds too basic to include even here, but many computers are set up so that the computer's actual power switch is always left in the "On" position and the computer is turned on or off by means of the switch on the surge protector or power strip. Many computer users are surprised to find out that their computers have an On/Off switch on the back of the cases.

✔ If you think your computer isn't plugged in but it looks like it is, listen for the fan. If the fan is turning, the computer is getting power and the problem is more serious than an unplugged power cord. (If the fan isn't running but the computer is plugged in and power is on, it could be that the fan is out to lunch.)

✔ If the computer is plugged in, turned on, and still not running, plug a lamp into the outlet to make sure that power is getting to the outlet. It could be that you need to reset a tripped circuit breaker.

✔ The monitor has a separate power cord and switch. Make sure that the monitor is plugged in and turned on.

✔ Your keyboard, monitor, mouse, and printer are all connected to the back of the computer by cables. Make sure that these cables are all plugged in securely.

✔ Make sure that the other ends of the monitor and printer cables are plugged in properly, too.

✔ Most monitors have knobs that you can use to adjust the contrast and brightness of the monitor's display. If the computer is running but your display is dark, try adjusting these knobs. They may have been turned all the way down.

Checking Your Network Connection

There's a saying among network gurus that 95 percent of all network problems are cable problems. The cable that connects your computer to the rest of the network is a finicky beast. It can break at a moment's notice, and by "break," I don't necessarily mean "physically break in two." Sure, sometimes the problem with the cable is that Eddie Haskel got to it with pruning sheers. But cable problems are not usually visible to the naked eye.

✔ If your network uses twisted-pair cable (the cable that looks something like phone wire and is sometimes called "10baseT" cable), you can quickly tell whether the cable connection to the network is good by looking at the back of your computer. A small light is near the place where the cable plugs in. If this light is glowing steadily, the cable is good. If the light is dark or if it's flashing intermittently, you have a cable problem.

If the light is not glowing steadily, try removing the cable from your computer and reinserting it. This action may cure the weak connection.

✔ Detecting a cable problem in a network that's wired with coax cable, the kind that looks like cable-TV cable, is more difficult. The connector on the back of the computer forms a T. The base end of the T plugs into your computer. One or two coax cables plug into the outer ends of the T. If only one coax cable is used, a special plug called a *terminator* must be used in place of a cable at the other end of the T. If you can't find a terminator, try conjuring one up from the 23rd century. ***Warning:*** Do not do this if your name happens to be Sarah Connor.

Don't unplug a coax cable from the network while the network is running. Data travels around a coax network the way the baton travels around the track in a relay race. If one person drops it, the race is over. The baton never gets to the next person. Likewise, if you unplug the network cable from your computer, the network data never gets to the computers that are "down the line" from your computer. (Well, actually, Ethernet — see Chapter 9 — isn't dumb enough to throw in the towel at the first sign of a cable breakage. You can disconnect the cable for a few seconds without permanently scattering network messages across the galaxy, and you can disconnect the T connector itself from the network card so long as you don't disconnect the cables from the T connector. But don't attempt either unless you have a good reason and a really good bribe for the network manager, who is sure to find out that you've been playing with the cables.)

✔ Some networks are wired so that your computer is connected to the network with a short (six feet or so) patch cable. One end of the patch cable plugs into your computer, and the other end plugs into a cable connector mounted on the wall. Try quickly disconnecting and reconnecting the patch cable. If that doesn't do the trick, try to find a spare patch cable that you can use.

If you can't find a spare patch cable, try borrowing a fellow network user's patch cable. If the problem goes away when you use your neighbor's patch cable, you can assume that yours has gone south and needs to be replaced.

✔ If you come in late at night while no one is around, you can swap your bad patch cable with someone else's good cable, and no one will ever know. The next day, that neighbor will want to borrow this book from you so that he or she can find out what's wrong with the network. The day after that, someone else will need the book. You may never get your book back. You'd better buy a copy for everyone now.

Notice: Neither the author nor the publisher endorses such selfish behavior. We mention it here only so that you'll know what happened when one day someone down the hall has a network problem, and you suddenly have a network problem the next day.

✔ In some networks, computers are connected to one another via a small box called a *concentrator,* or *hub*. The concentrator is prone to cable problems, too — especially those concentrators that are wired in a "professional manner" involving a rat's nest of patch cables. Don't touch the rat's nest. Leave problems with the rat's nest to the rat — er, that is, the network guru.

A Bunch of Error Messages Flew By!

Did you notice any error messages on your computer screen when you started your computer? If so, write them down. They are invaluable clues that can help the network guru solve the problem.

✔ Don't panic if you see lots of error messages fly by. Sometimes a simple problem that's easy to correct can cause a plethora of error messages when you start your computer. It may look as if your computer is falling to pieces, but the fix may be very simple.

✔ If the messages fly by so fast that you can't see them, press your computer's Pause key. Your computer comes to a screeching halt, giving you a chance to catch up on your error-message reading. After you've read enough, press the Pause key again to get things moving. (On some computers, the Pause key is labeled "Hold." On computers that don't have a Pause key, pressing Ctrl+Num Lock or Ctrl+S does the same thing.)

✔ If you missed the error messages the first time, restart your computer and watch them again.

✔ Better yet, press F8 when you see the message Starting MS-DOS or Starting Windows. This processes each line of your CONFIG.SYS and AUTOEXEC.BAT files separately, enabling you to see the messages displayed by each command before proceeding to the next command.

Time to Experiment

If you can't find some obvious explanation for your troubles — like the computer's unplugged — you need to do a little experimenting to narrow down the possibilities. Design your experiments to answer one basic question: Is this a network problem, or is the problem local to your computer?

✓ Try performing the same operation on someone else's computer. If no one on the network can access a network drive or printer, something is probably wrong with the network. On the other hand, if you're the only one having trouble, the problem is with your computer alone. Your computer may not be reliably talking to the network or it isn't configured properly for the network, or the problem may have nothing to do with the network at all.

✓ If you're able to perform the operation on someone else's computer without problems, try logging on to the network with someone else's computer but using your own user ID. Then see whether you can perform the operation without error. If you can, your network guru will want to know.

✓ Try the operation without using the network. Log off the network using the Start⇨Logoff command. Then try the operation again.

If the symptoms of the problem remain the same whether your computer is logged onto the network or not, the problem is probably not with the network.

✓ What if the operation simply can't be done without the network? For example, what if the data files are on a network drive? Try copying the files to your local drive. Then log off the network and try the operation again, this time using the files on your local drive.

How to Restart Your Computer

Sometimes trouble gets your computer so tied up in knots that the only thing to do is reboot. In some cases, your computer just starts acting weird. Strange characters appear on the screen, or Windows goes haywire and won't let you exit a program. Sometimes your computer gets so confused it can't even move. It just sits there, like a deer staring at oncoming headlights. It won't move, no matter how hard you press the Esc key or the Enter key.

When your computer starts acting like this, it's time to reboot. The following procedure lists the steps for restarting your computer:

1. **Save your work if you can.**

   Use the File⇨Save command if you can to save any documents or files you were editing when things started to go haywire. If you can't use the menus, try clicking the Save button in the toolbar. If that doesn't work, try pressing Ctrl+S — the standard keyboard shortcut for the Save command.

2. **Close any running programs if you can.**

   Use the File⇨Exit command, or click the Close button in the upper right corner of the program window. Or press Alt+F4.

3. **Choose the Start⇨Shut Down command from the taskbar.**

    The Shut Down Windows dialog box appears.

4. **Select the Restart option and then click OK.**

    Your computer restarts itself.

 If restarting your computer doesn't seem to fix the problem, you may need to turn your computer all the way off, then turn it on again. To do so, follow the previous procedure until Step 4. Choose the Shut Down option instead of the Restart option and then click OK. Depending on your computer, Windows 95 will either turn off your computer or display a message that says It is now safe to turn off your computer. If Windows 95 doesn't turn the computer off for you, flip the On/Off switch to turn your computer off. Wait a few seconds and then turn the computer back on.

> ✔ If your computer refuses to respond to the Start⇨Shut Down command, try pressing the Ctrl, Alt, and Del keys at the same time. This is called the "three-finger salute." It's appropriate to say "Queueue" as you do it.
>
> When you press Ctrl+Alt+Del, Windows 95 and 98 display a dialog box that allows you to close any program that is running or shut down your computer entirely. In Windows 3.1 and Windows for Workgroups, pressing Ctrl+Alt+Del automatically restarts your computer.
>
> ✔ If Ctrl+Alt+Del doesn't do anything, you've reached the last resort. The only thing left to do is press the button labeled Reset on your computer.

> ✔ Pressing the Reset button (or, in Windows 3.1 or Windows for Workgroups, pressing Ctrl+Alt+Del) is a drastic action that you should take only after your computer has become completely unresponsive. Any work you haven't yet saved to disk is lost. (Sniff.)

> ✔ If at all possible, save your work before restarting your computer. Any work you haven't saved is lost. Unfortunately, if your computer is totally tied up in knots, you probably can't save your work. In that case, you have no choice but to jump off the digital cliff.

How to Restart the Network

If you think the network is causing your trouble, you can restart the network to see whether the problem goes away.

 Restarting a NetWare or Windows NT server is not a good idea unless your network administrator has shown you how to do it and has given you permission to do so. If you don't know what you're doing, you may not be able to get the server running again. In that case, you'll have to tuck your tail between your legs, call the network administrator, and apologize profusely for messing with the network when you know you shouldn't have.

Here is the basic procedure for restarting a network. Keep in mind that for NetWare or Windows NT servers, additional steps may be needed to get things going again. Check with your network administrator to be sure.

1. **Have all the users log off the network and turn off their computers.**

2. **After you're sure the users have logged off the network and shut down their computers, shut down the network server (assuming you have a dedicated server).**

   You want to do this like a good citizen if possible, decently and in order. If you use Novell NetWare, type DOWN at the server's keyboard and then reboot the server. For Windows NT Server, use the Start⇨Shut Down command.

3. **Reboot the server computer, or turn it off and then on again. Watch the server start up to make sure that no error messages appear.**

4. **Turn on each computer one at a time, making sure that each computer starts up without error.**

Remember the following when you consider restarting the network:

- ✔ Restarting the network is even more drastic than restarting your individual computer. Make sure that everyone saves his or her work and logs off the network before you do it! You can cause major problems if you blindly turn off the server computer while users are logged on.

- ✔ Obviously, restarting the network is a major inconvenience to every network user. Better offer treats.

- ✔ Restarting the network is a job for the network guru. Don't do it yourself unless the network guru isn't around, and even then, do it only after asking his or her permission in writing, preferably in triplicate.

The Care and Feeding of Your Network Guru

Your most valuable asset when something goes wrong with the network is your network guru. If you've been careful to stay on good terms with your guru, you'll be way ahead of the game when you need his or her help.

Make an effort to solve the problem yourself before calling in the cavalry. Check the network connection. Try rebooting. Try using someone else's computer. The more information you can provide the guru, the more appreciation you get.

Be polite, but assertively tell your guru what the problem is, what you tried to do to fix it, and what you think may be causing the problem (if you have a clue). Say something like this:

"Hi, Joe. I've got a problem with the network: I can't log in from my computer. I tried a few things to try to figure out the problem. I was able to log in from Wally's computer using my user ID, so I think the problem may be just with my computer.

"To be sure, I checked some other things. The green light on the back of my computer where the network cable plugs in is glowing, so I don't think it's a cable problem. I also rebooted my computer, but I still couldn't log on. Then I had everyone log off, and I restarted the server, but still no luck. My guess is that something may be wrong with my computer's network driver."

Blow into your guru's ear like that, and he'll follow you anywhere. (Of course, that may be an undesirable result.)

- Always remember your manners. No one likes to be yelled at, and even computer geeks have feelings (believe it or not). Be polite to your network guru even if you're mad or you think it's his fault. This may sound obvious, but you want your guru to like you.

- Don't call your guru every time the slightest little thing goes wrong. Computer experts hate explaining that the reason the computer is only printing in capital letters is that you've pressed the Caps Lock key.

- Read the manual. It probably won't help, but at least your guru thinks you've tried. Gurus like that.

- Humor your network guru when he tries to explain what's going on. Nod attentively when he describes what the bindery is or when he says something is wrong with the File Allocation Table. Smile appreciatively when he tries to simplify the explanation by using a colorful metaphor. Wink when he thinks you understand.

- Mimick your guru's own sense of humor, if you can. Say something like, "It's Joe, fixin' the network. Crimpin' the cable. Jumpin' Joe, the Net-o-Rama, rentin' an apartment at eight oh two dot three Ethernet Lane. Captain Joe of the Good Ship NetWare, goin' down with the server." Don't worry if it's not funny. He'll think it is.

Computer Bribes for Serious Network Trouble

A ...*For Dummies* book wouldn't be complete without a bribe list. You probably know already about the common foodstuffs most computer gurus respond to: Chee-tos, Doritos, Jolt Cola, Diet Coke (I wish they made Diet Jolt — twice the caffeine, twice the NutraSweet), Twinkies, and so on.

Bribes of this sort are suitable for small favors. But if you're having a serious problem with your network, you may need to lay it on a bit thicker. More serious bribes include the following:

- ✔ Computer games, especially 3-D shoot-em-ups. Quake is best.

- ✔ Videotapes of any Pink Panther, Monty Python, or Mel Brooks movie.

- ✔ T-shirts with strange stuff written on them or T-shirts from computer companies.

- ✔ Star Trek paraphernalia. A high percentage of computer gurus are also Trekkies, or as they sometimes prefer to be called, Trekers. Most of them like the original *Star Trek, The Next Generation,* and *Deep Space Nine*. Most don't care for *Voyager.*

If you want to really impress them, use the three-letter acronyms for each series: *TOS* for The Original Series, *TNG* for *The Next Generation,* and *DS9* for *Deep Space Nine.* (*VOY* is for *Voyager,* but since nobody likes *Voyager,* it doesn't matter.)

- ✔ Digitized sounds, if your guru has a sound card. You can never have enough digitized sounds. Anything from a Pink Panther movie ("Does your dog bite?"), *Saturday Night Live* ("All right, have a beer, make some copies, havin' a party!"), or *Home Improvement* ("Say, Al, do you suppose they call these coping saws because they're good at handling stress?") will do. Clips from a favorite Star Trek show are good bribes, too.

Don't give him a digitized recording of the famous "I've fallen and I can't get up" line. He already has five of those.

You can find an ample supply of digitized sounds on the Internet. If you don't have access to the Internet, it may be worth the cost just for the constant supply of bribes these files can provide.

Part II
Building Your Own Network

The 5th Wave — By Rich Tennant

"NOW JUST WHEN THE HECK DID I INTEGRATE THAT INTO THE SYSTEM?"

In this part . . .

You discover how to build a network yourself, which includes planning it and installing it. You find out what choices are available for cable types, network operating systems, and all the other bits and pieces that you have to contend with.

Yes, some technical information is included in these chapters. But fear not! I bring you tidings of great joy! Lo, a working network is at hand, and you, yea even you, can design it and install it yourself.

Chapter 6

The Bad News: You Have to Plan Ahead

*O*kay, so you're convinced you need to network your computers. What now? Do you stop by Computers-R-Us on the way to work, install the network before morning coffee, and expect the network to be fully operational by noon?

I don't think so.

Networking your computers is just like any other worthwhile endeavor: To do it right requires a bit of planning. This chapter is designed to help you think your network through before you start spending money. It shows you how to come up with a networking plan that's every bit as good as the plan a network consultant would charge you $1,000 for. See? This book is already saving you money!

Making a Network Plan

If you were to pay a consultant to study your business and prepare a networking plan, the result would be a 500-page proposal with the sole purpose, aside from impressing you with bulk, of preventing you from understanding just exactly what the consultant is proposing.

Truth is, you don't have to be a computer science major to make a good network plan. Despite what computer consultants want you to think, designing a small computer network isn't rocket science. You can do it yourself.

- ✔ Don't rush through the planning phase. The most costly networking mistakes are the ones you make before you put the network in. Think things through and consider alternatives.

- ✔ Write down the network plan. The plan doesn't have to be a fancy, 500-page document. (If you want to make it look good, pick up a ¹/₂-inch 3-ring binder. The binder is big enough to hold your network plan with room to spare.)

- ✔ Ask someone else to read your network plan before you buy anything, preferably someone who knows more about computers than you do.

Taking Stock

One of the most challenging parts of planning a network is figuring out how to work with the computers you already have. In other words, how do you get there from here? Before you can plan how to get "there," you have to know what "here" is. In other words, you have to take a thorough inventory of your current computers.

What you need to know

You need to know the following information about each of your computers:

- ✔ **The processor type and, if possible, its clock speed.** Hope that all your computers are 200MHz Pentiums or better. But in most cases, you find a mixture of Pentium and 486 processors with perhaps even some archaic 386, 286 and (heaven forbid) 8088 processors, with clock speeds ranging anywhere from 25MHz to 200MHz.

  Sometimes you can't tell what kind of processor you have just by looking at the box. Most computers, however, display the processor type when you turn them on or reboot them by pressing Ctrl+Alt+Del. For example, have a look at the screen shown in Figure 6-1. From this screen, you can tell that this poor user is stuck with a 33MHz 486 processor and should upgrade soon. (If the information on the startup screen scrolls away too quickly for you to read it, try pressing the Pause key to freeze the information. When you're finished reading it, press the Pause key again so that your computer can continue booting.)

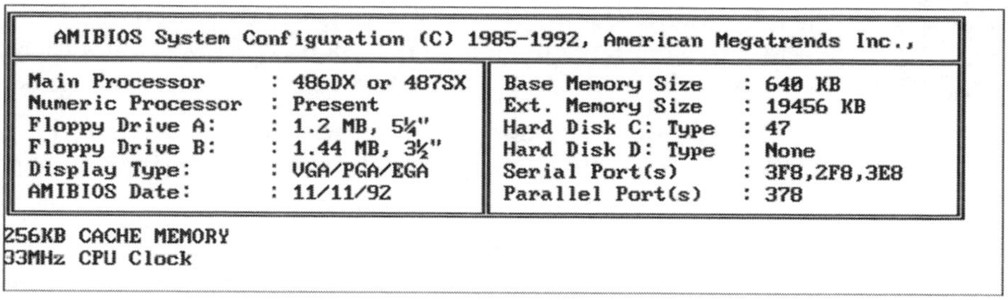

Figure 6-1:
A typical
start-up
screen
showing
useful
information
about the
computer.

```
AMIBIOS System Configuration (C) 1985-1992, American Megatrends Inc.,

Main Processor      : 486DX or 487SX   Base Memory Size    : 640 KB
Numeric Processor   : Present          Ext. Memory Size    : 19456 KB
Floppy Drive A:     : 1.2 MB, 5¼"      Hard Disk C: Type   : 47
Floppy Drive B:     : 1.44 MB, 3½"     Hard Disk D: Type   : None
Display Type:       : VGA/PGA/EGA      Serial Port(s)      : 3F8,2F8,3E8
AMIBIOS Date:       : 11/11/92         Parallel Port(s)    : 378

256KB CACHE MEMORY
33MHz CPU Clock
```

✔ **The size of the hard disk and the arrangement of its partitions.** Some really old computers have a 40MB hard disk divided into two partitions, so that the partitions appear to be two separate hard disks. That's okay, as long as you know how the partitions are set up.

On a Windows 95 or Windows 98 computer, you can find out the size of a hard disk by opening a My Computer window, right-clicking the drive icon, and choosing the Properties command from the shortcut menu that appears.

If your computer runs MS-DOS (with or without Windows), run the CHKDSK command from a DOS command prompt to find the size of your disk drives. When you run the CHKDSK command, it displays a whole bunch of numbers. For example:

```
Volume DOS  created on 09-15-1992 2:04p
Volume Serial Number is 16EA 0958
  44363776  bytes total disk space
  79872 bytes in 2 hidden files
  40960 bytes in 15 directories
  19443712  bytes in 569 user files
  20480 bytes in bad sectors
  24778752  bytes available on disk
  2048  bytes in each allocation unit
  21662 total allocation units on disk
  12099 available allocation units on disk
  655360     total bytes memory
  584512     bytes free
```

The two numbers that you're interested in here are the bytes of total disk space (44363776, about 44 million, or 44MB) and the bytes available on disk (24778752, about 24 million, or 24MB).

With DOS 6.2, Microsoft finally realized that most mortals can't quickly tell whether the number 44363776 is 443 thousand or 44 million, so Microsoft added commas to the numbers. Now, 44363776 appears as 44,363,776. Who says DOS isn't user friendly?

✓ **The amount of memory.** In Windows 95, you can find this out easily enough by right-clicking the My Computer desktop icon and choosing the Properties command. The amount of memory on your computer is displayed in the resulting dialog box.

If you're working with an older DOS-based computer, you have to fuss with three different kinds of memory: conventional, expanded, and extended. Use the CHKDSK command to find out how much conventional memory a computer has. If you have DOS 4.0 or a later version of DOS, you can type MEM to find out how much extended memory you have.

Expanded memory is found most often on older 8088 or 286 computers and doesn't affect the network much. Don't worry about it.

✓ **The version of DOS you're using.** Type VER to find out. To use a network, running at least version 3.3 is best. Network life is simpler if all your computers use the same DOS version.

✓ **What version of Windows you're running (if you're running Windows).** In Windows 3.*x,* choose the Help⇨About command from Program Manager to find out the Windows version. If you're using Windows 95, right-click the My Computer desktop icon and choose the Properties command.

✓ **What kind of monitor the computer has — monochrome, CGA, EGA, or VGA.** Often you can find out by reading the messages that appear when you turn on your computer.

✓ **What kind of printer, if any, is attached to the computer.**

✓ **What software is used on the computer.** Microsoft Office? WordPerfect? Lotus 1-2-3? Make a complete list, including version numbers.

Programs that gather information for you

Gathering information about your computers is a lot of work if you have more than a few computers to network. Fortunately, several software programs are available to automatically gather the information for you. These programs inspect various aspects of a computer, such as the CPU type and speed, amount of RAM, and the size of the computer's disk drives. Then they show the information on the screen and give you the option of saving the information to a disk file or printing it.

Windows 98 comes with just such a program, called *Microsoft System Information*. Microsoft System Information gathers and prints information about your computer. You'll find Microsoft System Information in the Start⇨Programs menu under Accessories.

When you fire up the Windows 98 Microsoft System Information program, you'll see a window similar to the one shown in Figure 6-2. Initially, Microsoft System Information displays basic information about your computer, such as the version of Microsoft Windows you are using, the processor type, the amount of memory on the computer, and the free space on each of the computer's disk drives. You can obtain more detailed information by clicking Resources, Components, or Software Environment in the left side of the window.

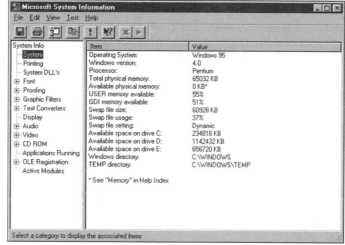

Figure 6-2: Microsoft System Information displays information about your computer.

If you don't have Windows 98 yet, don't panic. You may have an older version of Microsoft System Information anyway: Microsoft included it free with Office 95 and Office 97. To start Microsoft System Information from any of the Office programs (Word, Excel, or PowerPoint), choose the Help⇨About command. When the About dialog box appears, click the System Info button.

MS-DOS 6 (including 6.0, 6.2, and 6.22) includes a similar program called *MSD,* which stands for *Microsoft Diagnostics.* To run it, just type **MSD** at a DOS command prompt and press Enter.

Why Do You Need a Network, Anyway?

An important step in planning your network is making sure that you understand why you want the network in the first place. Here are some of the more common reasons for needing a network, all of them quite valid:

- ✔ My coworker and I exchange files using a floppy disk just about every day. With a network, we could trade files without using the floppies.

- ✔ I don't want to buy everyone a laser printer when I know the one we have now just sits there taking up space most of the day. Wouldn't buying a network be better than buying a laser printer for every computer?

- ✔ Someone figured out that we're destroying seven trees a day by printing interoffice memos on real paper, so we'd like to set up an e-mail system.

- ✔ Business is so good that one person typing in orders eight hours each day can't keep up. With a network, I could have two people entering orders, and I wouldn't have to pay either one overtime.

- ✔ My brother-in-law just put in a network at his office, and I don't want him to think I'm behind the times.

Make sure that you identify all the reasons you think you need a network and write them down. Don't worry about winning the Pulitzer Prize for your stunning prose. Just make sure that you've written down what you expect a network will do for you.

If you were making a 500-page networking proposal, you'd place the description of why a network is needed in a tabbed section labeled "Justification." In your $1/2$-inch network binder, file it under "Why."

As you consider the reasons you need a network, you may come to the conclusion that you don't need a network after all. That's okay. You can always use the binder for your stamp collection.

Three Basic Network Decisions You Can't Avoid

When you plan a computer network, you're confronted with three inescapable network decisions. You can't install the network until you've made these decisions. The decisions are weighty enough that I've devoted a separate section in this chapter to each one.

Stupid stuff about printer switches

If your only reason for networking is to share a printer, a cheaper way may exist: Buy a switch box instead of a network. Switch boxes let two or more computers share a single printer. Instead of running a cable directly from computer to printer, you run cables from each computer to the switch box and then run one cable from the switch box to the printer. Only one of the computers has access to the printer at a time; the switch decides which one.

You can find two kinds of printer switches:

Manual printer switches have a knob on the front that enables you to select which computer is connected to the printer. When you use a manual switch, you first must make sure that the knob is set to your computer before you try to print. Turning the knob while someone else is printing probably will cost you a bag of doughnuts.

Automatic printer switches have a built-in electronic ear that listens to each computer. When it hears one of the computers trying to talk to the printer, the electronic ear automatically connects that computer to the printer. The switch also has an electronic holding pen called a *buffer* that can hold printer output from one computer if another computer is using the printer. Automatic switches aren't foolproof, but they work most of the time.

Naturally, a good automatic switch costs more than a manual switch. For example, a manual switch that can allow four computers to share one printer costs about $20. A decent automatic switch to enable four computers to share a printer can set you back about $75. Still, that's a lot cheaper than a full-blown network.

It's been a long time since I've introduced a new TLA (three-letter acronym), so call these basic network decisions BNDs, which stands for — you guessed it — "basic network decisions."

BND #1: What network operating system will you use?

You have many network operating systems from which to choose, but from a practical point of view, your choices are limited to the following:

 ✔ Novell NetWare, the most popular network operating system for large networks. NetWare requires that you dedicate at least one computer to act as a network server, and it can be a challenge for a novice user to install. With NetWare, the client computers can run DOS or any version of Windows. Plus, you can easily connect Macintosh computers to a NetWare network.

✔ Windows NT Server, a special version of Windows which, like NetWare, requires that you dedicate one or more computers to act as network servers. Windows NT Server is best used when all the client computers run some version of Windows — preferably Windows 95. However, Windows NT Server can be made to work with DOS and Macintosh client computers.

✔ If you don't want to dedicate a computer to function as a server, you can build the entire network using Windows 95 or Windows for Workgroups on your client computers.

✔ Artisoft's LANtastic offers many peer-to-peer networking features that aren't provided by Windows 95 or Windows for Workgroups. You may want to consider using LANtastic, if you want to set up a sophisticated peer-to-peer network that can share printers, disk drives, and other devices such as modems or fax machines, or if many of your computers run DOS but not Windows.

✔ You can start with a simple peer-to-peer network using Windows 95 and Windows for Workgroups now and then upgrade to NetWare or Windows NT Server later. All the networks listed in this section use the same cable, network interface cards, hubs, and so on. Changing from one to another is a matter of reconfiguring the software. (Of course, to change from a peer-to-peer network to NetWare or Windows NT Server, you must have a dedicated server computer.)

✔ You can also build a peer-to-peer network using Windows 95 or Windows for Workgroups and then upgrade to LANtastic later. If all your computers run Windows 95, I recommend this approach. After all, in Windows 95 you already have all the software you need to get a network up and running. Spend your time and money getting the network interface cards and cables working. Then you can add LANtastic later if you find that Windows 95 networking isn't enough for your needs.

✔ Chapter 7 describes the advantages and disadvantages of each of these systems so that you can decide which is the best choice for your network.

BND #2: What arrangement of server computers will you use?

Peer-to-peer networks like Windows 95 or Windows 98, Windows for Workgroups, and LANtastic don't require you to use dedicated server computers. This doesn't mean that dedicated server computers can and should be used only with NetWare or Windows NT Server. On the contrary, if you can possibly afford it, a dedicated server computer is almost always the way to go, no matter what network operating system you use.

✔ Using a dedicated server computer even on a peer-to-peer network makes the network faster, easier to work with, and more reliable. Consider what happens when the user of a server computer doubling as a workstation decides to turn the computer off, not realizing that someone else is accessing files on his or her disk drive.

✔ You don't necessarily have to use your biggest and fastest computer as your server computer. I've seen networks where the slowest computer on the network is the server. This is especially true when the server is used mostly to share a printer.

✔ When you plan your server configuration, you must also plan how your data and program files will be dispersed on the network. For example, will all users have copies of Microsoft Office on their local drives, or will one copy of Office be stored on the server drive? (Within the limits of your software license, of course.)

✔ Planning your server configuration also means assigning network drive letters for computers requiring you to map drive letters to network drives. Be consistent about this so that a particular network drive is accessed by using the same drive letter from every computer.

✔ Server configuration is heady enough to merit its own chapter: Chapter 8.

BND #3: How will you cable the network?

The third basic networking decision is how to connect your computers.

✔ You must choose between two basic types of network cabling: Twisted-pair cable (called UTP or 10baseT) and standard coax cable (called thinnet). Advantages and disadvantages exist to each, and using a mixture of both is possible and sometimes desirable. (For information about the differences between these two types of cables, refer to the section "What Makes it Tick?" in Chapter 1. Or, skip ahead to Chapter 9 for even more gory details.)

✔ You must also pick the network interface cards to install in each computer. Using the same card in each computer is best, although it's also possible to mix and match. The card you select must be compatible with the cable you select.

✔ If you use twisted-pair cable, you also need a network hub.

✔ As you plan your network cabling, you need to draw a floor plan showing the location of each computer and the route the cables will follow.

✔ The details of network cabling are covered in Chapter 9.

Networks to Go: Using a Network Starter Kit

For me one of the most fun parts of building a network is going to my local computer store and filling a shopping cart full of stuff. I love to wander the aisles and pick out a network hub, network interface cards, cables, connectors, and other goodies.

If shopping isn't your bag, you can buy all the pieces you need to network two or three computers in a single box. A typical network starter kit for three computers includes three Ethernet network interface cards, a hub, three twisted pair cables with connectors already attached so you can connect all three computers to the hub, and instructions for hooking everything up. A kit of this sort costs between $300 and $350, depending on where you purchase it and who manufactures the individual components placed in the kit.

One important piece of the networking puzzle that is missing from these kits is the network operating system itself. To use a starter kit, you must first have Windows 95 or another network-ready operating system (such as Windows for Workgroups, Windows NT Workstation, or LANtastic) installed on your computer.

The starter kit accommodates the first two or three computers in your network. For each additional computer you want to connect, you purchase an add-on kit that contains a network interface card and a cable.

> ✔ The cable that comes with the starter kit is generally 25 feet long. If your computers are farther apart than that, you have to buy a separate cable.

> ✔ Network kits typically come with moderately priced network interface cards. You often can save money by purchasing the components separately so that you can buy a less-expensive interface card.

> ✔ Artisoft — the company that makes LANtastic — also sells starter kits which include the hardware necessary to network two computers plus two copies of the LANtastic network operating system. You can get a two-computer starter kit for about $250 and single-computer add-on kits for about $150 each.

A Sample Network Plan

Consider a typical family business: Cleavers' Baseball Card Emporium, which buys and sells valuable as well as worthless baseball cards and other baseball memorabilia.

The Cleavers' computer inventory

The Cleavers have four computers:

- Ward's computer is a brand-new 266MHz Pentium II with 64MB of RAM and a 6GB disk drive. Ward runs Microsoft Windows 98 for spreadsheet analysis (Excel) and occasional word processing (Word). He also has a laser printer.

- June's computer is a 33MHz 486 with 4MB of RAM and a 300MB hard disk. June runs Windows 3.1 and does most of the company's word processing work with an old version of Word for Windows. She has a near-letter-quality dot-matrix printer but would like to use Ward's laser printer to print letters.

- Wally's computer is a 386 with 2MB of RAM and an 80MB hard drive. Wally keeps the company's inventory records on his computer by using a database program called Q&A.

- The Beave's computer is a genuine IBM AT computer with a 286 processor, 512K of RAM, and a 20MB hard disk. Beaver's computer also includes a modem. Beaver uses the computer mostly to communicate with an on-line service for market research and to play Pong.

Why the Cleavers need a network

The Cleavers want to network their computers for two simple reasons:

1. So that everyone can access the laser printer.

2. So that everyone can access the inventory database.

If it weren't for reason 2, a network wouldn't be necessary. The Cleavers could share the laser printer by purchasing a simple printer sharing switch that would enable all four computers to access the printer (see the sidebar "Stupid stuff about printer switches" earlier in this chapter). But to give everyone access to the inventory database, a network is required.

Network operating system

None of the Cleavers is a computer whiz, so they've opted for a simple peer-to-peer network operating system: LANtastic. It enables them to share the printer and the disk drive containing the inventory database — so it adequately meets their needs.

Ward wanted to use Windows 98 networking because he heard the hearts game is great on a network. But he backed off when he remembered that Wally's and Beave's computers can't run Windows 98. They ruled out both NetWare and Windows NT Server because the family can't afford a separate server computer (see the "Server configuration" section).

Server configuration

Because the Cleavers can't afford a separate computer to use as a server, two of the computers do double duty as both clients and servers. Ward's computer is set up as a client/server so that everyone can access his printer, and Wally's computer is set up as a client/server so that everyone can access the inventory database.

After the network is up and running, Wally is considering moving the inventory database to Ward's computer. That way, only one server computer has to be managed. Because Ward doesn't use his computer often, he probably won't mind the small reduction in performance as other users access his disk. (Of course, since Ward is both company CEO and the head of the household, he wouldn't consider trading his high-powered computer with June, who uses her computer six or seven hours every day. Sigh.)

Network cabling

For simplicity, the Cleavers have opted to wire their network with thinnet coax cable. All four computers are located in the spacious den, so the floor plan presents no unusual wiring problems. To simplify shopping, the Cleavers decided to purchase a LANtastic starter kit for two of the computers and two one-computer add-on kits for the other two.

Figure 6-3 shows the floor plan for the Cleavers' network setup. You can see how they plan to run the cable.

After the Cleavers have their network plan in hand, setting up the network is a simple matter of buying the necessary network cards and cable and the LANtastic networking software and then setting everything up. It won't take them more than a couple of hours to get their network up and running.

Chapter 7 takes you on an informal tour of the various options for creating your own network — Windows 95, Windows 98, Windows NT Server, NetWare, Windows for Workgroups, and LANtastic — and gives you the information to decide which network is the right one for you.

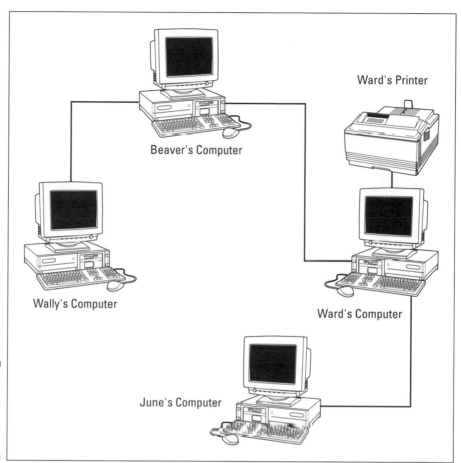

Figure 6-3:
Floor plan
for the
Cleavers'
network.

Chapter 7

Choose Your Weapon (or, Which Network Should I Use?)

*O*ne of the basic choices you must make before you go too far is which network operating system you'll use as the foundation for your network. This chapter provides an overview of the advantages and disadvantages of the most popular network operating systems. It starts with Novell IntranetWare, the most popular network operating system. A description of Novell's chief competitor, Windows NT server, comes next. Then the chapter describes three peer-to-peer networks: Microsoft Windows 95 (soon to be Windows 98), Windows for Workgroups, and Artisoft's LANtastic.

Novell's NetWare (Oops, I Mean IntranetWare)

IntranetWare is the latest incarnation of Novell's popular NetWare network operating system. IntranetWare is based on version 4.11 of NetWare and includes a number of extra goodies which add Internet capabilities to your LAN. You can use IntranetWare to create networks consisting of hundreds of computers, but it's also suitable for smaller networks.

IntranetWare includes NetWare 4.11. If you prefer, you can purchase NetWare 4.11 separately. However, IntranetWare and NetWare 4.11 are priced the same. Since the extra Internet goodies that come with IntranetWare are essentially free, it makes little sense to buy NetWare 4.11 by itself.

Mumbo jumbo about why NetWare is slicker than DOS

Because NetWare doesn't rely on the primitive file management of DOS, it's free to use more efficient file-handling techniques. A survey of NetWare's standard efficiency techniques reads like a syllabus for a graduate-level computer science class.

Caching means keeping a copy of recently read disk data in memory with the hope that the same data will be needed again. If it is, disk access can be avoided. DOS uses caching too, but NetWare's caching features are much more sophisticated than the primitive caching provided by DOS.

Directory hashing is an efficient way to locate directory files on disk. Because of directory hashing, NetWare can find a file much faster than DOS can.

Elevator seeking is a way to improve disk access for a busy file server. Picture the way an elevator works and you'll get the idea. Suppose that three people get on an elevator. The first person presses the button for the 10th floor, the second for the 4th floor, and the third for the 7th floor. The elevator doesn't go to floor 10, then come back to floor 4, then go up to floor 7. Instead, it stops at the floors in order: 4, then 7, then 10. If three people request disk access at nearly the same time, DOS services the requests in the order in which they were received. NetWare, on the other hand, rearranges the requests so that they can be serviced as efficiently as possible.

Novell also still sells version 3.12 of NetWare, mostly for those who have large NetWare 3.12 networks already in place and want to expand them. If you're building a new network, opt for IntranetWare rather than NetWare 3.12, especially considering the fact that NetWare 3.12 is actually more expensive than the newer IntranetWare.

In this book, I use the term *NetWare* to refer to the NetWare operating system, regardless of the version. I use the term *IntranetWare* only when I want to refer specifically to the combination of NetWare 4.11 and the Internet tools that come along with the IntranetWare package.

What's so great about NetWare?

Throughout this book, I've pounded NetWare a bit for being overly complicated. However, a lot can be said in favor of NetWare. NetWare can be complicated to set up and administer, but it's far and away the most popular network operating system in use. There must be something good to say about it!

✔ When Novell set out to design NetWare way back in the 1980s, it recognized that the old DOS operating system just didn't cut it when networking. Rather than live with the limitations of DOS, Novell decided to bypass DOS altogether. NetWare file servers don't run DOS; instead, NetWare itself is the operating system for the file server. This frees NetWare from the many built-in limitations of DOS.

✔ Because NetWare servers don't run DOS, NetWare servers must be dedicated as servers. In other words, you can't have a NetWare server double as a user's workstation. This setup costs more because you must purchase a separate server computer. However, it's more efficient because the server computer can concentrate on servicing the network.

✔ Clients on a NetWare network can be DOS- or Windows-based computers, computers running OS/2, or Macintoshes. If you have a mix of PCs and Macintoshes, NetWare may be your best choice.

✔ The NetWare file server uses a more efficient structure for organizing files and directories than DOS. With NetWare, you can divide each disk drive into one or more volumes, which are similar to DOS logical drives.

Novell volumes have names rather than single drive letters. To access a NetWare volume from a DOS client computer, a drive letter is assigned to the volume. But you can access a NetWare volume from a Windows 95 client using the volume's name.

✔ NetWare provides a special filing system called Btrieve. Btrieve is used mostly by specialized application programs that you can buy for your business. For example, if your business is a video store, you can buy specialized video-store software that uses Btrieve. If you run a farming operation, you can buy specialized agricultural software that uses Btrieve. But general-purpose software, such as word processing and spreadsheet programs, doesn't use Btrieve.

If you work with specialized software that uses Btrieve, that software runs more efficiently on NetWare than on a peer-to-peer network.

✔ All versions of NetWare provide features for System Fault Tolerance (SFT), which are designed to keep the network running even if a hardware failure occurs.

✔ NetWare 4.11 can support very large networks. Here's the run-down on just how large a NetWare 4.11 network can get:

- Up to 1,000 users.

- Up to 100,000 files open simultaneously on each server.

- Up to 16 million files per volume.

- Up to 64 disk volumes per server. (This means that the theoretical maximum number of files per server is 16 million times 64, which works out to a little over one billion. Novell should put up a sign that says "Over One Billion Files Served.")

- Each volume can be chopped into as many as 1,024 logical drives.

- Each server can support a total of 32,768GB of disk storage.

- A single file can be as large as 4GB.

The disadvantages of NetWare

NetWare is among the best networking systems available, but that doesn't mean it's the best choice for your network. There are a number of disadvantages to using NetWare for small networks.

✔ A NetWare network is definitely more complicated to set up than a peer-to-peer network based on Windows 95. The learning curve is steep. Windows 95 comes with an instruction manual that's so small you can almost call it a pamphlet. NetWare comes with thousands of pages of manuals.

If you learn computer stuff pretty quickly, you can probably handle NetWare. Otherwise, using NetWare probably means you'll have to hire a consultant to install it for you. That's not necessarily a bad thing; just remember that installing NetWare is not a do-it-yourself project unless you're pretty good with computers.

✔ The hardware for a NetWare system costs more than for a peer-to-peer network because you must dedicate at least one computer as a file server. (However, the networking components — adapter cards, cable, and so on — don't cost any more. And if you use a dedicated file server for your peer-to-peer network, the hardware costs are the same.)

✔ Then, there's the cost of NetWare itself. If you build a peer-to-peer network based on Windows 95, you don't have to pay extra for the networking software because networking is built in to Windows 95. But if you opt for NetWare, you have to purchase the NetWare software for your server.

The price of the NetWare server software varies depending on how many client computers your network will have. Unfortunately, you can't buy NetWare client licenses one at a time. Instead, you purchase the NetWare software along with a licensing option that enables you to use it for 5, 10, 25, 50, 100, 250, 500, or 1,000 users. If your network has 6 users, you must pay for the 10-user version. If you have 11 users, you must buy the 25-user version.

Table 7-1 shows the prices for IntranetWare as of November, 1997. The pricing for NetWare 4.11 was the same. As you can see, the cost per user is smaller for larger networks. (Note that you can probably purchase IntranetWare at a discount from mail order suppliers, a software store, or most any software reseller.)

This pricing scheme isn't so bad for larger networks. But because peer-to-peer networks are usually sold one copy per user, they're often cheaper for small networks.

Table 7-1	The Cost of IntranetWare	
Number of Users	*Price*	*Cost Per User*
5	$1,095.00	$219.00
10	$2,095.00	$209.50
25	$3,695.00	$147.80
50	$4,995.00	$99.90
100	$6,995.00	$69.95
250	$12,995.00	$51.98
500	$24,995.00	$49.99
1,000	$47,995.00	$47.99

I don't get a penny for promoting *Networking with NetWare For Dummies*

If you think NetWare is the networking system for you, be sure to get a copy of IDG Books Worldwide's *Networking with NetWare For Dummies,* 3rd Edition, by Ed Tittel, Deni Connor, and Earl Follis. This is a great book that shows you how to install, use, and manage your network and keep your sanity.

I thought I should get like a 2 percent commission or something for promoting *Networking with NetWare For Dummies,* 3E here, but no such luck. Bummer. Get the book anyway.

TIP

Do you have the savvy to install NetWare?

How do you know whether you have what it takes to contend with NetWare? Try this little self test. If you know all (or most) of the answers to these questions, you probably have enough computer savvy to figure out NetWare. If not, don't feel bad. As it says (sort of) in the Good Book, "Some are prophets, some are evangelists, some are teachers, some are NetWare administrators, some are Computer Dummies. . . ."

1. What command do you use to copy all the files, including files in subdirectories, from drive A to the current directory?

   A. FDISK
   B. DELETE A:*.*
   C. FORMAT C:
   D. XCOPY A:*.* /S

2. Which of these files is processed every time you start your computer?

   A. LETSGETGOING.BAT
   B. GETUPYOULITTLESLEEPY HEAD.COM

   C. YOURANG.LURCH
   D. AUTOEXEC.BAT

3. Which of the following bribes are appropriate when enlisting the help of a computer guru?

   A. Chee-tos
   B. Doritos
   C. Doughnuts
   D. All the above

4. Who is the most dangerous man in all of France?

   A. Jacques Cousteau
   B. Marcel Marceau
   C. Big Bird
   D. Chief Inspector Jacques Clouseau

If you answered D to three or more of these questions, you probably have the savvy to install NetWare yourself, unless the one you missed was #3, in which case you don't have a prayer.

Network Directory Service (A.k.a. NDS)

In previous versions of NetWare, information about the resources that were available on each server and the users that could log on were stored in a special file called the *bindery* on the server. Each server's bindery contained information only about the resources on that particular server. The bindery meant that as a user, you had to log on separately to each server that contained resources you wanted to use.

With NetWare version 4.11, the bindery has been replaced by a feature called the Network Directory Service, or NDS. NDS is like a super bindery for the entire network. With NDS, you don't have to log on to individual servers. Instead, you log on to the network just once to gain access to any of the network's resources.

NDS isn't particularly important for small networks with only one server. For large networks with dozens of servers, though, NDS is a major improvement because it dramatically simplifies management of the servers.

How much computer do you need for NetWare 4.11?

Novell claims that NetWare 4.11 can run on any 386-based computer with at least 8MB of RAM and 55MB of free disk space. This may be possible, but I sure wouldn't want to try it. A more realistic minimum setup for a NetWare 4.11 server computer is something like this:

- ✔ Pentium Processor, at least 100MHz.
- ✔ 32MB of RAM. 64MB is better.
- ✔ 2G of disk space.

This setup gives you enough computing horsepower, RAM, and disk space to make NetWare run decently for a small network. For a larger network, you have to allow more RAM and disk space.

Novell has a complicated formula that can help you estimate the memory needed for a Netware server. If you're interested in such things, you can find it on the Internet by going to the following Web address:

```
http://developer.novell.com/research/appnotes/1997/march/
01/04.html
```

What about NetWare 3.12?

NetWare 3.12 is an older version of NetWare which is often used for smaller networks. Although NetWare 3.12 can support up to 250 users, it's best for networks with just a few dozen users. If you have more than 250 users, you must use NetWare 4.11 instead. Novell says that NetWare 3.12 can run on a server computer with as little as 6MB of RAM, but that's not enough. I wouldn't do it with less than 16MB of RAM on the server.

Although you can still purchase NetWare 3.12, you may be surprised to discover that IntranetWare is actually slightly less expensive than NetWare 3.12. In addition, IntranetWare is a bit easier to install and manage than NetWare 3.12 because IntranetWare sports a nice graphical user interface, whereas NetWare 3.12 relies more on cryptic commands. I'd go with IntranetWare rather than NetWare 3.12, even for small networks.

Windows NT Server 4.0

Windows NT Server is Microsoft's answer to NetWare. For the longest time, Microsoft played second fiddle to Novell. Recently, however, Windows NT Server has gained ground on NetWare, and today it's a toss-up as to which server to choose. If you want to stay with an all-Microsoft network, Windows NT Server is the way to go.

The newest incarnation of Windows NT Server is version 4.0. NT Server 4.0 uses the popular and friendly user interface of Windows 95. As a result, if you know how to use Windows 95, you'll have no trouble working with NT Server 4.0.

Similar to Novell IntranetWare, Windows NT Server 4.0 also comes with a bunch of free Internet tools. These tools enable you to connect to the Internet and set up your own Internet Web site. In addition, you can use the Internet tools to set up an Intranet, which is simply a Web site that can be accessed only from the computers that are on your LAN.

Here's a summary of NT's more pertinent features:

- NT Server supports an unlimited number of users.
- The server processor must be at least a 486, with at least 16MB of memory. Yeah, right. I wouldn't try it on anything smaller than a 100MHz Pentium with 32MB of RAM.
- Here are some of the file-system limits:
  - Max number of users: unlimited
  - Number of volumes: 25
  - Max size of a volume: 17,000GB
  - Max disk space for server: 408,000GB
  - Largest file: 17 billion GB (Wow! That's more than the maximum disk space for a server, which is impossible!)
  - Max amount of RAM in server: 4GB
  - Max number of open files: unlimited
- NT Server is priced differently than NetWare. For NT Server, you buy the server with 5 client licenses for $809 or 10 client licenses for $1,129. Then you can add additional client licenses for $39.95 apiece, or you can buy client licenses 20 at a time for $659 (which works out to $32.95 per client). For the sake of comparing prices with NetWare, Table 7-2 shows the price of NT Server for 5, 10, 25, 50, 100, 250, 500, and 1,000 users.

✔ Another price consideration for NT Server: Microsoft doesn't have a "Suggested Retail Price." Retailers who sell NT Server can charge whatever they want for it, so you have to shop around for the best price. The prices shown in Table 7-2 are Microsoft's own estimates of the actual retail price for NT Server based on a survey of actual retailers.

Table 7-2		The Cost of Windows NT Server 4.0	
Number of Users	*Price*	*Explanation*	*Cost Per User*
5	$809	5-user Server	$161.00
10	$1,129	10-user Server	$112.90
25	$1,468	5-user Server + 20-user client	$58.72
50	$2,447	10-user Server + 2 20-user clients	$48.94
100	$4,104	5-user Server + 5 20-user clients	$41.04
250	$9,037	10-user Server + 12 20-user clients	$36.15
500	$17,284	5-user Server + 25 20-user clients	$34.57
1,000	$33,759	5-user Server + 50 20-user clients	$33.76

✔ Windows NT Server is part of a family of products from Microsoft called Microsoft BackOffice. Besides NT Server, BackOffice includes the following:

- Microsoft SQL Server, a database program
- Microsoft Exchange Server for improved electronic mail
- Microsoft Site Server for creating advanced Internet Web sites
- Microsoft SNA Server to connect to mainframe computers
- Microsoft System Management Server to manage large networks

Anticipating Windows NT Server 5.0

At the time of this writing, Microsoft is preparing to release a new version of Windows NT Server, known as version 5.0. It will sport a variety of new features, including:

✔ Active Directory, which provides a single directory of all network resources and enables program developers to incorporate the directory into their programs. Active Directory will integrate various directory services such as Novell's NDS and NT's own directory services and enable you to manage all the directory information on your network using a single interface which resembles the Internet's World Wide Web.

(continued)

(continued)

✔ Each user on the network will automatically be given a "My Documents" folder on an NT server for managing personal documents. My Computer is the default storage location for user documents.

✔ A new set of administration Wizards simplifies the task of managing the network.

✔ Support for up to 32GB of RAM on a server computer.

NT Server 5.0 includes many other features as well. It will undoubtedly be a big hit when it comes out.

OS/2 Warp Server

Although NetWare and NT Server are the two most popular choices for network operating systems, IBM's OS/2 Warp Server is one operating system that you shouldn't overlook. It's comparable in many ways to both NetWare and NT Server. OS/2 Warp Server offers advanced file and print server features and supports DOS, Windows 3.x, Windows 95, and Macintosh client computers.

OS/2 Warp Server comes in two versions. The basic OS/2 Warp Server is designed for smaller networks and can support up to 120 users per server. In addition, the server doesn't have to be dedicated. OS/2 Warp Server costs $559.

For larger networks, you can opt for OS/2 Warp Server Advanced. This $1,179 package includes more advanced networking features and can support up to 1,000 users on a single server.

One of OS/2 Warp Server's biggest limitations is its lack of a global directory service, such as NetWare's NDS or the Active Directory feature that will be available with Windows NT Server 5.0.

Peer-to-Peer Networks

If you're not up to the complexity of NetWare or NT, you may want to opt for a simpler network such as Windows 95 (or the soon-to-be-released Windows 98), Windows for Workgroups, or LANtastic.

Why peer-to-peer networks are easier to use

Peer-to-peer networks are easier to set up and use than NetWare or NT mainly because they don't require you to jettison your familiar DOS or Windows operating system in favor of a specialized network operating system. Instead, peer-to-peer networks just add network capabilities to your existing DOS- or Windows-based computers.

Although DOS and Windows limit the capabilities of these networks, these networks are easier to use because you don't have to find out the ins and outs of a foreign operating system. Everything you already know about DOS and Windows — even if that's not very much — can help you when you set up a peer-to-peer network.

✔ Peer-to-peer networks don't require that you use a dedicated server computer. Any computer on the network can function both as a network server and as a user's workstation. (However, you can configure a computer as a dedicated server if you want to. This results in better performance.)

✔ One reason peer-to-peer networks are easier to set up and use is that they don't provide as many advanced features as NetWare or NT. Peer-to-peer networks don't provide the same fault tolerance features, their security systems aren't as advanced, and they don't provide as many options for tweaking performance. With fewer variables to worry about, mastering the equation is easier.

Drawbacks of peer-to-peer networks

Yes, peer-to-peer networks are easier to install and manage than NetWare or NT, but they aren't without their drawbacks.

✔ Because peer-to-peer networks are DOS- or Windows-based, they're subject to the inherent limitations of DOS and Windows. DOS and Windows just aren't designed with a network server in mind, so they can never manage a file server as efficiently as a real network operating system.

✔ If you don't set up a dedicated network server, someone (hopefully not you) may have to live with the inconvenience of sharing his or her computer with the network. With NetWare or NT Server, the server computers are dedicated to network use so that no one has to put up with this inconvenience.

✔ Although a peer-to-peer network may have a lower cost per computer for smaller networks, the cost difference between peer-to-peer networks and NetWare or NT is less significant in larger networks (say, 20 or more clients).

Windows 95

Windows 95, the current version of Windows at the time I wrote this, includes everything you need to set up a peer-to-peer network. If all your computers are running Windows 95, you only have to purchase network cards and cable to build a network.

Here are the more salient features of Windows 95 networking:

- ✔ Windows 95 automatically detects most networking cards and configures itself to work with them.

- ✔ Windows 95 enables you to access the network through a desktop icon called Network Neighborhood. It's child's play.

- ✔ Windows 95 can connect to other Windows 95 computers or to Windows for Workgroups, Windows NT Server, or NetWare servers.

- ✔ Windows 95 includes a great Hearts game that can be played with other network users.

Anticipating Windows 98

At the time I wrote this, Microsoft was preparing to release a new version of Windows, to be called Windows 98. Windows 98 will build on Windows 95 in several ways, the most important being that Microsoft's Internet browser program, called Internet Explorer, will be integrated into Windows itself so that the distinction between resources on your computer, your local area network, and the Internet will be blurred. Windows 98 will enable you to view the files and folders on your computer's local hard drives and on your network servers as if they're a part of the World Wide Web. In fact, folders displayed by My Computer or Network Neighborhood windows resemble Web documents.

I love the irony in all of this. Back in 1995, when Microsoft sprang Windows 95 on the world, Microsoft also introduced a brand new online service called The Microsoft Network. One of the chief selling points of the Microsoft Network was that it used the same user interface

as Windows 95, so you didn't have to learn two different user interfaces: one to use your computer, the other to use your online service (which included Internet access). In essence, the design of Windows 95 and The Microsoft Network was an attempt to make the Internet look like Windows. The attempt fell flat on its face.

Now, with Windows 98, Microsoft has done a complete about-face. Instead of trying to make the Internet look like Windows, it's trying to make Windows look like the Internet.

Apart from Internet features, the networking features of Windows 98 are basically the same as the networking features that were built in to Windows 95. Microsoft has made minor improvements here and there, but no major new networking features have been added. Windows 95 and Windows 98 computers can coexist peacefully on the same network.

Windows for Workgroups

Although Microsoft wants you to believe that Windows 95 (soon to be replaced by Windows 98) is the ultimate version of Windows, many computer users are still quite happy with Windows 3.1. If you're one of them, the good news is that you don't have to upgrade to Windows 95 to network your Windows computers. Instead, you can upgrade to a special networking version of Windows called Windows for Workgroups. Unlike Windows 95, Windows for Workgroups doesn't require that you switch to the newfangled Windows 95 desktop interface just to add networking capabilities.

Here are the interesting features of Windows for Workgroups:

- ✔ Windows for Workgroups includes an enhanced version of File Manager that provides menu functions for managing network disk drives and an enhanced version of Print Manager for managing network printers.

- ✔ One of the most interesting features of Windows for Workgroups is the network clipboard, which enables you to cut or copy data from an application on one computer and paste it into an application on another.

- ✔ Windows for Workgroups also comes with Microsoft Mail, a sophisticated electronic mail program, and a scheduling program that enables you to schedule meetings with other network users.

- ✔ Windows for Workgroups works best on networks where all the computers run Windows. To use a non-Windows computer with a Windows for Workgroups network, you must purchase a separate program called Workgroup Connection. A DOS computer running Workgroup Connection can access resources on a Windows for Workgroups server but can't act as a server itself.

- ✔ Windows for Workgroups can be integrated with a NetWare network or a Windows NT Server network. That task, however, is best left to a professional.

Artisoft's LANtastic

Artisoft's LANtastic was once the most popular peer-to-peer network operating system. Ever since Microsoft decided to include peer-to-peer networking for free with Windows 95, LANtastic has become somewhat less popular. It's ideal for networks of 2 to 25 computers but can also be used on larger networks of 100 or more computers.

✔ LANtastic is easy to install. The entire program comes on one disk and can be installed in just a few minutes.

✔ LANtastic includes an option that enables you to dedicate a computer for use as a server. Although a dedicated LANtastic server won't operate as efficiently as a dedicated NetWare or NT server, it's more efficient than a Windows 95 or Windows for Workgroups server.

✔ Artisoft also manufactures top-quality network interface cards, and you can purchase the LANtastic software in kits bundled with Artisoft's cards.

✔ You can use LANtastic with network interface cards made by other vendors, as long as the cards are NE2000 compatible (I explain what that means in Chapter 8). To use another vendor's network card with LANtastic, you must purchase a copy of the Adapter Independent version of the LANtastic software (known as LANtastic AI) for each computer. You often can save $25–$50 per computer by purchasing a less-expensive network adapter card and LANtastic AI rather than purchasing an Artisoft adapter card.

✔ LANtastic runs on DOS, Windows, or Windows 95. A version that runs with Windows NT is expected soon. However, no Macintosh version of LANtastic is available. If you need to mix PCs and Macs in your network, LANtastic is probably not a good choice.

✔ Unlike Windows 95 or Windows for Workgroups networking, LANtastic can share modems and an Internet connection. If you want to enable your network users to connect to the Internet through a shared modem, LANtastic is the way to go.

✔ Artisoft also makes an e-mail program called XtraMail which enables you to exchange e-mail with other users on a LANtastic network as well as Internet users. With XtraMail, you don't have to use separate e-mail programs for LAN and Internet mail.

Chapter 8
Planning Your Servers

- -

- -

*O*ne of the key decisions you must make when networking your computers is how you make use of server computers. Even if you use a peer-to-peer network system such as Windows 95, you must still deal with the question of servers.

This chapter helps you to make the best use of your network server, first by convincing you to use a dedicated server if possible and then by suggesting ways to use the server efficiently.

To Dedicate or Not to Dedicate

In case you haven't noticed, I'm a big believer in dedicated server computers, even if you use a peer-to-peer network. Yes, one of the strengths of a simple Windows 95 network is that you can use any computer on the network as both a server computer and a user's workstation. Does that mean it's a good idea to make every computer a server? No way.

You give up a lot when your desktop computer doubles as a network server:

🖛 The network software required to make your computer work as a server takes up valuable RAM (random access memory), leaving less memory for your own work.

🖛 Every time someone accesses data on your hard disk, your own work is temporarily suspended. If your hard disk is popular, you'll become annoyed with the frequent delays.

✔ You lose the sense of privacy that comes with having your own computer. Remember that nasty memo about your boss? You'd better not leave it lying around on your disk . . . someone else may lift it off the network. (You can set up your disk so that you have some private space where other users can't snoop about. But make sure that you set it up right, and remember to store confidential files in private space. And make sure that you know more about the networking software than anyone else in the office. Someone who knows more about networking than you do can probably figure out a way to thwart your security measures.)

✔ You lose the independence of having your own computer. You have to leave your computer on all day even when you're not using it because someone else may be. Want to turn off your computer because the noise it makes interrupts your afternoon nap? You can't. Want to delete some unnecessary files to free up some hard disk space? You can't, if the files don't belong to you.

✔ Your computer isn't immune to damage caused by other network users. What if someone accidentally deletes an important file on your disk? What if someone copies a 100MB file onto your hard disk while you aren't looking, so that no free space is available when you try saving the spreadsheet you've been working on all afternoon?

I hope that you're convinced. If you can at all afford it, set aside a computer for use as a dedicated server. Beg, borrow, or steal a computer if you must.

✔ Peer-to-peer networks enable you to adjust certain configuration options for network servers. If you use a computer as both a server and a client, you must balance these options so that they provide reasonable performance for both server and client functions. But if you dedicate the computer as a server, you can skew these options in favor of the server functions. In other words, you're free to tweak the server's configuration for peak network performance. Details on doing this are found in Chapter 13.

✔ As a general rule, try to limit the number of servers on your network. Having one server sharing a 2GB drive is better than two servers each sharing a 1GB drive.

✔ In a larger network, you may want to use two dedicated server computers: one as a file server and the other as a print server. This improves the performance for file operations and network printing.

✔ If you're the greedy type, offer to donate your old 66MHz 486 computer as the network server if the company will purchase a new 266MHz Pentium II computer for your desktop.

Actually, this idea has merit: The file server doesn't have to be the fastest computer on the block, especially if it's used mostly to store and retrieve word processing, spreadsheet, and other types of document files rather than for intensive database processing.

How Much Disk Space?

The general rule for a network is that you never have enough disk space. No matter how much you have, you'll eventually run out. Don't delude yourself into thinking that 4GB is twice as much space as you'll ever need. Make that space available to the network, and it fills up in no time.

What then? Should you just keep adding a new disk drive to your file server every time you run out of space? Certainly not. The key to managing network disk space is just that — managing it. Someone has to sign on the dotted line that he or she will keep tabs on the network disk and let everyone know when it's about to burst its seams. And every network user must realize that disk storage on the server is a precious resource, to be used judiciously and not squandered.

✔ If you use a peer-to-peer network, consider installing DOS 6.22 or Windows 95 on the file server and activating its DriveSpace feature. To set up DriveSpace properly, you first must quote from *Wayne's World*: Say "Ex-squeeze me," and DriveSpace will politely compress the data on your hard disk so that the disk's capacity is effectively doubled. And it really, really works. Only trouble is, it slows down the server a bit. For the best server performance, you're better off purchasing a larger disk drive and not compressing it.

I wrote an entire book about DriveSpace, published by another publisher, but I'm afraid that if I mention it here, my IDG editor will lay a curse upon me, and my family will never hear from me again. So I won't mention it here at all.

✔ Make sure that all network users are encouraged to remember that their computers have local disk drives in addition to the network drives. Just because you have a network doesn't mean that everything has to be stored on a network drive!

✔ Don't try to cut costs by using *diskless clients*. Some networks are set up so that the clients have no local drives at all. For this to work, a special chip is required in the network interface card so that the computer can boot without a disk drive. Diskless clients are cheaper, but they force the user to store everything on the network. In addition, they bog down the network because routine disk accesses, such as locating DOS program files, have to travel across the network cable.

What to Put on a File Server

Of course, the only way to really predict how much network disk space you'll need is to plan what files you're going to store on the server. You need enough space to accommodate the network itself, shared data files, private data files, and shared application programs.

The network itself

Not all the space on the network server's disk can be made available to network users; some of it's required for the network operating system itself. It's not unreasonable to set aside 100MB of disk space for the network operating system, print spool files, sealing wax, and other fancy stuff.

- ✔ For NetWare, allow 55MB of disk space for the network operating system itself. For Windows NT Server, allow 100MB.

- ✔ If you go the peer-to-peer route with Windows 95 or Windows for Workgroups, the network support is built in to the operating system so that you don't have to allow for additional disk space. The operating systems require a hefty amount of disk space, though. Windows 95 easily fills 70MB of disk space, and the combination of MS-DOS and Windows for Workgroups takes up a good 20MB. If you decide to go with LANtastic, allow an additional 10MB beyond the disk space required for MS-DOS and Windows.

- ✔ If the server can support a printer, allow an additional 20MB for spool files. If you routinely print large graphics files on the network printer, you may have to allow even more spool space.

- ✔ Allow space for any additional programs that you may want to have available on the server, such as a utility program like Norton Utilities.

Shared data files

Allow sufficient space on the file server for data files that network users share. Most of this space may be taken up by one large database file, or it can consist of hundreds or even thousands of small word processing or spreadsheet files. Either way, don't skimp on space here.

Estimate the amount of space you need for shared files. The only way you can do this is to add up the size of the files that will be shared. Double the result. If you can afford to, double it again.

Private data files

Every user wants access to network disk space for private file storage — perhaps because their own disks are getting full, or they want the security of knowing that their files are backed up regularly, or they just want to try out the network.

You have two approaches to providing this private space:

✔ Create a subdirectory for each network user on a shared network drive. For example, the Cleavers set up the following private directories:

Ward   \WARD

June   \JUNE

Wally   \WALLY

Beaver \BEAVER

Now, just tell each network user to store private files in his or her own subdirectory. The problem with this setup is that these directories aren't really private; there's nothing to keep Beaver from looking at files in Wally's directory.

To make these directories more secure, you can password protect them by using the security features that are available with your network operating system.

✔ Create a separate network drive mapping for each private directory. For example, you can map drive P to each network user's private directory. Then you can tell each user to store private files on his or her P drive. For Wally, the P drive refers to the \WALLY directory, but for Beaver, P refers to \BEAVER. This setup keeps Beaver out of Wally's files.

The net effect (groan, sorry) of this setup is that each user seems to have a separate P drive on the server. In reality, these drives are merely subdirectories on the server drive.

Estimating the disk space required for private file storage is more difficult than estimating shared file storage. After your users figure out that they have seemingly unlimited private storage on the network server, they'll start filling it up.

Shared programs

If several users use the same application program, consider purchasing a network version of the program and storing the program file on the network server. The advantage of doing this rather than storing a separate copy of the program on each user's local disk is that you have to manage only one copy of the software. For example, if a new version of the software comes out, you have to update just the copy on the server rather than separate copies on each workstation.

✔ The network version of most programs enables each network user to set the program's options according to his or her preferences. Thus, one user may run the program using the default setup with boring colors, while another user may prefer to change the screen colors so that the program displays magenta text on a cyan background. Stalin probably would have outlawed network versions.

✔ Many application programs create temporary files that you're not aware of and don't normally need to worry about. When you use these programs on a network, be sure to configure them so that the temporary files are created on a local drive rather than on a network drive. This configuration not only gives you better performance, but also ensures that one user's temporary files don't interfere with another's.

Planning Your Network Drive Mapping

If you're working with MS-DOS or Windows for Workgroup client computers, you must scope out the drive letters that you'll use to access network drives over the network. Here are some general rules to follow:

✔ Be consistent. If a network drive is accessed as drive Q from one workstation, map it as drive Q from all workstations that access the same drive. Don't have one user referring to a network drive as drive Q and another using the same drive but with a different letter.

✔ Use drive letters that are high enough to avoid conflicts with drive letters that are used by local drives. For example, suppose that one of your computers has three disk partitions, a CD-ROM drive, and a RAM drive. This computer would already have drive letters C through G assigned. I usually start network drive assignments with drive M and continue with N, O, P, and so on.

✔ Novell NetWare usually begins drive assignments at drive F.

✔ If you use DriveSpace, be aware that DriveSpace causes drive letter crashes if you're not careful. To protect yourself, start your network before you install DriveSpace so that DriveSpace can find its way around your network drive assignments. And always wear a helmet and safety goggles when using DriveSpace.

✔ With Windows 95, keep in mind that drive letter mapping isn't a requirement. Users can access any shared network drive via the Network Neighborhood that appears on the Windows 95 desktop.

Using a Separate Print Server

If you have a larger network (say, eight or more computers) and shared printing is one of the main reasons you're networking, you may want to consider using two dedicated server computers: one as a file server and the other as a print server.

If you read this, your dog will die

NetWare decides which drive letter to assign to the first network drive by peeking inside that scariest-of-all DOS files, CONFIG.SYS. NetWare looks in CONFIG.SYS to see whether it contains a line that looks like this:

```
LASTDRIVE=E
```

This CONFIG.SYS line tells DOS how many drive letters to set aside for local use. NetWare knows its ABCs, so it picks the next letter in the alphabet after the LASTDRIVE letter to use for the first network drive letter. If LASTDRIVE is set to E, NetWare uses F for the first network drive. If LASTDRIVE is set to G, NetWare uses H. You get the idea.

Not all CONFIG.SYS files have a LASTDRIVE line. If LASTDRIVE is missing, DOS assumes that E is the highest drive letter in use. That's why NetWare usually picks F for the network drive.

You can change LASTDRIVE if you want, but this is heady DOS stuff that requires a pocket protector.

✔ Most network operating systems have configuration options that enable you to balance disk performance against printer performance. By using separate computers for your file server and print server, you can set these options accordingly. If the same computer works as both a file server and a print server, you must set these options somewhere in the middle, compromising performance one way or the other.

✔ It the printer is a dot-matrix printer or a laser printer used exclusively for text output, the print server can be the slowest computer on the network and you still won't notice any performance delay. If you do a lot of graphics printing on a high-quality laser printer, however, don't use a dog computer for the print server. I've seen 10-minute print jobs slowed to an hour or more by a cheap print server.

✔ As an alternative to dedicating a separate computer to use as a print server, most printers can be connected directly to the network via an inexpensive print server device. The most commonly used device of this type is called the HP JetDirect, made by Hewlett-Packard (the same folks who make all those great printers). An external HP JetDirect is a small box which contains an Ethernet port (RJ-45 for twisted-pair, BNC for thinnet, or both) and a parallel port to which you can attach a printer. Internal HP JetDirect cards are designed to be installed in Hewlett-Packard printers, enabling you to connect the printer directly to the network. An External HP JetDirect can be purchased for under $150.

Buying a Server Computer

If you have a spare computer lying around that you can use as a server, great. Most of us don't have spare computers in the closet, though. If you plan to buy a new computer to use as a network server, here are some tips for configuring it properly:

✔ A network server computer need not have the latest in high-resolution color monitors. Monochrome is fine. After all, the server just sits there all day with the same boring display. No need to spend $600 on a 17-inch monitor when a $200 monochrome monitor can do just as well. (Unless, of course, you're running Windows for Workgroups, Windows 95, or Windows NT Server, which require the server to run Windows. Still, a large 17-inch monitor isn't necessary. A cheaper 14-inch monitor can do the job.)

✔ On the other hand, don't scrimp when it comes to the processor and memory. Buy the fastest Pentium II processor you can afford and equip it with at least 32MB of RAM. 64 megabytes is better. Every last byte of extra memory can be put to good use on a server.

✔ Buy the biggest disk drive you can afford. The price of disk storage has dropped so much in recent years that there's little reason to outfit a server computer with fewer than 5GB of disk storage. (Heck, the desktop computer I used to write this book has a 5GB disk.)

✔ While you're at it, buy SCSI disks instead of IDE disks. SCSI offers much better performance for network servers, where several users are accessing the disk simultaneously. SCSI is more expensive than IDE, but the performance benefit is worth the increased cost.

✔ Have the computer built in a tower-style case that has plenty of room for expansion: several free bays for additional disk drives and a more-than-adequate power supply. You want to make sure that you can expand the server when you realize you didn't buy enough disk space.

Keeping the Power On

One feature people often overlook when setting up a network server is the power. You can simply plug the server computer into the wall, or you can plug it into a surge protector to smooth out power spikes before they damage your computer. Using a surge protector is good, but even better is connecting your server computer to a device called an *uninterruptible power supply,* or UPS.

Inside the UPS box is a battery that is constantly charged and some electronics that monitor the condition of the power coming from the wall outlet. If a power failure occurs, the battery keeps the computer running. The battery can't run the computer forever, but it can keep it running long enough — anywhere from 10 minutes to more than an hour, depending on how much you paid for the UPS — to shut things down in familiar Presbyterian fashion (decently and in order). For most small networks, a UPS that keeps you going for 10 minutes is enough. You just want to make sure that any disk in progress (I/O) has time to finish. A decent UPS can be had for about $150.

✔ Using a UPS can prevent you from losing data when a power outage occurs. Without a UPS, your server computer can be shut down at the worst of times, such as while it's updating the directory information that tracks the location of your files. With a UPS, the computer can stay on long enough for such meticulous operations to be completed safely.

✔ In a true UPS, power is always supplied to the computer from the battery; the current from the wall outlet is used only to keep the battery charged. Most inexpensive UPS devices are actually stand-by power supplies (SPSs). An SPS runs the computer from the wall-outlet current but switches to battery within a few gazillionths of a second if a power failure occurs. With a true UPS, you have no delay between the power failure and the battery takeover. SPSs are less expensive than UPSs, though, so they're more commonly used.

✔ The ultimate power-failure protection is to attach a UPS to every computer on the network. That gets a bit expensive, though. But at least protect the server.

✔ If a power outage occurs and your server is protected by a UPS, get to the server as quickly as you can, log everyone off, and shut down the server. It's also a good idea to go to each computer and turn off the power switch. Then, when power is restored, you can restart the server, restart each workstation, and assess the damage.

Location, Location, and Location

The final network server consideration to address in this chapter is where to put the server. In the old days, you put the network server in a room with glass windows all around, had a full-time lab technician in a white coat tending to its every need, and gave it a name like "ARDVARC" or "SHADRAC."

Nowadays, the most likely location for a file server is in the closet. No reason exists that says the server has to be in a central location; it can be in the closet down at the end of the hall, atop the filing cabinets in the storage room, or in the corner office. The server can be almost anywhere, as long as it's near an electrical outlet and network cable can be routed to it.

Of course, a print server is different. It should be near the printer, which should be in an accessible location with storage space for paper, toner (for laser printers), a place to leave printouts that belong to other users, and a box to drop wasted paper so that it can be recycled.

Some bad locations for the server:

- ✔ In the attic. Too dusty.
- ✔ In the bathroom. Too much moisture.
- ✔ In the kitchen. Your computer gurus will raid your refrigerator every time you call them. They'll start showing up spontaneously "just to check."
- ✔ In your boss's office. You don't want him or her to think of you every time the server beeps.

The good news is that you still get to name your server computer. You can call it something boring like SERVER1, or you can give it an interesting name like BERTHA or SPOCK.

Chapter 9

Oh, What a Tangled Web We Weave (Cables, Adapters, and Other Stuff)

· ·

In This Chapter

▶ Finding out what Ethernet is

▶ Checking out the different types of network cable

▶ Using coax cable

▶ Using twisted-pair cable

▶ Mixing coax and twisted pair on the same network

▶ Selecting your network interface cards

▶ Adding professional touches to your cabling

▶ Reading a network mail-order advertisement

· ·

*I*f you've ever installed an underground sprinkler system, you'll have no trouble cabling your network. Working with network cable is a lot like working with sprinkler pipe: You have to use the right size pipe (cable), the right valves and headers (hubs and repeaters), and the right sprinkler heads (network interface cards).

Network cables have one compelling advantage over sprinkler pipes: You don't get wet when they leak.

This chapter tells you far more about network cables than you probably need to know. You're introduced to Ethernet, the most common system of network cabling for small networks. Then you find out how to work with the cables used to wire an Ethernet network. You also find out how to select the right network interface cards that enable you to connect the cables to your computers.

What Is Ethernet?

Ethernet is a standardized way of connecting computers together to create a network. You can think of Ethernet as kind of like a municipal building code for networks: It specifies what kind of cables to use, how to connect the cables together, how long the cables can be, how computers transmit data to one another using the cables, and more.

You may have heard of two other popular network building codes: Token Ring and ARCnet. Ethernet is more commonly used than Token Ring because it's less expensive. Ethernet is used more than ARCnet because ARCnet is slower.

Some people treat Ethernet, Token Ring, and ARCnet like religions that they're willing to die for. To a Token Ring zealot, Ethernet represents the Antichrist. Ethernet fanatics often claim that you can hear satanic messages if you send data backwards through a Token Ring network. Ethernet and Token Ring fanatics both treat ARCnet users as if they were a cult, possibly because there have been reports of ARCnet disciples giving away flowers at airports. Don't engage an Ethernet, Token Ring, or ARCnet Pharisee in a discussion about the merits of his or her network beliefs over opponents' beliefs. It's futile.

Without regard to the technical merits of Ethernet, Token Ring, or ARCnet, the fact is that the vast majority of small networks use Ethernet. 'Nough said.

- ✔ *Ethernet* is a set of standards for the infrastructure on which a network is built. All the network operating systems I discuss in this book — NetWare, Windows NT Server, Windows 95, Windows for Workgroups, and LANtastic — can operate on an Ethernet network. If you build your network on a solid Ethernet base, you can easily change network operating systems later.

- ✔ Ethernet is often referred to by network gurus as 802.3 (pronounced eight-oh-two-dot-three) because this is the official designation used by the IEEE (pronounced Eye-triple-ee), a group of electrical engineers who wear bow ties and have nothing better to do than argue about inductance all day long. It's a good thing, though, because if it weren't for them, you wouldn't be able to mix and match Ethernet components made by different companies.

- ✔ Standard Ethernet transmits data at a rate of 10 million bits per second, or 10Mbps. Because 8 bits are in a byte, that translates into roughly 1.2 million bytes per second. In practice, Ethernet can't move information that fast because data must be transmitted in packages of no more than 1,500 bytes, called *packets*. So a 150K file would have to be split into 100 packets.

Stop me before I tell you about Token Ring!

Just in case you do get into an argument about Ethernet with a Token Ring fanatic, here's where he or she's coming from. Ethernet can get bogged down if the network gets really busy and messages start colliding like crazy. Token Ring uses a more orderly approach to sending packets through the network. Instead of sending a message whenever it wants to, a computer on a Token Ring network must wait its turn. In a Token Ring network, a special packet called the token is constantly passed through the network from computer to computer. A computer can send a packet of data only when it has the token. In this way, Token Ring ensures that collisions won't happen.

Sometimes, a computer with a defective network interface card accidentally swallows the token. If the token disappears for too long, the network assumes it's been swallowed, so the network generates a new token.

Two versions of Token Ring are in use. The older version runs at 4Mbps. The newer version runs at 16Mbps, plus it allows two tokens to exist at once, which makes the network even faster.

Oh, in case you're wondering, ARCnet uses a similar token-passing scheme.

> This speed has nothing to do with how fast electrical signals move on the cable. The electrical signals themselves travel at about 70 percent the speed of light, or as Picard would say, "Warp factor point-seven-oh. Engage."

✔ A new version of Ethernet exists, called Fast Ethernet, which moves data ten times as fast as normal Ethernet. Because Fast Ethernet moves data at a whopping 100Mbps and utilizes twisted pair cabling, it's often called 100BaseT. Although it's more expensive than standard 10Mbps Ethernet, the cost of Fast Ethernet is coming down. If you're interested in speed, you may want to check out Fast Ethernet for your network. However, 10Mbps is plenty fast for most small networks.

Three Types of Ethernet Cable

A 10Mbps Ethernet network can be constructed using three different types of cable: thick coax (called yellow cable because it's usually yellow), thin coax (called thinnet because it's thinner than the yellow stuff or cheapernet because it's cheaper than the yellow stuff), or twisted pair, which looks like phone cable. Twisted-pair cable is sometimes called UTP or 10baseT cable, for reasons I'll try hard not to explain later.

The yellow stuff isn't used much for small networks, but I'll describe it anyway. The real choice you must make is between thinnet cable and twisted pair.

Who cares what CSMA/CD stands for?

Besides specifying the mechanical and electrical characteristics of network cables, Ethernet specifies the techniques used to control the flow of information over the network cables. The technique Ethernet uses is called CSMA/CD, which stands for "carrier sense multiple access with collision detection." This is a mouthful, but if we take it apart piece by piece, you get an idea of how Ethernet works (as if you want to know).

Carrier sense means that whenever a computer wants to send a message on the network cable, it first listens to the cable to see whether anyone else is already sending a message. If it doesn't hear any other messages on the cable, the computer assumes that it's free to send one.

Multiple access means that nothing prevents two or more computers from trying to send a message at the same time. Sure, each computer listens before sending. But suppose that two computers listen, hear nothing and then proceed to send their messages? Picture what happens when you and someone else arrive at a four-way stop sign at the same time. You wave the other driver on, he or she waves you on, you wave, he or she waves, you all wave, and then you both end up going at the same time.

Collision detection means that after a computer sends a message on the network, it listens carefully to see whether it crashed into another message. Kind of like listening for the screeching of brakes at the four-way stop. If the computer hears the screeching of brakes, it waits for a random period of time and tries to send the message again. Because the delay is random, two messages that collide are sent again after different delay periods, so a second collision is unlikely.

Wasn't that a waste of time?

The yellow stuff

The original Ethernet networks were wired with thick, heavy cable called thick coax, or yellow cable, because of its color. Thick coax isn't used much anymore, especially for small networks, because it's expensive, heavy, and not very flexible (I mean that literally: It's difficult to make yellow cable bend around tight corners).

- The yellow stuff is less susceptible to interference from mongo-magnets and motors and what not, so it's still used sometimes in factories, warehouses, nuclear test sites, Frankenstein laboratories, and so on.
- Yellow cable can be strung for greater distances than other types of Ethernet cable. A single run of yellow cable (called a segment) can be as long as 500 meters.

Worthless filler about network topology

A networking book wouldn't be complete without the usual textbook description of the three basic "network topologies." The first type of network topology is called a *bus,* in which network nodes (that is, computers) are strung together in a line, like this:

A bus is the simplest type of topology, but it has its drawbacks. If the cable breaks somewhere in the middle, it splits the network into two.

The second type of topology is called a *ring*.

A ring is very much like a bus, except there's no end to the line: The last node on the line is connected to the first node, forming an endless loop.

The third type of topology is called a *star*.

In a star network, all the nodes are connected to a central hub. In effect, each node has an independent connection to the network, so a break in one cable doesn't affect the others.

Ethernet networks are based on a bus design. However, fancy cabling tricks make it appear to be wired as a star when twisted-pair cable is used.

✔ The way yellow cable is attached to individual computers is weird. Usually, a long length of yellow cable is run along a path that takes it near each computer on the network. Each computer must be connected to the yellow cable via a device called a *transceiver*. The transceiver usually includes a device called a *vampire tap*, a clamp-like thingamabob that taps into the yellow cable without cutting and splicing it. The transceiver is connected to the network interface card by means of an AUI cable. (AUI stands for attached unit interface, not that it matters.)

✔ I think you can see why the yellow stuff isn't used much anymore.

✔ It's really too bad. The yellow stuff would coordinate so well with this book.

Thinnet

A more practical type of cable for Ethernet networks is thin coaxial cable, usually called thinnet. Thinnet is less expensive than yellow cable, not only because the cable itself is less expensive, but also because separate transceivers aren't required to attach computers to the cable. (Thinnet does use transceivers, but the transceiver is built into the adapter card.) Figure 9-1 shows a typical thinnet cable:

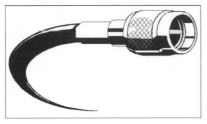

Figure 9-1:
A thinnet
cable.

- ✔ Thinnet is about ¹/₅ of an inch in diameter, so it's much lighter and more flexible than the yellow stuff. You can easily wrap it around corners, drape it over doorways, around potted plants, and so on.

- ✔ You attach thinnet to the network interface card by using a goofy twist-on connector called a BNC connector. You can purchase preassembled cables with BNC connectors already attached in lengths of 25 or 50 feet, or you can buy bulk cable on a big spool and attach the connectors yourself by using a special tool.

- ✔ Whereas yellow cable is usually wired with a single length of cable that's tapped into using vampire taps, thinnet is run with separate lengths of cable. At each computer, a tee-connector is used to connect two cables to the network interface card. Figure 9-2 shows a typical thinnet arrangement. One length of thinnet connects Ward's computer to June's, a second length connects June's to Wally's, and a third length connects Wally's to Beaver's.

- ✔ A special plug called a *terminator* is required at each end of a series of thinnet cables. In Figure 9-2, a terminator is required at Ward's computer and at Beaver's. The terminator prevents data from spilling out the end of the cable and staining the carpet.

- ✔ The cables strung end to end from one terminator to the other are collectively called a *segment*. The maximum length of a thinnet segment is 185 meters. You can connect as many as 30 computers on one segment. To span a distance greater than 185 meters or to connect more than 30 computers, you must use two or more segments with a funky device called a repeater to connect each segment.

Unshielded twisted-pair (UTP) cable

A popular alternative to thinnet cable is unshielded twisted-pair cable, or UTP. UTP cable is even cheaper than thin coax cable, and best of all, many modern buildings are already wired with twisted pair because this type of wiring is often used with modern phone systems. Figure 9-3 shows a twisted-pair cable.

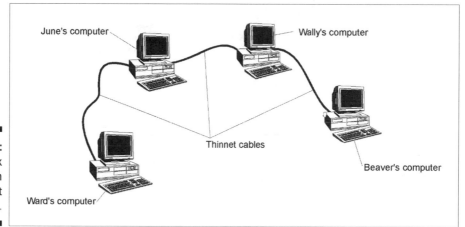

Figure 9-2:
A network
wired with
thinnet
cable.

June's computer

Wally's computer

Thinnet cables

Beaver's computer

Ward's computer

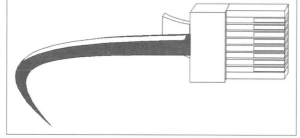

Figure 9-3:
Unshielded
twisted pair
cable.

When you use UTP cable to construct an Ethernet network, you connect the computers in a star arrangement, as Figure 9-4 illustrates. In the center of this star is a device called a hub. Depending on the model, Ethernet hubs enable you to connect from 4 to 24 computers using twisted-pair cable. Most hubs have connectors for 8 or 12 cables. Hubs are sometimes called concentrators.

An advantage of this star arrangement is that if one cable goes bad, only the computer attached to that cable is affected; the rest of the network continues to chug along. With thinnet, a bad cable affects not only the computer that it's connected to, but all computers unfortunate enough to lie beyond the bad cable.

  ✔ UTP cable consists of pairs of thin wire twisted around each other; several such pairs are gathered up inside an outer insulating jacket. Ethernet uses two pairs of wires, or four wires all together. The number of pairs in a UTP cable varies but is often more than two.

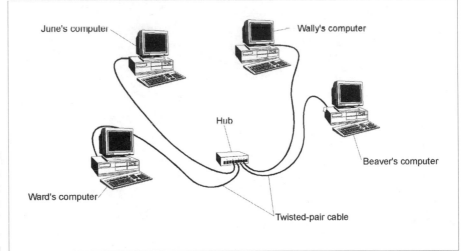

Figure 9-4:
A network
wired with
twisted-pair
cable.

✓ UTP cable comes in five grades, category 1 through category 5. The higher the category number, the greater the amount of protection the cable provides from outside electrical interference. Of course, higher-category cables are also more expensive. Ethernet networks should be cabled with category 3 or better. Cagetory 5 is preferable.

✓ If you want to sound like you know what you're talking about, say "cat 5" instead of "category 5."

✓ UTP cable connectors look like modular phone connectors but are a bit larger. UTP connectors are officially called RJ-45 connectors.

✓ Like thinnet, UTP cable is also sold in prefabricated lengths. However, RJ-45 connectors are much easier to attach to bulk UTP cable than BNC cables are to attach to bulk coax cable. As a result, I suggest you buy bulk cable and connectors unless your network consists of just two or three computers. A basic crimp tool to attach the RJ-45 connectors will cost about $50.

✓ The maximum allowable cable length between the hub and the computer is 100 meters.

Working with Hubs

The biggest difference between using thinnet and UTP cable is that when you use UTP, you also must use a separate device called a *hub*. Working with a hub isn't difficult, but it is one extra piece of an already complicated puzzle, so many do-it-yourself networkers opt for thinnet to avoid dealing with hubs altogether.

Ten base what?

The IEEE, in its infinite wisdom, has decreed that the following names shall be used to designate the three types of cable used with 802.3 networks (in other words, with Ethernet):

✔ 10base5 is thick coax cable (the yellow stuff).

✔ 10base2 is thin coax cable (thinnet).

✔ 10baseT is unshielded twisted-pair cable (UTP).

In each moniker, the 10 means that the cable operates at 10Mbps, and *base* means the cable is used for baseband networks as opposed to broadband networks (don't ask). The 5 in 10base5 is the maximum length of a yellow cable segment: 500 meters; the 2 in 10base2 stands for 200 meters, which is about the 185-meter maximum segment length for thinnet (for a group of engineers, the IEEE is odd; I didn't know the word "about" is in an engineer's vocabulary); and the T in 10baseT stands for "twisted."

Of these three official monikers, 10baseT is the only one that's frequently used; 10base5 and 10base2 are usually just called thick and thin.

If your network has more than 6 or 8 computers, you may find it's worth it to purchase a hub and use UTP instead of thinnet, especially if it's likely that your networking needs change periodically. With UTP, it's easier to add new computers to the network, to move computers, to find and correct cable problems, and to service computers that need to be removed from the network temporarily.

If you do decide to use UTP, you need to know some of the ins and outs of using 10baseT hubs:

✔ Because you must run a cable from each computer to the hub, find a central location for the hub to which the cables can be easily routed.

✔ The hub requires electrical power, so make sure that an electrical outlet is handy.

✔ When you purchase the hub, purchase one with at least twice as many connections as you need. Don't buy a four-port hub if you want to network four computers; when (and not if) you add the fifth computer, you'll have to buy another hub.

✔ You can connect hubs to one another as shown in Figure 9-5; this is called *daisy-chaining*. When you daisy-chain hubs, you connect a cable to a standard port on one of the hubs and the daisy-chain port on the other hub. Be sure to read the instructions that came with the hub to make sure that you daisy-chain them properly.

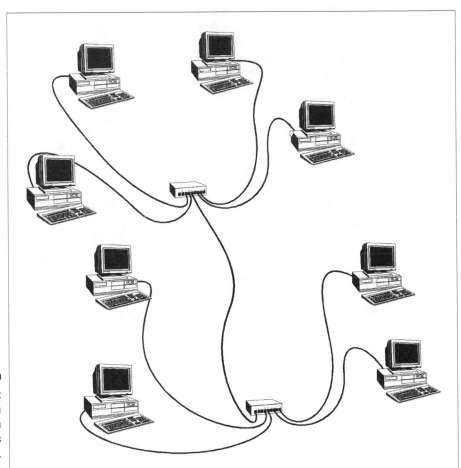

Figure 9-5:
You can
daisy-chain
hubs
together.

✔ You can daisy-chain no more than three hubs together. If you have more computers than can be accommodated by three hubs, don't panic. Most hubs have a BNC connection on the back so that you can connect them together via thinnet cable. The three-hub limit doesn't apply when you connect the hubs using thinnet cable.

✔ When you shop for network hubs, you may notice that the expensive ones have network-management features that support something called SNMP. These are called *managed hubs*. Unless your network is very large and you know what SNMP is, don't bother with the more expensive managed hubs. You'd be paying for a feature you'd never use.

Network Interface Cards

Now that you know far more about network cable than you really need to, I want to point out a few things about network interface cards to consider before you buy:

- ✔ The network interface cards you use must have a connector that matches the type of cable you use. If you plan on wiring your network with thinnet cable, make sure that the network cards have a BNC connector. For twisted pair wiring, make sure that the cards have an RJ45 connector.

- ✔ Some network cards provide two or three connectors. I've seen them in every combination: BNC and AUI, RJ-45 and AUI, BNC and RJ-45, and all three. Selecting a card that has both BNC and RJ-45 connectors isn't a bad idea. That way, you can switch from thinnet to twisted pair or vice versa without buying new network cards. You can get both types of connectors for a cost of only $5-$10 more per card. Don't worry about the AUI connector, though. You'll probably never need it.

- ✔ The standard of compatibility for network interface cards is the NE2000, which used to be manufactured by Novell but is now made by Eagle. If a card is NE2000 compatible, you can use it with just about any network.

- ✔ When you purchase a network card, make sure that you get one that's compatible with your computer. Most computers can accommodate cards designed for the standard 16-bit ISA bus. Newer Pentium-based computers can also accommodate cards with 32-bit PCI bus. For a Pentium computer, PCI cards are well worth the extra few bucks.

- ✔ Make sure that the computer in which you're going to use the card has an available slot of the type you purchase. For example, suppose your computer has four ISA bus slots and three PCI bus slots, but all three of the PCI slots are already in use while two of the ISA slots are available. In this case, get an ISA card.

- ✔ Make sure that the card is Plug and Play compatible. This enables Windows 95 to automatically configure the card so that you won't have to go through a bunch of tedious configuration gyrations just to get the card working.

- ✔ Network cards can be a bit tricky to set up — even Plug and Play cards. Each different card has its own nuances. You can simplify your life a bit if you pick one card and stick with it. Try not to mix and match network cards.

- ✔ If you see Ethernet cards advertised on late-night television for an unbelievably low price (like $9.95 or free with Proof of Purchase seals from three cereal boxes), make sure that the cards are 16-bit cards. You won't be satisfied with the slow performance of bargain-basement 8-bit cards unless your computer is also of the bargain-basement variety. If you have a 486 or Pentium computer, don't even think about using 8-bit cards.

- ✔ If you're stuck in the dark ages with an ancient 8088-based computer (such as an original IBM PC or XT), you have two alternatives: (1) You can purchase an 8-bit network adapter card or (2) you can sell the computer to Sanford & Son (like for $9.95 or in exchange for an old toaster). Don't get a 16-bit network adapter card, though, because it won't work. 8088-based computers don't have a 16-bit bus, so they can't accommodate 16-bit cards.

Professional Touches

If most of the stuff I've presented so far makes sense to you, and if you want to impress your friends, consider adding the following extra touches to your network installation. They make the job look like it was done by a professional. (If you've found this chapter to be hopelessly confusing so far, you should probably concentrate on just getting your network up and running. Worry about making it look pretty later.)

These professional touches are shown in Figure 9-6:

- ✔ Use 10baseT wiring; that's what most network pros are doing these days.

- ✔ Run the wiring through the ceiling and walls instead of along the floor, and mount a wall jack near each computer. Then plug each computer into the wall jack by using a short (10-foot or so) patch cable. Be sure to use top-quality Category 5 jacks, and make sure each pair of wires inside the cable is twisted right up to the point where the wires attach to the jack. In other words, don't untwist the wires any more than absolutely necessary to make them easier to work with.

- ✔ When you run the wiring through the walls and ceiling, take special care to avoid power cords, florescent lamps, and other electrical devices which may interfere with the signals traveling inside the network cable. And don't kink the cable: curve it gently around corners.

- ✔ To really do it right, run 10baseT cable to every possible computer location in your office, even if you don't yet have a computer there. That way, when you do move a computer to that location, the hard wiring (up in the ceiling and through the wall) is already done. All you'll have to do is attach the computer to the wall jack with a patch cord.

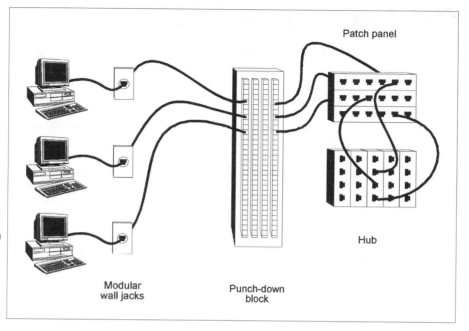

Figure 9-6:
A pro-
fessional
touch.

✔ Designate a corner of a closet or storeroom to be your wiring closet. Bundle all the cables together and attach them to a punch-down block. Run wires from the punch-down block to a patch panel, which is nothing more than a series of RJ-45 jacks mounted neatly in a row.

✔ Connect the appropriate jacks in the patch panel to your network hub with short patch cables. The whole thing will look a bit like a rat's nest, but you'll be able to easily reconfigure the network at a moment's notice. If someone changes locations, all you have to do is adjust the patch cables in the wiring closet accordingly.

✔ A full-fledged patch panel like this is usually used only with large networks. For smaller networks, you can get small self-contained units that contain a punch-down block that's already connected to six or eight RJ-45 blocks. These boxes are a slick way to give a professional look to a small network setup.

✔ Be careful about making your network look too good. People may assume that you're a network geek, and start offering you Chee-tos to solve their problems.

Reading a Network Ad

If you're willing to purchase your network components from a mail-order supplier, you can probably save a bunch of money. Just go to the supermarket and pick up a copy of Computer Shopper and browse through it until you find several companies that specialize in networking products.

You can probably figure out most ads, but I want to point out a few things:

- ✔ The lines that have two prices (generally separated by a slash) are either listing the price if you buy one item or the price if you buy five or more, or the price for two similar items configured differently. For example, the Fancy Dance 2000 ISA network card may be $79.95 if you buy one, but $69.95 each if you buy five or more.

- ✔ Some prices change too often to print, so you have to call to find out.

- ✔ Most mail-order networking companies are very willing to answer questions on the phone. If you're not sure what you need, give the company a call.

- ✔ Make sure that you understand the shipping costs and the conditions for returning damaged goods. Before you buy anything, make sure that they have the product in stock and can ship it the same day, or the next day if you call late.

Chapter 10

Putting It Together (or, Insert Tab A into Slot B)

. . . .

In This Chapter

▶ Deciding what tools you need to install a network

▶ Installing a network card

▶ Finding out about IRQs, I/O addresses, and DMA channels

▶ Crimping cable

▶ Installing network software

▶ Checking out your installation

. . . .

*N*ow comes the fun part: putting your network together. Get ready to roll up your sleeves and dig into the bowels of your computers. Make sure that you scrub thoroughly first.

Tools You'll Need

Of course, to do a job right, you must have the right tools.

Start with a basic set of computer tools, which can be had for about $15 from any computer store or large office-supply store. These kits include the right screwdrivers and socket wrenches to open up your computers and insert adapter cards. (If you don't have a computer tool kit, make sure that you have several flathead and Phillips screwdrivers of various sizes.)

If all your computers are in the same room, and you're going to run the cables along the floor, and you're using prefabricated cables, the computer tool kit should contain everything you need.

If you're using bulk cable and plan on attaching your own connectors, you need the following tools in addition to the tools that come with the basic computer tool kit:

- ✔ **Wire cutters.** Big ones for thinnet cable; smaller ones are okay for 10baseT cable. If you're using yellow cable, you need the Jaws of Life.

- ✔ **A crimp tool appropriate to your cable type.** You need the crimp tool to attach the connectors to the cable.

- ✔ **Wire stripper.** You need this only if the crimp tool doesn't include a wire stripper. For thinnet, a special wire-stripper-doohickey is required because the cable's inner conductor, outer conductor, and outer insulation must be cut at precise lengths.

If you plan on running cables through walls, you need additional tools:

- ✔ **A hammer.**

- ✔ **A keyhole saw.** This is useful if you plan on cutting holes through walls to route your cable.

- ✔ **A flashlight.**

- ✔ **A ladder.**

- ✔ **Possibly a *fish tape*.** A fish tape is a coiled-up length of stiff metal tape. To use it, you feed the tape into one wall opening and *fish* it towards the other opening, where a partner is ready to grab it when the tape arrives. Next, your partner attaches the cable to the fish tape and yells something like "Let 'er rip!" or "Bombs away!" Then you reel in the fish tape and the cable along with it. (Fish tape can be found in the electrical section of most well-stocked hardware stores.)

If you plan on routing cable through a concrete subfloor, you need to rent a jackhammer and a backhoe and hire someone to hold a yellow flag while you work.

Configuring and Installing Your Network Cards

You have to install a network card in each of your computers before you can connect the network cables. Installing a network card is a manageable task, but you have to be willing to roll up your sleeves.

Fortunately, most network cards sold these days are of the Windows 95 (soon to be Windows 98) "Plug and Play" variety. This means that you can slap them into your computer and, the next time you start up your computer, Windows 95 or 98 automatically configures itself to use the card. If any of the card's settings conflict with settings used by other cards already installed in your computer, Windows 95 or 98 adjusts the settings automatically to eliminate the conflict.

Would that all network cards were Plug and Play cards. Unfortunately, not all of them are. Some network cards (especially cheaper ones) still require that you use a special installation or configuration program that comes with the card. And if you're installing a hand-me-down network card you got from your brother-in-law, you may have to contend with setting switches or jumper blocks on the card itself. Bother.

And, of course, Plug and Play is a Windows 95 and 98 feature. If you're stuck with DOS or Windows for Workgroups, you have to configure the network cards the old-fashioned way. If you're lucky enough to have Plug and Play cards in an all-Windows 95 network, you can boldly skip ahead to the section "Installing the Network Interface Card." Otherwise, read on.

Configuring network cards is probably the most confusing part of installing a network, and it's also the most troublesome if you don't get it just right. So be sure to pay attention when you're configuring your network cards. Make sure that you've had your morning coffee.

✔ It's not your fault that configuring cards is so confusing. Blame it on the guys and gals who designed the original IBM PC many moons ago. They had no idea that so many companies would make so many different kinds of add-on devices for the PC, such as modems, scanners, tape drives, CD-ROM drives, mice, and, of course, network cards. So they didn't put enough engineering muscle into the design of the PC's expansion slots. The result is that you have to manually configure your network card to make sure that its electronic signals don't crash into electronic signals used by the other manually configured cards already in your computer.

✔ On some cards, configuration settings are made by changing special switches called *DIP switches* or moving a *jumper block*. Figure 10-1 shows what a DIP switch and jumper block look like. The switch or block must be set *before* you install the card into your computer.

✔ A straightened-out paper clip is the ideal tool for setting DIP switches.

✔ To change a jumper block, you move the *plug* from one set of wires to another. You need fingernails to do it properly. Or a good set of tweezers.

✔ If you're lucky, your network cards have been preconfigured for you with the most likely settings. You need to double-check, though, because (1) the factory settings are not always appropriate, and (2) sometimes they make mistakes at the factory and configure the card incorrectly.

✔ If you're even luckier, your cards don't use DIP switches or jumper blocks at all. These cards still have to be configured, but the configuration is done with software rather than with a paper clip or your fingernails.

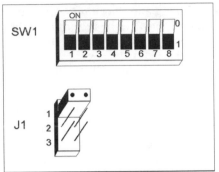

Figure 10-1:
A DIP
switch and
a jumper
block.

✓ Most network cards have two configuration settings: IRQ number and I/O port address. Some cards also enable you to configure a DMA channel. These settings are described under separate headings on the next few pages. It's technical and boring, so make sure that you're wide awake.

✓ Network cards that support more than one type of cable connector also have to be configured for the proper cable type. For example, if your card supports both 10baseT and AUI connectors, you have to configure the card depending on the type of cable you use. Normally, the card is configured at the factory for thinnet or 10baseT (if the card supports both thinnet and 10baseT, it's usually configured for thinnet). So you have to change the configuration only if you're not using the preconfigured cable type.

✓ When you configure a network card, write down the settings you select. You need these settings later when you install the client software. Store your list of network card settings in your network binder.

✓ It would be too easy to add a joke about DIP switches here. Insert your own joke if you're so inclined.

Configuring those irksome IRQ numbers

IRQ stands for "Interrupt ReQuest." You don't need to know that; I tell you only because I think it's funny that the Q is capitalized in the middle of the word. Each computer has 16 different IRQ numbers, and each I/O device — such as a printer port, modem, mouse, and so on — must be assigned a separate IRQ number. Finding an IRQ number that's not already used isn't always easy. (On old XT computers, only eight IRQ numbers exist. That makes avoiding IRQ conflicts even harder.)

The trick to setting the IRQ number is knowing what IRQ numbers are already being used by the computer. Table 10-1 shows the usual IRQ settings.

Table 10-1	Typical IRQ Assignments
IRQ Number	*What It's Used For*
IRQ0	The computer's internal timer
IRQ1	The keyboard
IRQ2	Not usable
IRQ3	Serial port COM2, often a mouse or modem
IRQ4	Serial port COM1, often a mouse or modem
IRQ5	Parallel port LPT2
IRQ6	Floppy disk
IRQ7	Parallel port LPT1
IRQ8	Internal clock
IRQ9-13	Usually available
IRQ14	Hard disk
IRQ15	Usually available

✔ Some network interface cards support only a few IRQ numbers, such as IRQ3, IRQ4, or IRQ5. IRQ5 is usually a safe choice unless the computer has two printers. However, if you've installed a device such as a CD-ROM drive or a scanner, make sure that IRQ5 isn't already in use.

✔ IRQ3 and 4 are used by the serial ports COM1 and COM2. If you have a modem and a serial-port mouse, don't use IRQ3 or 4 for the network card.

✔ If your computer is loaded up with extra devices, check which IRQs are available *before* you buy your network cards. Make sure that the cards you buy can be configured to an IRQ number you can use.

✔ If you're not sure what IRQ numbers are in use and you have DOS version 6.0 or 6.2 or Windows 3.1, run the MSD program. Press Q to display the IRQs that are in use.

✔ Plug and Play in Windows 95 and 98 automatically assigns an IRQ number that doesn't conflict with other devices in your computer. Isn't that special?

Configuring the I/O port address

The I/O port address is a doorway the network card uses to transfer information to and from the network. It's usually set to a number such as 300, 310, 320, and so on. The only trick to setting the I/O port is making sure that it doesn't conflict with the port setting used by another device.

- Unlike IRQ lines, I/O port conflicts are less common. You have lots of I/O port addresses to choose from, so avoiding conflicts is easier. It's likely that the factory I/O port address setting is acceptable.

- The factory certainly won't ship out a network card with an I/O port setting that conflicts with your printer port, mouse, disk drive, or other common components. You're likely to see a conflict only if you have other stuff attached to your computer, such as a sound card, CD-ROM drive, or scanner. When you configure a network card, just make sure that the I/O port setting isn't the same as the setting you used for some other device.

- I/O port addresses are hexadecimal numbers that include the letters A-F along with the digits 0-9. For example, 37C is a valid I/O port address number. Be thankful that you don't have to understand hexadecimal numbering to set the port address correctly; just follow the instructions that come with the card and the hex monsters won't bite you.

- The *h* that's sometimes added to the end of the I/O address — like 300h or 37Ch — is just to remind you that the number is hexadecimal, as if it mattered.

- Plug and Play in Windows 95 and 98 automatically assigns an I/O address that doesn't conflict with the address used by any other device.

Configuring the DMA channel

Some network cards use DMA channels for faster performance. (DMA stands for "Direct Memory Access," but that's not important now.) If your card uses a DMA channel, you may have to change the default setting to avoid conflicting with some other add-on card that also may use DMA, such as a CD-ROM adapter or a scanner. You'll have to check the manual that came with your card to find out if the card uses DMA.

Not all network cards use DMA. If yours doesn't, you get to skip this step.

Installing the Network Interface Card

If you've installed one adapter card, you've installed them all. In other words, installing a network card is just like installing a modem, a new video controller card, a sound card, or any other type of card. If you've ever installed one of these cards, you can probably install a network card blindfolded.

If you haven't installed a card, here's a step-by-step procedure:

1. **Turn the computer off and unplug it.**

   Never work in your computer's insides with the power on or the power cord plugged in!

2. **Remove the cover from your computer.**

   Figure 10-2 shows the screws you must typically remove to open the cover. Put the screws someplace where they won't wander off.

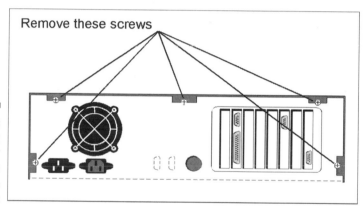

Figure 10-2:
Removing
your
computer's
cover.

3. **Find an unused expansion slot inside the computer.**

   The expansion slots are lined up in a neat row near the back of the computer; you can't miss 'em. Most computers have at least five slots known as ISA slots. Each of these slots consists of two adjacent receptacles, one slightly longer than the other. The cards have two corresponding connectors which slide into the receptacles.

   Newer computers of the Pentium variety have two or three high-speed *PCI slots.* These slots are usually used for high-speed video or disk controllers, but they can also be used for network-interface cards, provided that you purchase a network-interface card that is designed for use in a PCI slot. The PCI slots are smaller than the regular ISA slots, so that you can't accidentally insert a PCI card into an ISA slot or vice versa.

   Some really old computers have both 8-bit slots and 16-bit slots. You can tell the difference by looking at the connectors: Each 16-bit slot has two connectors, whereas 8-bit slots have only one connector. Since 16-bit cards have two connectors, you can't possibly put a 16-bit card into an 8-bit slot. If you have an 8-bit card and your computer has both an 8-bit slot and a 16-bit slot free, slide the card into the 8-bit slot. There's no point in wasting a perfectly good 16-bit slot on a wimpy 8-bit card if you can avoid it.

Some computers also have other types of slots — mainly VESA and EISA slots. Standard ISA or PCI networking cards won't fit in these slots, so don't try to force them.

4. **When you've found a slot that doesn't have a card in it, remove the metal slot protector from the back of the computer's chassis.**

A small retaining screw holds the slot protector in place. Remove it, pull the slot protector out, and put the slot protector in a box with all your other old slot protectors. Don't lose the screw. (After a while, you collect a whole bunch of slot protectors. Keep them as souvenirs.)

5. **Insert the network card into the slot.**

Line up the connectors on the bottom of the card with the connectors in the expansion slot and then press the card straight down. Sometimes you have to press uncomfortably hard to get the card to slide into the slot.

6. **Secure the network card with the screw you removed in Step 4.**

7. **Put the computer's case back together.**

Watch out for the loose cables inside the computer; you don't want to pinch them with the case as you slide it back on. Secure the case with the screws you removed in Step 2.

8. **Turn the computer back on.**

If you're using a Plug and Play card with Windows 95, the card automatically is configured after you start the computer again. Otherwise, you may need to run an additional software installation program. See the installation instructions that came with the network interface card for details.

Working with Cable

The hardest part about working with network cable is attaching the cable connectors. That's why the easiest way to wire a network is to buy prefabricated cables, with the connectors already attached. Thinnet cable is commonly sold in prefabricated lengths of 25, 50, or 100 feet. Twisted-pair cable can be purchase prefabricated, or you can attach the connectors yourself (it isn't hard to do).

Before I show you how to attach cable connectors, here are a few general tips for working with cable:

✔ Always use more cable than you need, especially if you're running cable through walls. Leave plenty of slack.

✔ When running cable, avoid sources of interference like fluorescent lights, big motors, and so on. The most common source of interference for cables run behind fake ceiling panels are fluorescent lights; be sure to give light fixtures a wide berth as you run your cable. Three feet should do it.

✔ If you must run cable across the floor where people walk, cover the cable so that no one trips over it. Inexpensive cable protectors are available from most hardware stores.

✔ When running cables through walls, label each cable at both ends. Most electrical supply stores carry pads of cable labels that are perfect for the job. These pads contain 50 sheets or so of precut labels with letters and numbers. They look much more professional than wrapping a loop of masking tape around the cable and writing on it with a marker.

✔ When several cables come together, tie them with plastic cable ties. Avoid masking tape if you can; the tape doesn't last, but the sticky glue stuff does. It'll be a mess a year later. Cable ties are available from electrical supply stores.

✔ Cable ties have all sorts of useful purposes. On my last backpacking trip, I used a pair of cable ties to attach an unsuspecting buddy's hat to a high tree limb. He wasn't impressed with my innovative use of the cable ties, but my other hiking companions were.

Attaching a BNC connector to thinnet cable

Properly connecting a BNC connector to thinnet cable is an acquired skill. You need two tools: A wire stripper that can cut through the various layers of the coax cable at just the right location and a crimping tool that crimps the connector tightly to the cable after you get it into position. BNC connectors have three separate pieces, as shown in Figure 10-3.

Here's the procedure, in case you ignore my advice and try to attach the connectors yourself:

1. **Slide the hollow tube portion of the connector (lovingly called the *ferrule*) over the cable.**

   Let it slide back a few feet to get it out of the way.

2. **Cut the end of the cable off cleanly.**

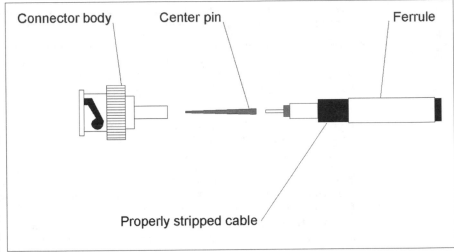

Connector body   Center pin   Ferrule

Properly stripped cable

Figure 10-3:
Attaching
a BNC
connector
to thinnet
cable.

3. **Use the stripping tool to strip the cable.**

   Strip the outer jacket back $1/2$ inch from the end of the cable, strip the braided shield back $1/4$ inch from the end, and strip the inner insulation back $3/16$ inch from the end.

4. **Twist the strands of the center conductor tightly and then insert them into the center pin.**

   Slide the center pin down until it seats against the inner insulation.

5. **Use the crimping tool to crimp the center pin.**

6. **Slide the connector body over the center pin and inner insulation but under the braided shield.**

   After you've pushed the body back far enough, the center pin clicks into place.

7. **Now slide the ferrule forward until it touches the connector body.**

   Crimp it with the crimping tool.

Don't get sucked into the trap of trying to use easy "screw-on" connectors. They aren't very reliable.

Attaching an RJ-45 connector to UTP cable

RJ-45 connectors for UTP wiring are much easier to connect than thinnet connectors. The only trick is making sure that you attach each wire to the correct pin. Each pair of wires in a UTP cable has complementary colors.

One pair consists of one white wire with an orange stripe and an orange wire with a white stripe, and the other pair has a white wire with a green stripe and a green wire with a white stripe.

Here are the proper pin connections:

Pin Number	Proper Connection
Pin 1	White/orange wire
Pin 2	Orange/white wire
Pin 3	White/green wire
Pin 6	Green/white wire

Figure 10-4 shows an RJ-45 plug properly connected.

Here's the procedure for attaching an RJ-45 connector:

1. **Cut the end of the cable to the desired length.**

   Make sure that you make a square cut, not a diagonal cut.

2. **Insert the cable into the stripper portion of the crimp tool so that the end of the cable is against the stop.**

   Squeeze the handles and slowly pull the cable out, keeping it square. This strips off the correct length of outer insulation without puncturing the insulation on the inner wires.

3. **Arrange the wires so that they lay flat in the following sequence from left to right: white/orange, orange/white, white/green, green/white.**

   Pull the green/white wire a bit to the right and then insert the cable into the back of the plug so that each wire slides into the channel for the correct pin.

4. **Make sure that the wires are in the correct pin channels; especially make sure that the green/white cable is in the channel for pin 6.**

5. **Insert the plug and wire into the crimping portion of the tool and squeeze the handles to crimp the plug.**

   Remove the plug from the tool and double-check the connection.

   ✔ The pins on the RJ-45 connectors are not numbered, but you can tell which is pin 1 by holding the connector so that the metal conductors are facing up, as in Figure 10-4. Pin 1 is on the left.

   ✔ Some people wire 10baseT cable differently, using the green and white pair for pins 1 and 2 and the orange and white pair for pins 3 and 6. This doesn't affect the operation of the network (the network is color-blind), _so long as the RJ-45 connectors on both ends of the cable are wired the same!_

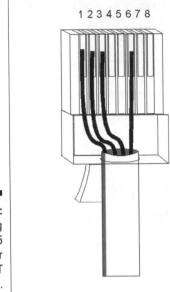

1 2 3 4 5 6 7 8

Pin connections:

Pin 1 - White/Orange
Pin 2 - Orange/White
Pin 3 - White/Green
Pin 6 - Green/White

Figure 10-4:
Attaching
an RJ-45
connector
to 10baseT
cable.

✔ Yes, I know that any normal person would have set up the RJ-45 connectors using pins 1 through 4, not pins 1, 2, 3, and 6. But remember, computer people aren't normal in any particularly relevant sense, so why would you expect the fourth wire to connect to the fourth pin? That's pretty naive, don't you think?

✔ If you're installing cable for a fast Ethernet system, you should be extra careful to follow the rules of category 5 cabling. That means, among other things, to make sure that you use category 5 components throughout: The cable and all connectors must be up to category 5 specs. When you attach the connectors, do not untwist more than $1/2$ inch of cable. And do not try to stretch the cable runs beyond the 100 meter maximum. When in doubt, it is best to have cable for a 100MHz Ethernet system professionally installed.

Installing the Network Software

Having installed the network cards and cable, all that remains is installing the network software. The procedures for doing this task vary considerably depending on the network you're using, so you need to consult your network software's manual for the details. I'll just describe some general things to keep in mind here.

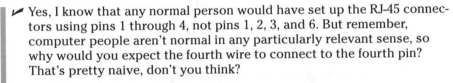

Installing the server software

Start by setting up your network server. It's the centerpiece of your network, and you won't know whether your workstations are working until you have a working server they can log on to.

If you're using NetWare, installing the server software is the most difficult part of setting up the network. Read the manual carefully, place it ceremoniously on your highest bookshelf, and pick up a copy of *NetWare For Dummies,* Second Edition by Ed Tittel, Deni Connor, & Earl Follis (IDG Books Worldwide, Inc.).

Installing the server software for Windows NT Server can be tedious as well. Fortunately, the installation for peer-to-peer networks such as Windows for Workgroups, Windows 95, and LANtastic is easier. In fact, for Windows 95 and Windows for Workgroups, you have no separate installation process for installing the server software; after you've set up Windows, the server is ready to go. As for LANtastic, server software setup is simply a matter of inserting the installation disk, typing **SETUP**, and following the instructions that appear on the screen.

- ✔ After you've installed the network software, you must define the server resources that will be shared on the network. This is where you assign the network names for your shared disk drives and printers.

- ✔ You also must build the user list. For each user on the system, you supply the user ID, password (if any), and access rights. More information about setting up the user list and managing network security is found in Chapter 12.

- ✔ If you're using LANtastic, you also modify the server computer's AUTOEXEC.BAT file so that the network is started automatically every time the computer starts. That way, if a power failure occurs, the network automatically resumes after power is restored. With other network operating systems, the network software restarts automatically when power comes back on. (If a power failure does occur, it's a good idea to turn off all the computers. When the power comes back on, restart the server first. Wait until the server has come back on-line before turning the workstations back on.)

Installing client software

Installing network software for a client is easier than installing server software, especially if you're using Windows 95 or Windows 98. If the client computer uses DOS or Windows for Workgroups, you'll have to follow the instructions that came with your networking card to configure your computer to recognize the card. Then you'll have to follow the instructions that came with your network software to add the client support software so that your computer can access the network. These chores are complicated enough to make your hair stand on end.

If you're using Windows 95 or its soon-to-be-available successor Windows 98, setting up the client computer for the network is child's play. For starters, Windows 95 (and Windows 98) automatically recognizes your network interface card when you start up your computer. All that remains to connect to the network in Windows 95 is to make sure that Windows installed the network protocols and client software properly. To do so, follow these steps:

1. **Choose the Start⇨Settings⇨Control Panel command to summon the Control Panel. Then double-click the Network icon.**

   The Network dialog box appears, as shown in Figure 10-5.

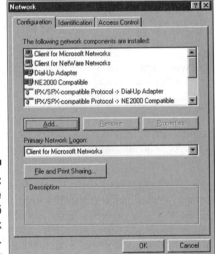

Figure 10-5:
The Windows 95 Network dialog box.

2. **Make sure that the network protocol you're using appears in the list of network resources.**

   If you're creating a Windows-based network using Windows 95, Windows 98, Windows for Workgroups, or Windows NT Server, make sure that you have the NETBEUI protocol listed. For a NetWare network, make sure that the IPX/SPX-Compatible Protocol is listed. To enable access to the Internet or an Intranet server, also make sure that TCP/IP is listed.

3. **If a protocol you need isn't listed, click the Add button and add the protocol you need.**

This displays a dialog box asking if you want to add a network client, adapter, protocol, or service, as shown in Figure 10-6. Click protocol and then click Add. A list of available protocols appears. Select the one you want to add and then click OK. (You may be asked to insert a disk or the Windows 95 CD-ROM.)

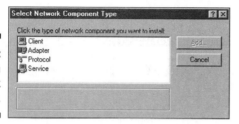

Figure 10-6: Adding a network component.

4. **Make sure that the network client you want to use appears in the list of network resources.**

   For a Windows-based network, make sure that "Client for Microsoft Networks" is listed. For a NetWare network, make sure that "Client for NetWare Networks" appears.

5. **If the client you need isn't listed, click the <u>A</u>dd button and add the client you need.**

   The dialog box that was shown in Figure 10-6 appears again. This time, click Client and then click Add. Select the network client you want to add and then click OK.

6. **Click OK to dismiss the Network dialog box.**

If your client computer is running DOS or Windows 3.*x*, you must manually install the network software. This process involves installing two programs. One is the *network shell,* or redirector, which keeps an eye on application programs and jumps in when they do something that requires access to the network. The other is a driver program that can communicate directly with your network card to access the network.

✔ With NetWare, the network shell is called NETX.EXE, and the driver is called IPX.EXE. You must generate a specific IPX.EXE file for each computer by running the WSGEN program and supplying it with information about your network card, including the IRQ number, I/O address, and so on. This stuff probably doesn't make any sense to you here, but that's okay. *NetWare For Dummies,* Second Edition by Ed Tittel, Deni Connor, & Earl Follis (IDG Books Worldwide, Inc.) explains all.

✔ To install the client software for Windows for Workgroups, just insert the first installation disk in drive A: and run the SETUP program. SETUP asks for the information it needs to configure your network card and install the necessary software.

Testing Your Network Installation

Your network isn't finished until you've tested it to make sure that it works. Hold your breath as you fire up your computers, starting with the server and then proceeding to the clients. Watch for error messages as each computer starts up. Then log on to the network to see whether it works.

- ✔ If you have a problem, the first culprit to suspect is your network cable. Check all your connections, especially any connections you crimped yourself. If you're using thinnet, make sure that the terminators are attached properly. If you're using UTP, make sure that the hub is plugged in and turned on.

- ✔ If you're using UTP, you can find a bad cable by checking the light on the back of each network card and each hub connection. The light should be glowing steadily; if it's not glowing at all or if it's glowing intermittently, replace the cable or reattach the connector.

- ✔ Double-check your network card configuration to make sure that you don't have any conflicts with other devices. Also, make sure that your network software configuration agrees with the way your network cards are actually set.

Part III
The Dummies Guide to Network Management

The 5th Wave   By Rich Tennant

UNDER PRESSURE TO INCREASE PRODUCTIVITY, THE SYSTEMS MANAGER AT MONDO CORP. READS THAT COMPUTER CHIPS RUN FASTER AT COLDER TEMPERATURES...

OK, BOB, THE PRINTER'S ON LINE!

In this part . . .

You discover that there's more to networking than installing the hardware and software. After you get the network up and running, you have to keep it up and running. That's called network management.

The chapters in this section show you how to set up your network's security system, how to improve its performance, and how to protect your network from disaster. I include a bit of technical stuff here, but no one said life was easy.

Chapter 11

Help Wanted (A Network Manager's Job Description)

*H*elp wanted. Network manager to help small business get control of a network run amok. Must have sound organizational and management skills. Only moderate computer experience required. Part-time only.

Does this sound like an ad that your company should run? Every network needs a network manager, whether the network has 2 computers or 200. Of course, managing a 200-computer network is a full-time job, whereas managing a 2-computer network isn't. At least, it shouldn't be.

This chapter introduces you to the boring job of network management. Oops . . . you're probably reading this chapter because you've been elected to be the network manager, so I'd better rephrase that: This chapter introduces you to the wonderful, exciting world of network management! Oh boy! This is going to be fun!

The Network Manager: A Closet Computer Geek

Most small companies can't afford and don't need a full-time computer geek. So the network manager is usually just a part-time computer geek. The ideal network manager is a closet computer geek: Someone who has a secret interest in computers but doesn't like to admit it.

The job of managing a network requires some computer skills, but it isn't entirely a technical job. Much of the work done by the network manager is routine housework. Basically, the network administrator dusts, vacuums, and mops the network periodically to keep it from becoming a mess.

- The network manager should be an organized person. Conduct a surprise office inspection and place the person with the neatest desk in charge of the network. (Don't warn them in advance, or everyone will mess up their desks intentionally the night before the inspection.)

- Allow enough time for network management. For a small network (such as 3 or 4 computers), an hour or two each week is enough. More time is needed up front as the network manager settles into the job and finds out about the ins and outs of the network. But after an initial settling-in period, network management for a small office network doesn't take more than an hour or two per week. (Of course, larger networks take more time to manage.)

- Make sure that everyone knows who the network manager is and that your network manager has authority to make decisions about the network — such as what files can and cannot be stored on the server, how often backups are done, and so on.

- In most cases, the person who installs the network is also the network manager. That's as it should be because no one understands the network better than the person who designed and installed it.

- The network manager makes sure that he or she has an understudy, someone who knows almost as much about the network, is eager to make a mark, and smiles when the worst network jobs are "delegated."

- The network manager has some sort of official title, like Network Boss, Network Czar, Vice President in Charge of Network Operations, or Dr. Network. A badge, a personalized pocket protector, or a set of Spock ears helps too.

Throw the Book at It

One of the network manager's main jobs is keeping the network book up-to-date. In Chapter 6, I suggested that you keep all the important information about your network in a $\frac{1}{2}$-inch binder. Call this binder your *Network Bible* or *The Good Book*.

✔ Include an up-to-date diagram of the network. This diagram can be in the form of a detailed floor plan, showing the actual location of each computer, or it can be in a more abstract, Picasso-like format. Any time you change the network layout, update the diagram. And include a detailed description of the change, the date the change was made, and the reason for the change.

✔ A detailed inventory of your computer equipment. Here is a sample form that you can use to keep track of your computer equipment:

Computer Equipment Checklist

Computer location: _____

User: _____

Manufacturer: _____

Model number: _____

Serial number: _____

Date purchased: _____

CPU type & speed: _____

Memory: _____

Hard disk size: _____

Video type: _____

Printer type: _____

Other equipment: _____

DOS version: _____

Software & version: _____

Network card type: _____

Connector (BNC/RJ45): _____

IRQ: _____

I/O Port Address: _____

DMA Channel: _____

- ✔ Keep a detailed list of network resources and drive assignments in the binder.

- ✔ If you use LANtastic, keep a copy of each computer's STARTNET.BAT file in the binder. For NetWare, keep copies of the login scripts.

- ✔ Keep in the binder whatever other information you think will be useful, such as details about how a particular application program must be configured to work with the network and copies of every network component's original invoice in case something breaks and you need to seek warranty service.

Managing the Network

The most obvious duty of the network manager is managing the network itself. The network's hardware — the cables, network adapter cards, hubs, and so on — needs oversight, as does the network operating system. On a big network, these responsibilities can become full-time jobs. Large networks tend to be volatile: Users come and go, equipment fails, cables break, and life in general seems to be one crisis after another.

Smaller networks are much more stable. After you get your network up and running, you probably won't have to spend much time managing its hardware and software. An occasional problem will pop up, but with only a few computers on the network, problems should be few and far between.

- ✔ The network manager must put on the pocket protector whenever a new computer is added to the network. It's the network manager's job to consider what changes need to be made to the cabling configuration, what computer name and user ID is assigned to the new user, what security rights the user has, and so on.

- ✔ Every once in a while, your trusty network vendor releases a new version of your network operating system. It's the network manager's job to read about the new version and decide whether its new features are beneficial enough to warrant an upgrade. Keep in mind that switching to an upgraded network version is often an all-or-nothing proposition: You can't have some computers running version X and others running version Y. Upgrading to a new network version is a bit of a chore, so you need to carefully consider the advantages the new version can bring.

- ✔ One of the easiest traps to get sucked into is the quest for network speed. The network is never fast enough, and your users always blame the hapless network manager. So the manager spends hours and hours tuning and tweaking the network to squeeze out that last two percent of performance. You don't want to get caught in this trap, but in case you do, Chapter 13 can help. It clues you in to the basics of tuning your network for best performance.

Routine Stuff You Hate to Do

Much of the network manager's job is routine stuff, the equivalent of vacuuming, dusting, and mopping. It's boring, but it has to be done.

✔ It's the network manager's job to make sure that the network is properly backed up. If something goes wrong and the network isn't backed up, guess who gets the blame? On the other hand, if disaster strikes but you're able to recover everything from yesterday's backup with only a small amount of work lost, guess who gets the pat on the back, the fat bonus, and the vacation in the Bahamas? Chapter 14 describes the options for network backups. You'd better read it soon.

✔ Chapter 14 also describes another routine network chore: checking for computer viruses. If you don't know what a virus is, read Chapter 14 to find out.

✔ Users think the network server is like the attic: They want to throw files up there and leave them there forever. The network manager gets the fun job of cleaning up the attic once in a while. Oh, joy. The best advice I can offer is to constantly complain about how messy it is up there and warn your users that spring cleaning is coming up.

Managing Network Users

Managing network technology is the easiest part of network management. Computer technology can be confusing at first, but computers are not nearly as confusing as people. The real challenge of managing a network is managing the network's users.

The difference between managing technology and managing users is obvious: You can figure out computers, but you can never really figure out people. The people who use the network are much less predictable than the network itself.

✔ Training is a key part of the network manager's job. Make sure that everyone who uses the network understands it and knows how to use it. If the network users don't understand the network, they'll do all kinds of weird things to it without meaning to.

✔ Never treat your network users like idiots. If they don't understand the network, it's not their fault. Explain it to them. Offer a class. Buy them each a copy of this book and tell them to read the first five chapters. Hold their hands. But don't treat them like idiots.

✔ Make up a network cheat sheet that has everything the users need to know about using the network on one page. Make sure that everyone gets a copy.

 ✔ Be as responsive as you can when a network user complains of a network problem. If you don't fix the problem soon, the user may try to fix it. You probably don't want that.

Tools for Network Managers

Network managers need certain tools to get their jobs done. Managers of big, complicated, and expensive networks need big, complicated, and expensive tools. Managers of small networks need small tools.

Some of the tools the manager needs are hardware tools like screwdrivers, cable crimpers, and hammers. But the tools I'm talking about here are software tools.

 ✔ Many of the software tools you need to manage a network come with the network itself. As the network manager, you should read through the manuals that come with your network software to see what management tools are available. For example, LANtastic comes with a program called LANCHECK, which you can use to make sure that all the computers on a network are able to communicate with one another.

 ✔ The Microsoft System Information program that comes with Microsoft Office, as well as its MS-DOS counterpart, MSD, is a useful utility for network managers.

 ✔ I suggest that you get one of those 100-in-1 utility programs like Norton Utilities or PC Tools. Both of these utility packages include invaluable utilities for repairing damaged disk drives, rearranging the directory structure of your disk, gathering information about your computer and its equipment, and so on. These programs are useful on NetWare and Windows NT networks, but they're even more useful on peer-to-peer networks because you can use them on the server computer as well as on the clients.

 ✔ More software tools are available for NetWare and Windows NT networks than for peer-to-peer networks — not only because NetWare and Windows NT are more popular than peer-to-peer networks, but also because NetWare and Windows NT networks tend to be larger and more in need of software management tools than peer-to-peer networks.

Chapter 12

Who Are You? (or, Big Brother's Guide to Network Security)

*B*efore you had a network, computer security was easy. You just locked your door when you left work for the day. You could rest securely in the knowledge that the bad guys would have to break down the door to get to your computer.

The network changes all of that. Now, anyone with access to any of the computers on the network can break into the network and steal *your* files. Not only do you have to lock your door, but you also have to make sure that everyone else locks their doors, too.

Fortunately, just about every network operating system known to humankind has built-in provisions for network security. This situation makes it difficult for someone to steal your files even if they do break down the door. The networks covered in this book all provide security measures that are more than adequate for all but the most paranoid users.

And when I say *more* than adequate, I mean it. Most networks have security features that would make even Maxwell Smart happy. Using all these security features is kind of like Smart insisting that the Chief lower the "Cone of Silence." Sure, no one else can hear them talking. But they can't hear each other, either! Don't make your system so secure that even the good guys can't get their work done.

Do You Need Security?

Most small networks are in small businesses or departments where everyone knows and trusts everyone else. They don't lock up their desks when they take a coffee break, and although everyone knows where the petty cash box is, money never disappears.

Network security isn't necessary in an idyllic setting such as this, is it? You bet it is. No network should be set up without at least some minimal concern for security.

✔ Even in the most friendly of office environments, some information is and should be confidential. If this information is stored on the network, store it in a directory that's available only to authorized users.

✔ Not all security breaches are malicious. A network user may be routinely scanning through his or her files and discover a file whose name isn't familiar. The user then may call up the file, only to discover that it contains confidential personnel information, juicy office gossip, or your résumé. Curiosity rather than malice is often the source of security breaches.

✔ Sure, everyone at the office is trustworthy now. But what if someone becomes disgruntled, a screw pops loose, and he or she decides to trash the network files before jumping out the window? Or what if that same person decides to print a few $1,000 checks before packing off to Tahiti?

✔ Sometimes the mere opportunity for fraud or theft can be too much for some people to resist. Give people free access to the payroll files, and they may decide to vote themselves a raise when no one is looking.

✔ Finally, remember that not everyone on the network knows enough about how DOS and the network work to be trusted with full access to your network disks. One careless use of DEL *.* can wipe out an entire directory of network files. One of the best reasons for activating your network's security features is to protect the network from mistakes made by users who don't know what they're doing.

User Accounts

The first level of network security is the use of *user accounts* to allow only authorized users access to the network. Without an account, a computer user can't log in and therefore can't use the network.

- ✔ Each account is associated with a *user ID*, which the user must enter when logging in to the network.

- ✔ Each account also has other network information associated with it, such as the user's password, the user's full name, and a list of *access rights* that tell the network what the user is and isn't allowed to do on the network. More about access rights later.

- ✔ Both IntranetWare and Windows NT Server enable you to specify that certain users can log in only during certain times of the day. This feature enables you to restrict your users to normal working hours so that they can't sneak in at 2:00 a.m. to do unauthorized work. It also prevents your users from working overtime, so use this feature judiciously.

- ✔ Windows NT Server and IntranetWare enable you to create *group accounts* which you can use to set up several accounts that have identical access rights. When you use a group account, each user still has an individual account with a user ID and password. In addition, the user accounts indicate which group or groups the user belongs to. All user accounts that belong to a particular group "inherit" the group account's access rights.

- ✔ Group accounts are the key to managing your user accounts. Set up group accounts for each different type of network user your network has. For example, you may create one type of group account for the accounting department and another for the sales department. Then you can easily configure the group accounts so that the accounting users can't mess with the sales users' files and vice versa.

- ✔ In older versions of NetWare (3.12 and before), each server computer has its own set of user accounts. This arrangement is a hassle for both network administrators and users. Administrators are bothered by having to manage a separate set of user accounts for each server. And if a user wants to access files on more than one server, he or she must log in separately to each server. Both NetWare 4.1 and with Windows NT Server keep a single list of user accounts that applies to the entire network. Thus, the administrator has but one set of accounts to keep up to date, and users who want to access more than one server don't have to log in to each server separately.

Passwords

One of the most important aspects of network security is the use of passwords. User IDs are not usually considered secret. In fact, it's often necessary that network users know one another's user IDs. For example, if you use your network for electronic mail, you have to know your colleagues' user IDs in order to address your mail properly.

Passwords, on the other hand, are top secret. Your network password is the one thing that keeps an impostor from logging in to the network using your user ID and therefore receiving the same access rights that you ordinarily do. *Guard your password with your life.*

✔ Don't use obvious passwords, such as your last name, your kid's name, or your dog's name. Don't pick passwords based on your hobbies, either. A friend of mine is into boating, and his password is the name of his boat. Anyone who knows him can guess his password after a few tries. Five lashes for naming your password after your boat.

✔ Store your password in your head, not on paper. Especially bad: writing your password down on a stick-on note and sticking it on your computer's monitor. Ten lashes for that. (If you must write your password down, write it on digestible paper that you can swallow after you've memorized the password.)

✔ Don't put your password in a batch file, either. Sure, you save time because you don't have to type it every time you log in. But if you put your password in a batch file, you may as well not have a password. Anyone can display the batch file to see your password, or easier still, run the batch file to log in as you. Twenty lashes for adding your password to a batch file.

✔ Most network operating systems enable you to set an expiration time for passwords. For example, you can specify that passwords expire after 30 days. When a user's password expires, the user must change it. Your users may consider this process a hassle, but it helps limit the risk of someone swiping a password and then trying to break into your computer system later.

✔ Some network managers opt against passwords altogether. Not using passwords is often appropriate on small networks where security is not a major concern. This is especially true when sensitive data isn't kept on a file server or when the main reason for the network is to share access to a printer. (Even if you don't use passwords, imposing basic security precautions such as limiting certain users' access to certain network directories is still possible. Just remember that if passwords aren't used, nothing prevents a user from signing on using someone else's user ID.)

A Password Generator for Dummies

How do you come up with passwords that no one can guess but that you can remember? Most security experts say that the best passwords don't correspond to any words in the English language but consist of a random sequence of letters, numbers, and special characters. But how in the heck are you supposed to memorize a password like *DKS4%DJ2?* Especially when you have to change it three weeks later to something like *3PQ&X(D8.*

Here's a compromise solution that enables you to create passwords that consist of two four-letter words back to back. Take your favorite book (if it's this one, you need to get a life) and turn to any page at random. Find the first four-letter word on the page. Say that it's WHEN. Then repeat the process to find another four-letter word; say you pick MOST the second time. Now combine the words to make your password: WHENMOST. I think you'll agree that WHENMOST is easier to remember than 3PQ&X(D8 and is probably just about as hard to guess. I probably wouldn't want the folks at NORAD using this scheme, but it's good enough for most of us.

✔ If the words end up being the same, pick another word. And pick different words if the combination seems too commonplace, like WESTWIND or FOOTBALL.

✔ For an interesting variation, pick one four-letter word and one three-letter word and randomly pick one of the keyboard's special characters (like *, &, or >) to separate the words. You end up with passwords such as INTO#CAT, BALL$AND, or TREE>DIP.

✔ If your network allows you to use passwords that are longer than eight characters, use longer words. For example, if your passwords can be 10 characters long, use a five-letter word, a four-letter word, and a separator, as in RIGHT)DOOR, HORSE!GONE, or CRIME^MARK.

✔ To further confuse your friends and enemies, use medieval passwords by picking words from Chaucer's *Canterbury Tales*. Chaucer is a great source for passwords because he lived before the days of word processors with spelling checkers. He wrote *seyd* instead of said, *gret* instead of great, *welk* instead of walked, *litel* instead of little. And he used lots of seven- and eight-letter words suitable for passwords: *glotenye* (gluttony), *benygne* (benign), and *opynyoun* (opinion).

✔ If you use any of these password schemes and someone breaks into your network, don't blame me. You're the one who's too lazy to memorize *D#SC$H4@*.

User Rights

User accounts and passwords are only the front line of defense in the game of network security. After a user has gained access to the network by typing a valid user ID and password, the second line of security defense comes into play: rights.

In the harsh realities of network life, all users are created equal, but some are more equal than others. The Preamble to the Declaration of Network Independence contains the statement, "We hold these truths to be self evident, that *some* users are endowed by the network administrator with certain inalienable rights. . . ."

Network rights we'd like to see

The network rights allowed by most network operating systems are pretty boring. Here are a few rights I wish would be allowed:

Right	Description
Cheat	Provides a special option that enables you to see what cards the other players are holding when you're playing Hearts.
Complain	Automatically sends e-mail messages to other users that explain how busy, tired, or upset you are.
Set Pay	Grants you special access to the payroll system so that you can give yourself a pay raise.
Sue	In America, everyone has the right to sue. So this right should be automatically granted to all users.

The specific rights you can assign to users depends on the network operating system you use. Here is a partial list of the user rights which are possible with Windows NT Server:

- **Log on locally:** Enables the user to log on to the server computer directly from the server's keyboard.
- **Change system time:** The user can change the time and date registered by the server.
- **Shut down the system:** The user can perform an orderly shutdown of the server.
- **Back up files and directories:** The user can perform a backup of files and directories on the server.
- **Restore files and directories:** The user can restore backed up files.
- **Take ownership of files and other objects:** The user can take over files and other network resources that belong to other users.

File System Rights (Who Gets What)

User rights control what a user can do on a network-wide basis. File system rights enable you to fine-tune your network security by controlling specific file operations for specific users. For example, you can set up file system rights to allow users into the accounting department to access files in the server's \ACCTG directory. File system rights also can enable some users to read certain files but not modify or delete them.

Each network operating system manages access rights in a different way. Whatever the details, the effect is that each user can be given certain rights to certain files, directories, or network drives. Table 12-1 lists the file system rights that are available in NetWare 4.1. Windows NT Server and other networks have a similar list of rights.

Table 12-1	NetWare 4.1 File System Rights	
Right	*Abbreviation*	*What the User Can Do*
Read	R	The user can open and read the file.
Write	W	The user can open and write to the file.
Create	C	The user is enabled to create new files or directories.
Modify	M	The user is enabled to change the name or other properties of the file or directory.
File Scan	F	The user is enabled to list the contents of the directory.
Erase	E	The user is enabled to delete the file or directory.
Access Control	A	The user can set the access rights for the file or directory.
Supervisor	S	The user is granted all rights to the file.

These operations usually are controlled on a directory-by-directory basis, though you can apply them to a single file or to a group of files by specifying a wildcard file name (like **ACCT*.*** to refer to all files that begin with ACCT).

With most networks, rights specified for a directory are applied automatically to any of that directory's subdirectories, unless a different set of rights is explicitly specified for the subdirectory.

Breeze right past this stuff about DOS file attributes

DOS has always provided a very rudimentary form of access rights through its directory attributes. Every file stored on your disk has one or more of the following attributes:

Attribute	Definition
R	*Read-only.* The file may be read but not changed, renamed, or deleted.
H	*Hidden.* The file doesn't show up in DIR listings.
S	*System.* The file is a part of DOS and shouldn't be disturbed. System files usually also have the Hidden attribute.
A	*Archive.* The file has been modified since it was last backed up and should be backed up again.

You can change these attribute settings by using the DOS ATTRIB command, but you normally shouldn't. In particular, don't try to use the DOS attributes to make a file read-only. The read-only access right managed by your network software is much more flexible than the DOS read-only attribute.

The main difference between DOS file attributes and network file system rights is that after you assign a DOS attribute to a file, that attribute is in effect for everyone who uses the file. In contrast, network access rights to particular files are assigned on a user-by-user basis, so that a file may be read-only to one user, but another user can have full rights to the file.

God (A.k.a. the Administrator)

It stands to reason that at least one network user must have the authority to use the network without any of the restrictions imposed upon other users. This user is called the *administrator*. The administrator is responsible for setting up the network's security system; that's why the administrator is exempt from all security restrictions.

Many networks automatically create an administrator user account when you install the network software. The user ID and password for this initial administrator are published in the network's documentation and are the same for all networks that use the same network operating system. One of the first things you do after getting your network up and running is change the password for this standard administrator account. Otherwise, all your

If you didn't read the last one, you REALLY should skip this one

One of the reasons Novell decided to write NetWare from scratch rather than build it atop DOS is the limitations of DOS file attributes. NetWare provides 14 different file attributes rather than the 4 provided by DOS. You don't need to know what they are, but you wouldn't bother reading this sidebar if you didn't want to know. So here they are, just so you won't lie awake tonight wondering:

Attribute	Description
A	Archive needed (same as DOS)
C	Copy inhibit; the file can't be copied
D	Delete inhibit; the file can't be deleted
X	Execute only (program files)
H	Hidden file (same as DOS)
I	Indexed file
P	Purge when deleted
Ra	Read audit
Ro	Read only
R	Rename inhibit; the file cannot be renamed
S	Shareable
Sy	System (same as DOS S)
T	Transactional; the file uses NetWare's advanced transaction-tracking features to ensure accuracy
Wa	Write audit

elaborate security precautions are a farce; anyone who knows the default administrator user ID and password can access your system with full administrator rights and privileges, bypassing the security restrictions that you so carefully set up.

✔ Most network administrators use a boring user ID for the supervisor account, like ADMIN, MANAGER, or SUPRVSOR. Some network administrators like to pretend they're creative by using a more clever user ID for the supervisor account. Here are some suitable user IDs for your supervisor account:

GOD	R2D2
ALLAH	C3PO
ALADDIN	PICARD
GENIE	DATA
TITAN	BORG
ZEUS	BARNEY
SKIPPER	HAL
GILLIGAN	M5

✔ ***Don't forget the password for the supervisor account!*** If a network user forgets his or her password, you can log in as the supervisor and change that user's password. But if you forget the supervisor's password, you're stuck.

Too Many Lists! (How to Manage Multiple Servers)

One of the problems you encounter as your network grows is that each file server on the network has its own list of user accounts. If you set up a five-computer network in which every computer is both a client and a server, you have to keep a separate user account list on each server. These lists can quickly get out of control if you don't manage them properly.

✔ Be consistent with user IDs. If a user's user ID is BARNEY on one server, it should be BARNEY on all servers.

✔ Not every user needs access to every server. One of the best security techniques is to create accounts for users only on the servers they need to access.

✔ Some networks have a feature that enables you to copy the user list from one server to another. This feature makes managing user accounts on several servers easier. After you get your user list set up the way you want it, you just copy it to all your servers. When you need to change a user account, you change it on just one server and copy the updated user list to the rest of the servers.

✔ Some networks, such as NetWare 4.1 and Windows NT Server, maintain just one user list for the entire network. With these networks, you don't have to maintain a separate user list for each server.

Chapter 13

Fast as Fast Can Be (or, The Jackalope's Guide to Network Performance)

*I*t really is true that there's no such thing as a free lunch. When you network your computers, you reap the benefits of being able to share information and resources such as disk drives and printers. But you also have many costs. You have the cost of purchasing network cards, cable, and software, plus the cost of the time required to install the network, find out how to use it, and keep it running.

Another cost of networking exists that you may not have considered yet: the performance cost. No matter how hard you try, you can't hide the ugly truth that putting a computer on a network slows down the computer. Retrieving a word processing document from a network disk takes a bit longer than retrieving the same document from your local disk drive. Sorting that big database file takes a bit longer. And printing a 300-page report also takes a bit longer.

Notice that I've used the word "bit" three times now. Lest my editor chide me for Overuse of a Three-Letter Word, I'd better point out that I used the word three times to make a point. The network inevitably slows things down, but only a bit. If your network has slowed things down to a snail's pace — so that your users are routinely taking coffee breaks whenever they save a file — you've got a performance problem that you can probably solve.

What Exactly Is a Bottleneck?

The term *bottleneck* does not in any way refer to the physique of your typical computer geek. (Well, I guess it *could,* in some cases.) Rather, the phrase was coined by computer geeks when they discovered that the tapered shape of a bottle of Jolt Cola limited the rate at which they could consume the beverage. "Hey," a computer geek said one day, "the narrowness of this bottleneck limits the rate at which I can consume the tasty caffeine-laden beverage contained within. This draws to mind an obvious analogy to the limiting effect that a single slow component of a computer system can have upon the performance of the system as a whole."

"Fascinating," replied all the other computer geeks who were fortunate enough to be present at that historic moment.

The phrase stuck and is used to this day to draw attention to the simple fact that a computer system is only as fast as its slowest component. It's the computer equivalent of the old truism that a chain is only as strong as its weakest link.

For a simple demonstration of this concept, consider what happens when you print a word processing document on a slow dot-matrix printer. Your word processing program reads the data from disk and sends it to the printer. Then you sit and wait while the printer prints the document.

Would buying a faster CPU or adding more memory make the document print faster? No. The CPU is already much faster than the printer, and your computer already has more than enough memory to print the document. The printer itself is the bottleneck, so the only way to print the document faster is to replace the slow printer with a faster one.

- A computer system always has a bottleneck. Buying a faster printer makes the bottleneck less severe, but the printer may still be a bottleneck. In some extreme cases, a printer can process information faster than the computer can send it. In this case, the printer is not the bottleneck; the parallel port that the printer is attached to has become the bottleneck. The bottleneck still exists, but it's been moved around. Since you can't eliminate a bottleneck, the best you can do is limit its effect.

- One way to limit the effect of a bottleneck is to avoid waiting for the bottleneck. For example, you can use the Windows print spooling feature to avoid waiting for the printer. This feature doesn't speed up the printer, but it does free you up to do other work while the printer chugs along. Network print spooling works the same way.

- One of the reasons computer geeks are switching from Jolt Cola to Snapple is that Snapple bottles have wider necks.

Warning! Reading this may be hazardous to your sanity

Every computer has a *bus,* which is basically a row of slots into which you can plug expansion cards such as disk controllers, modems, video controllers, and network adapter cards. Four different types of buses are generally available today:

ISA. ISA stands for "Industry Standard Architecture." ISA bus is the most common type of expansion bus. It was designed many years ago when IBM introduced its first computers based on the 80286 processor. The ISA bus sends data between the CPU and the expansion cards 8 or 16 bits at a time, depending on whether you use it with 8- or 16-bit adapter cards. The ISA bus runs at 8MHz.

MCA. MCA stands for "MicroChannel Architecture." It was introduced by IBM for its PS/2 systems. MCA sends data 32 bits at a time. MCA never really caught on, though, so it's not used as much. MCA runs a bit faster than ISA, clocking in at 10MHz.

EISA. EISA, which stands for "Extended Industry Standard Architecture," is a 32-bit

version of the basic ISA bus with a few bells and whistles added in. It's widely available and is often used for network servers because the 32-bit bus can make a disk and network more efficient if special 32-bit disk controllers and network adapter cards are used. To stay compatible with standard ISA cards, the EISA bus runs at 8MHz.

PCI. Nearly all new computers include a high-speed bus called a PCI bus that overcomes the speed limitation inherent in the ISA bus design. These computers typically include four to six standard ISA slots and two or three PCI slots for high-speed devices. Usually, PCI slots are used for high-speed video and disk controllers, but PCI network controllers are also available.

VESA. VESA is an older-style high-speed bus which is found on many 486 systems. VESA was replaced by PCI around the same time Pentiums became the processor of choice for new PCs.

What Are the Eight Most Common Network Bottlenecks?

Funny you should ask. Here they are, in no particular order:

1. **The CPU in the file server**. If the file server is used extensively, it should have a powerful CPU — Pentium Pro is best. If you're using NetWare or Windows NT Server, look into getting a server computer that can house two or more processors for even better performance.

2. **The amount of memory in the file server**. You can never have too much memory in the server. With the cost of memory so cheap these days, why not upgrade to 64MB or even 128MB?

Just say no to technical stuff about drive interfaces

Disk drives come in several varieties, and not all of them are made equal. Here's the Lowe-down on the most common drive types:

ESDI. ESDI was a popular drive type during the early days of 386 computers, but its popu-larity was eclipsed by IDE drives. ESDI stands for "Enhanced System Device Interface," and it's pronounced EZ-dee or ES-dee.

IDE. IDE, which stands for "Integrated Drive Electronics" (as if that mattered), is the most common drive type used today. Don't embar-rass yourself by trying to pronounce this term in any way other than spelling out the letters.

EIDE. EIDE is a newer version of IDE that supports larger disk drives. Those 4GB that drives you see advertised for $299 are EIDE drives. EIDE not only allows larger drives, but it's faster than IDE, too.

SCSI. SCSI stands for "Small Computer Sys-tem Interface" but is pronounced Scuzzy. SCSI drives have several advantages over IDE drives but are also a bit more expensive. SCSI also wins the prize for Best Computer Acro-nym, hands down. Two newer, faster forms of SCSI are now available. Fast SCSI is twice as fast as basic SCSI, and fast-wide SCSI is twice as fast as fast SCSI, making it four times as fast as basic SCSI.

3. **The file server computer's bus**. Oops . . . this is kind of technical, so I'll put the details in a sidebar that you can skip. The nontechnical version is this: Make sure that your server computer has plenty of PCI slots.

4. **The network card.** Use 32-bit PCI network cards for the best network performance. Remember that the server computer uses the network a lot more than any of the clients.

5. **The file server's disk drives**. If possible, use EIDE or SCSI drives. Sorry! I went technical on you again. Time for another sidebar.

6. **The file server's disk controller card.** All disks must be connected to the computer via a controller card, and sometimes the bottleneck isn't the disk itself, but the controller card. A beefed-up controller card can do wonders for performance.

7. **The server's configuration options.** Even simple peer-to-peer networks have all sorts of options that you can configure. Some of these options can make the difference between a pokey network and a zippy network. Unfortunately, no hard-and-fast rules exist for setting these options. Otherwise, you wouldn't have options.

8. **The network itself.** If you have too many users, the network can become bogged down. The solution is to divide the network into two smaller networks connected with a cool little black box called a *bridge*.

The hardest part about improving the performance of a network is determining what the bottlenecks are. With sophisticated test equipment and years of experience, network gurus can make pretty good educated guesses. Without the equipment and experience, you can still make pretty good uneducated guesses.

The Compulsive Way to Tune Your Network

You have two ways to tune your network. The first is to think about it a bit, take a guess at what may improve performance, try it, and see whether the network seems to run faster. This is the way most people go about it.

Then you have the compulsive way, suitable for people who organize their sock drawers by color and their food cupboards alphabetically by food groups, or worse, alphabetically within food groups. The compulsive approach to tuning a network goes something like this:

1. **Establish a method for objectively testing the performance of some aspect of the network.**

   This method is called a *benchmark*. For example, if you want to improve the performance of network printing, use a stopwatch to time how long printing a fairly large document takes.

2. **Now, change one variable of your network configuration and rerun the test.**

   For example, if you think increasing the size of the disk cache can improve performance, change the cache size, restart the server, and run the benchmark test. Note whether the performance improved, stayed the same, or became worse.

3. **Repeat Step 2 for each variable you want to test.**

   ✔ If possible, test each variable separately — in other words, reverse the changes you've made to other network variables before proceeding.

   ✔ Write down the results of each test so that you have an accurate record of the impact that each change has on your network's performance.

   ✔ It's important that you change only one aspect of the network each time you run the benchmark. If you make several changes, you won't know which one resulted in the change. Or one change improved performance, but the other change worsened performance so that the changes canceled each other out — kind of like offsetting penalties in a football game.

- Make sure that no one else is using the network when you conduct the test; otherwise, the unpredictable activities of other network users can spoil the test.

- To establish your baseline performance, run your benchmark test two or three times to make sure that the results are repeatable. If the print job takes one minute the first time, three minutes the second time, and 22 seconds the third time, something is wrong with the test. A variation of just a few seconds is acceptable, though.

- Standardized benchmark tests are available from on-line services such as CompuServe. These tests aren't as good as tests that you devise yourself because the tests you come up with are likely to reflect the type of work you do on your network. Nevertheless, they're useful if you can't come up with any realistic tests on your own.

Tuning a Peer-to-Peer Server

When you use a peer-to-peer network, several options exist that you can fiddle around with to improve the performance of your server computers. The time spent is worthwhile to a point because the effect of a more efficient server computer is noticed by all users of the network.

When you first install your network, make no attempt to tune the server for efficient performance. In fact, do what you can to make sure that the server runs as inefficiently as possible. Then after the network has been running a week or two, announce that you're sick and tired of lackluster network performance and you're not going to take it any more. Apply the basic performance-tuning techniques described here and you'll be a hero.

Using a disk cache

The numero uno thing you can do to boost the performance of a server is to use a program feature called a *disk cache*. A disk cache dramatically improves the performance of your disk drives. Here's how it works. (This process is a bit complicated, so make sure that you're sitting down before you continue.)

It's a given that computer memory (that is, RAM) can be accessed faster than disk storage, right? A disk cache works by setting aside a portion of memory to hold disk data that's frequently accessed. Whenever a network user tries to read data from the disk, the cache program checks first to see whether the data is already in the cache memory. If so, the data is read directly from memory, much faster than if it had to be accessed from the disk.

The more memory you set aside for the cache, the more likely it is that when a network user needs to retrieve data from the server's disk, the data can be retrieved quickly from cache memory instead. So the general rule is this: Set aside as much memory as humanly possible for the disk cache. The cache is the reason you can never have too much memory in a network server.

✔ A disk-caching program isn't something you have to run out and buy. If you're using Windows 95, disk caching is built in, so that you don't have to do anything to use it. Windows for Workgroups comes with a disk-caching program called SMARTDRV. To use it, just make sure that the server's AUTOEXEC.BAT file contains a SMARTDRV command. LANtastic also comes with a disk-caching program.

✔ Windows NT Server and Netware have built-in caching.

✔ If you're using DOS 5.0 or an earlier version, the cache that came with your networking software is probably more sophisticated than your version of SMARTDRV. However, the DOS 6.0 and 6.2 versions of SMARTDRV are as powerful as LANcache or NLCACHE. Which one you use is a matter of preference.

✔ Computer geeks tend to have strong "opynyouns" about which cache is better. Although it's true that one cache program may achieve better scores in benchmark tests than another, the truth of the matter is that any cache is better than no cache, and the differences between caches are relatively minor. Don't fret too much over which cache to use, so long as you use one.

✔ A hot topic of debate among cache aficionados (called *cacheoholics*) is whether or not to enable the risky but speedy *delayed write* feature. This feature — found in both SMARTDRV and Windows 95 — caches disk *writes* as well as disk *reads*. This significantly speeds up disk performance but at some risk: If a power failure, an earthquake, or the rapture occurs between the time that data is written to the cache and the time that the cache program decides to write the data to disk, you have a good chance of losing data.

✔ If you use a DOS-based network, the command to start your disk cache should be included in the server computer's AUTOEXEC.BAT file. That way, the cache starts automatically when you turn on the server computer.

✔ If you use a disk-caching program such as SMARTDRV, reduce the BUFFERS setting in your CONFIG.SYS file to 3. Find the BUFFERS line in CONFIG.SYS and change it to this:

```
buffers=3
```

Stop! You already know too much about SMARTDRV!

If you have DOS Version 6.0, 6.2 or 6.22, you have the latest and greatest version of the Microsoft disk-caching program, affectionately known as SMARTDRV. To activate SMARTDRV, add a command to your AUTOEXEC.BAT like this one:

```
smartdrv
```

Place the command near the top of AUTOEXEC.BAT, preferably immediately after the PATH command.

SMARTDRV checks the amount of memory your computer has to decide how much memory to use for the cache. If your computer has 4MB of memory or less, SMARTDRV uses 1MB of memory for the cache. If more than 4MB is available, SMARTDRV creates a 2MB cache.

You can change the size of the cache SMARTDRV creates by typing the size of the cache you want to use on the command line:

```
smartdrv 4096
```

This command tells SMARTDRV to create a 4MB cache. (The number you type in this command specifies the number of kilobytes you want to use for cache memory; 4MB is the same as 4096K.)

SMARTDRV uses the risky delayed-write feature unless you specifically tell it not to. With DOS 6.0, you tell SMARTDRV to forget about the delayed-write feature by listing all the drives you want cached, following each drive letter with a plus sign. If you have two hard disks — C and D — you type the SMARTDRV command like this:

```
smartdrv c+ d+
```

Confusing? Yup. Microsoft saw the error of its ways and decided that DOS 6.2 would enable you to disable delayed-write simply by adding /x to the command:

```
smartdrv /x
```

Enabling 32-bit file access for Windows for Workgroups

If you're using Windows for Workgroups 3.11, you can improve the disk performance on your server computers by enabling a feature called *32-bit file access*, sometimes also known as *VFAT* (VFAT stands for Virtual File Allocation Table, but that won't be on the test). VFAT enables Windows for Workgroups to completely bypass MS-DOS when reading or writing on your disk drive. That means faster disk access.

To enable VFAT, open the Control Panel and double-click on the 386 Enhanced icon. Next, click the Virtual Memory button and then click the Change button. This brings up the dialog box shown in Figure 13-1. Click the Use 32-Bit Disk Access checkbox if it isn't already checked. Then set the Cache Size control to an appropriate amount. Finally, click OK.

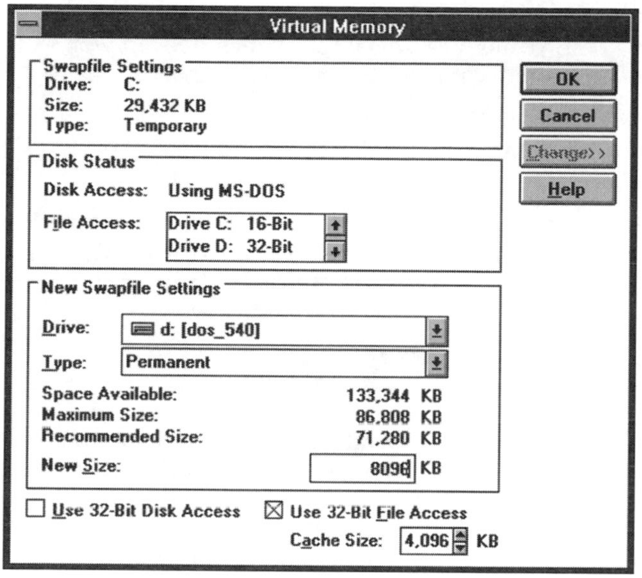

Figure 13-1:
Activating
32-bit file
access for
Windows
for
Workgroups.

How much memory do you allocate for the cache? No hard-and-fast rules exist, but the following list gives some reasonable suggestions based on how much RAM the computer has:

RAM	Cache size
4MB	1,024KB
8MB	2,048KB
12MB	3,072KB
16MB	4,096KB

Here are a few tidbits to ponder as you lie awake tonight:

✔ Microsoft claims that 32-bit file access improves disk performance by as much as 50 percent over Windows 3.1, and most benchmark tests support that claim. With 32-bit file access enabled, programs load faster, documents open faster, database queries run faster, Print Manager prints faster, and, well, you get the idea. Any Windows operation that depends on disk access runs faster when you turn on 32-bit file access.

✔ 32-bit file access provides its own disk caching, duplicating the function of SmartDrive. Therefore, remove the SMARTDRV command line from your AUTOEXEC.BAT file, unless you want to use it to cache diskettes or CD-ROM drives (32-bit file access works only for hard disks).

✔ If you don't remove the SMARTDRV command from your AUTOEXEC.BAT file, VFAT disables SMARTDRV but won't be able to reclaim the memory it used. So SMARTDRV becomes a real memory waster when VFAT is used.

✔ You can also remove the SHARE command from AUTOEXEC.BAT since 32-bit file access duplicates its function as well.

✔ VFAT is automatically used in Windows 95 (and Windows 98), so you don't have to worry about installing or configuring it.

Tuning a Windows 95 server

Windows 95 has a handy tuning feature that enables you to configure server options with a single click of the mouse. The following procedure shows how to tune a Windows 95 server computer:

1. **Choose Settings➪Control Panel from the Start menu and then double-click the System icon.**

   The System Properties dialog box appears.

2. **Click the Performance tab.**

3. **Click the File System button.**

   The dialog box shown in Figure 13-2 appears.

4. **Set the drop-down list box labeled Typical role of this machine to Network Server.**

   Your computer is now tuned as a network server.

5. **Click OK to dismiss the File System Properties dialog box.**

   You're returned to the System Properties dialog box.

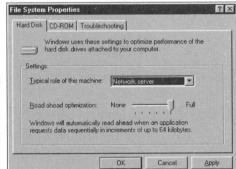

Figure 13-2:
Tuning a
Windows 95
server
computer.

> **6. Click OK to dismiss the System Properties dialog box.**

That's all there is to it.

Tuning a Windows 98 Server

Windows 98 includes the same basic tuning options as Windows 95, so you can follow the procedure listed in the section "Tuning a Windows 95 Server" to set the basic performance options for a Windows 98 server as well. In addition, Windows 98 offers several new features which can help you boost performance even more.

The most important performance improvement for Windows 98 is *FAT32,* an improved format for hard disks which uses the space on drives that are larger than 512MB more efficiently. With FAT32, you'll be able to store more data on your disk drives because less space will be wasted.

To convert your hard drive to FAT32, choose Start⇨Programs⇨Accessories⇨ System Tools⇨FAT32 Converter. The conversion will take a long time — perhaps an hour or more. You won't be able to use your computer during the conversion, so just before lunch may be a good time to start.

Unfortunately, FAT32 imposes some limitations on you:

- ✔ If you convert a drive to FAT32, you can't use Microsoft's disk compression program DriveSpace to compress the data on the drive.

- ✔ After you convert a drive to FAT32, you have no easy way to convert it back to the old format.

- ✔ If you've set up your computer using a feature called *dual boot,* which enables you to choose between two operating systems when you start your computer, the dual boot feature is disabled by FAT32.

- ✔ After you install FAT32, you won't be able to uninstall Windows 98.

In spite of these limitations, I recommend that you use FAT32 for any disk drives that will be used primarily as shared drivers on a Windows 98 network server.

Windows 98 includes another performance-tuning feature called Windows Tune-Up. Windows Tune-Up enables you to run several programs that optimize Windows' performance, including ScanDisk (which corrects errors on your disk drive), Disk Defragmenter, which juggles your disk data so that it's arranged efficiently on the disk, and a new program called Disk Cleanup, which removes unnecessary files from your computer.

The best thing about Windows Tune-Up is that it enables you to set up a schedule so that the tune-up programs are run automatically on a periodic basis. For example, you can use Windows Tune-Up to specify that Disk Defragmenter and ScanDisk should be run every night at midnight and Disk Cleanup should be run every Friday at noon. This feature can help ensure that your Windows 98 server computer is always maintained at peak performance.

You can find Windows Tune-Up buried in the Start menu, under Programs⇨ Accessories⇨System Tools.

Tuning a Windows NT Server

Tuning a Windows NT Server computer is more difficult than tuning a Windows 95 computer. Windows NT Server includes dozens of options that can affect server performance. You can spend hours tweaking these options to squeeze optimum performance out of NT.

On the other hand, Windows NT Server tends to be somewhat self-tuning. Turn it on and let it run for a few days and it soon adjusts itself to the pattern of usage it sees on your network. Soon the server is purring like a kitten. You only need to trouble yourself with tuning Windows NT if something appears drastically wrong with the network's performance — for instance, if users complain that opening a two-page document on the network server takes 10 minutes or that the print job they sent to the printer last Tuesday still hasn't printed.

To help monitor performance so that you can determine exactly where a performance problem lies, Windows NT Server comes with a program called Performance Monitor. Performance Monitor gathers statistics about all kinds of activity on your server computer, such as disk I/O, program execution, network traffic, and so on. By analyzing these statistics, you can determine the source of a network performance problem. Depending on the problem, you may be able to solve it by adjusting one of NT's configuration settings. Or, you may need to purchase additional hardware to correct the problem.

Using Performance Monitor is simple. But interpreting the statistics it gathers isn't. Unless you're really into counting cache hits and average disk seek times, you probably want to steer clear of Performance Manager if you possibly can.

Tuning a NetWare Server

Like Windows NT Server, NetWare is also a self-tuning system. Let it run for a few days to adjust to the usage patterns of your network, and it runs just fine. If you have a problem, you can always play with the server settings to try to improve performance.

Many NetWare configuration options are controlled with SET commands that you place in the AUTOEXEC.NCF file or the STARTUP.NCF file. For example, SET enables you to specify the amount of memory to use for file caching, the size of each cache buffer, the size of packet receive buffers, and a whole bunch of other stuff that's way too low-level and detailed to go into in a proud book such as this one.

Some of the best techniques for tuning NetWare are suitable only for larger networks. For example, you can dramatically improve disk performance by using a special type of disk-drive gizmo called *RAID* (which stands for "Redundant Array of Inexpensive Disks"). You improve server performance by using "superservers" that have more than one CPU. And NetWare networks are often tuned by using devices such as bridges and routers to manage "traffic" on the network.

Tuning a Client

The biggest network performance benefits are gained by tuning the network servers because the effort you spend tuning one computer results in improved performance for every user who uses that server. Still, you shouldn't neglect performance tuning for the individual clients on the network.

✔ All clients should use some sort of local disk cache: SMARTDRV for DOS-based computers or the disk caching built in to Windows 95. A local disk cache can't cache network drives, but it can still improve performance when accessing non-network drives.

✔ Speaking of local drives, you can reduce the traffic on the network dramatically by storing frequently used data on local disks rather than on a server disk. Of course, files that have to be shared should be stored on a server drive so that the users who share the file all have access to the same copy of the file. But many files don't actually have to be shared. For example, consider placing a copy of frequently used program files on each computer rather than forcing each user to access program files from the server. This arrangement can improve network performance considerably. (Of course, you must make sure that each user has a legal copy of the software.)

> ✔ Many application programs can be customized to specify the location of temporary files. Always set these programs up so that the temporary files are stored on a local drive. Doing so is especially important for database files that are used to sort information.

Chapter 14

Things That Go Bump in the Night (How to Protect Your Network Data)

∙∙

In This Chapter

▶ Planning for disasters

▶ Finding out why you should back up network data

▶ Figuring out how to do it

▶ Performing periodic maintenance for your network drives

▶ Realizing what a virus is and why networks are particularly vulnerable

▶ Protecting your network from virus attacks

∙∙

*I*f you're the hapless network manager, the safety of the data on your network is your responsibility. You get paid to lay awake at night worrying about your data. Will it be there tomorrow? If it's not, will you be able to get it back? And — most importantly — if you can't get it back, will you be there tomorrow?

This chapter covers the ins and outs of being a good, responsible, trustworthy network manager. They don't give out merit badges for this stuff, but they should.

Disaster Planning

On April Fool's Day about ten years ago, my colleagues and I discovered that some kook had broken into the office the night before and pounded our computer equipment to death with a crowbar. (I'm not making this up.)

Sitting on a shelf right next to the mangled piles of what used to be a Wang minicomputer system was an undisturbed disk pack that contained the only complete backup of all the information that was on the destroyed computer. The vandal didn't realize that one more swing of the crowbar would have escalated this major inconvenience into a complete catastrophe. Sure, we were up a creek until we could get the computer replaced. But after we had a new computer, a simple restore from the backup disk brought us right back to where we were on March 31. Without that backup, getting back on track would have taken months.

I've been paranoid about disaster planning ever since. Before then, I thought that disaster planning meant doing good backups. That's a part of it, but I'll never forget the day we came within one swing of the crowbar of losing it all. Vandals are probably much smarter now: They know to smash the backup disks as well as the computers themselves. There's more to being prepared for disasters than doing regular backups.

Don't think that it can happen to you? A few years back, the news was filled with stories of fires in Los Angeles that destroyed 400 homes. How many computers do you think were lost to Hurricane Andrew? to the floods along the Mississippi in 1993? to the San Francisco earthquake in 1989? (Not too many computers were lost in the 1906 earthquake.) And as I write this, El Niño is on its way.

Most disasters are of the less spectacular variety. Make at least a rudimentary plan for how you can get your computer network back up and running should a major or minor disaster strike.

- ✔ The cornerstone of any disaster/recovery plan is a program of regular backups. Much of this chapter is devoted to helping you get a backup program started. Keep in mind, though, that your backups are only one swing of the crowbar from being useless. Don't leave your backup disks or tapes sitting on the shelf next to your computer: Store them in a fireproof box or safe, and store at least one set at another location.

- ✔ Your network binder is an irreplaceable source of information about your network. You should have more than one copy of it. I suggest that you take a copy home so that if the entire office burns to the ground, you still have a copy of your network documentation. Then you're able to decide quickly what equipment you need to purchase and how you need to configure it so that you can get your network back up and running again.

- ✔ After your computers are completely destroyed by fire, vandalism, or theft, how can you prove to your insurance adjuster that you really had all that equipment? A frequently overlooked part of planning for disaster is keeping a detailed record of what computer equipment you own. Keep copies of all invoices for computer equipment and software in a safe place. And consider making a videotape or photographic record of your equipment, too.

✔ Another aspect of disaster planning that's often overlooked is expertise. In many businesses, one person takes charge of all the computers, and that one person is the only one who knows anything more than how to start WordPerfect and print a letter. What if that person becomes ill, decides to go work for the competition, or wins the Lottery and retires to the Bahamas? Don't let any one person at the office form a computer dynasty that only he or she can run. Spread the computer expertise around as much as possible.

Backing Up Your Data

The main goal of backups is simple: Make sure that no matter what happens, you never lose more than one day's work. The stock market may crash, and Ross Perot may run for president again, but you never lose more than one day's work if you stay on top of your backups.

Now that we agree on the purpose of backups, we can get to the good stuff: how to do it.

Use a decent backup program

DOS comes with a backup program called, appropriately, BACKUP. If your network has only a few megabytes of important data, BACKUP may be a reasonable program to use. If you have more than a few megabytes of data, however, BACKUP is unacceptable. Life is too short to spend it waiting for the BACKUP command to toss your data off to disk one byte at a time when programs that are four times as fast are readily available. Which would you prefer: spending 5 minutes backing up your data every day, or spending 20 minutes to do the same job?

✔ Besides being faster than BACKUP, other backup programs use special techniques to squeeze your data so that fewer floppy disks are required to store your backups. Compression factors of 2:1 are common, so a backup that takes 20 disks with the BACKUP command can be done with 10 disks using another backup program.

✔ MS-DOS 6.0, 6.2, and 6.22 came with an improved backup program called MSBACKUP. MSBACKUP isn't quite as good as backup programs you purchase separately, but it's good enough for most. The only drawback to MSBACKUP is that you can't use it with a tape drive. If you buy a tape drive, you have to use some other program.

✔ Windows 95 comes with a serviceable backup program, which can be accessed from the Start menu under Programs⇨Accessories⇨System Tools. Unlike older MS-DOS backup programs from Microsoft, this one supports garden-variety tape drives.

✔ Windows 98 comes with a vastly improved backup program. The new backup program has better options for selecting which files to back up and restore than the older Windows 95 backup program. Plus, it has better support for tape drives — including support for fast SCSI tape drives. Figure 14-1 shows the Windows 98 backup program in action.

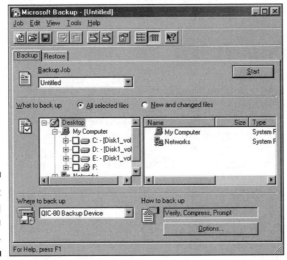

Figure 14-1:
Backing up with Windows 98.

✔ Both NetWare and Windows NT Server also come with backup programs. NetWare comes with a program called SBACKUP which can back up NetWare server data to tape or disk. Windows NT Server comes with a similar program.

✔ Better backup programs are available from utility vendors such as Symantec.

✔ If you buy a tape drive, you get backup software designed specifically for that drive. You can use the software that comes with the tape drive, or you can purchase other backup programs.

Why you should buy a tape drive

Diskettes are okay for backing up a few megabytes of data, but if you have a large amount of data to back up, use a tape drive. With an inexpensive tape drive, you can copy as much as 800MB of data to a single tape.

The beauty of a tape drive is that you can start your backups and leave. You don't have to baby-sit your computer, feeding it disk after disk and reading a bad novel in between disk swaps. A tape drive makes running your backups unattended possible. The labor savings can pay for the cost of the tape drive in the first week.

✔ The most popular style of tape backup for smallish networks is called *QIC,* which stands for "quarter-inch tape." The current QIC drives are also known as *Travan* and come in a variety of models with tape capacities ranging from 800MB to 8GB. You can purchase an 800MB Travan drive for under $100, and an 8GB unit can set you back about $500. QIC drives are slow, but they get the job done.

✔ For larger networks, you can get high-capacity and high-speed digital audiotape *(DAT)* drives. DAT drives are more expensive than QIC drives, but are much faster. An 8GB DAT drive can cost about $1,000.

You don't have to back up every file every day

If you have a tape drive and all your network data can fit on one tape, the best approach to backups is to back up all your data every day. If you have more data than can fit on one tape, or if you're using disks for backup and a complete backup takes more than a few disks, consider using *incremental* backups instead.

An incremental backup backs up only the files that you've modified since the last time you did a backup of any sort. Incremental backups are a lot faster than full backups because you probably only modify a few files each day. Even if a full backup takes 50 disks, you can probably fit each day's incremental backups on one or two disks.

✔ The easiest way to use incremental backups is to do a full backup every Monday and then do an incremental backup on Tuesday, Wednesday, Thursday, and Friday.

✔ When you use incremental backups, the complete backup consists of the full backup disks and all the incremental backup disks you've made since you did the full backup.

✔ A variation of the incremental backup idea is the *differential* backup. A differential backup backs up all the files that have been modified since the last time you did a *full* backup. When you use differential backups, the complete backup consists of the full backup disks plus the disks from your most recent differential backup.

Stop me before I get carried away

The Archive Bit is not an old Abbott & Costello routine ("All right, I wanna know who modified the archive bit." "What." "Who?" "No, what." "Wait a minute . . . just tell me what's the name of the guy who modified the archive bit!" "Right.").

The archive bit is a little flag that's tucked into each file's directory entry, right next to the file name. Any time that a program modifies a file, DOS sets the file's archive bit to the "ON" position. Then after a backup program backs up the file, it sets the file's archive bit to the "OFF" position.

Because backup programs reset the archive bit after they back up a file, they can use the archive bit to select just the files that have been modified since the last backup. Clever, eh?

Differential backups work because they don't reset the archive bit. When you use differential backups, each differential backup backs up all the files that have been modified since the last full backup.

Server versus client backups

When you back up on a peer-to-peer network, you have two basic approaches to running the back-up software: You can run the backup software on the file server itself, or you can run the backups from one of the network's clients. If you run the backups from the file server, you probably have to shut down the network in order to run backups. You can run backups from a client without taking down the server.

Even though you can run backups from a client while the network is running, doing backups while the network is being used isn't a good idea. The backup program skips over any files that have been opened by other users, so that your backup won't include those files. Ironically, those are the files that need backing up the most because they're the files that are being used and probably modified.

✔ Backing up from a workstation enables you to select network drives from more than one server. If you back up from the server and shut down the network, you're only able to access the drives on that server.

✔ You may think that backing up directly from the server would be more efficient than backing up from a client because data doesn't have to travel over the network. Actually, this usually isn't the case, because most networks are faster than most tape drives. The network probably won't slow down backups unless you back up during the busiest time of the day, when hordes of network users are storming the network gates.

✔ Setting up a special user ID for the user who does backups is best. This user ID requires access to all the files on the server. If you're worried about security, worry about this user ID. Anyone who knows it — and its password — can log in and bypass any security restrictions that you've placed on that user's normal user ID.

You can counter potential security problems by restricting the backup user ID to a certain client and a certain time of the day. If you're really clever (and paranoid), you can probably set up the backup user's account so that the only program it can run is the backup program.

(Windows NT Server provides a special user group which you can use to create backup users.)

How many sets of backups should you keep?

Don't try to cut costs by purchasing one backup tape and reusing it every day. What happens if you accidentally delete an important file on Tuesday and don't discover your mistake until Thursday? Because the file didn't exist on Wednesday, it won't be on Wednesday's backup tape. If you have only one tape that's reused every day, you're outta luck.

The safest scheme is to use a new backup tape every day and keep all your old tapes in a vault. Pretty soon, though, your tape vault can start looking like the warehouse where they stored the Ark of the Covenant at the end of *Raiders of the Lost Ark*.

As a compromise between these two extremes, most users purchase several tapes and rotate them. That way, you always have several backup tapes to fall back on in case the file you need isn't on the most recent backup tape. This technique is called *tape rotation,* and several variations are in common use.

✔ The simplest approach is to purchase three tapes and label them A, B, and C. You use the tapes on a daily basis in sequence: A, B, C, A, B, C, and so on. On any given day, you have three *generations* of backups: today's, yesterday's, and the day-before-yesterday's. Computer geeks like to call these the *grandfather, father,* and *son* tapes.

✔ Another simple approach is to purchase five tapes and use one each day of the week.

✔ A variation of this scheme is to buy eight tapes. Take four of them and write *Monday* on one label, *Tuesday* on another, *Wednesday* on the third, and *Thursday* on the fourth label. On the other four tapes, write *Friday 1, Friday 2, Friday 3,* and *Friday 4*. Now, tack a calendar up on the wall near the computer and number all the Fridays in the year: 1, 2, 3, 4, 1, 2, 3, 4, and so on.

On Monday through Thursday, you use the appropriate daily backup tape. When you do backups on Friday, you consult the calendar to decide which Friday tape to use. With this scheme, you always have four weeks' worth of Friday backup tapes, plus individual backup tapes for the past five days.

✔ If bookkeeping data lives on the network, making a back-up copy of all your files (or at least all your accounting files) immediately before closing the books each month and retaining those backups for each month of the year is a good idea. Does that mean you should purchase 12 additional tapes? Not necessarily. If you back up just your accounting files, you probably can fit all 12 months on a single tape. Just make sure that you back up with the "append to tape" option rather than the "erase tape" option so that the previous contents of the tape aren't destroyed. And treat this accounting backup as completely separate from your normal daily backup routine.

A word about tape reliability

From experience, I've found that although tape drives are very reliable, once in a while they run amok. Problem is, they don't always tell you they're not working. A tape drive can spin along for hours, pretending to back up your data, when in reality your data isn't being written reliably to the tape. In other words, a tape drive can trick you into thinking that your backups are working just fine, but when disaster strikes and you need your backup tapes, you may just discover that the tapes are worthless.

Don't panic! You have a simple way to assure yourself that your tape drive is working. Just activate the "compare after backup" feature of your backup software. Then as soon as your backup program finishes backing up your data, it rewinds the tape, read each backed up file, and compares it with the original version on disk. If all files compare, you know your backups are trustworthy.

✔ The compare function doubles the time required to do a backup, but that doesn't matter if your entire backup fits on one tape. You can just run the backup after hours. It doesn't matter whether it takes one hour or ten, as long as it's finished by the time you arrive at work the next morning.

✔ If your backups require more than one tape, you may not want to run the compare-after-backup option every day. But be sure to run it periodically to check that your tape drive is working.

✔ All back-up programs have a compare function, but not all of them have a "compare after backup" option that automatically compares data immediately after a backup. If yours doesn't, you can construct a batch file that has two commands: one to back up your data and the other to run the backup program's compare function. This setup can have the same effect. Such a batch file may look something like this:

```
TAPE C:\*.* /S /BACKUP
TAPE C:\*.* /S /COMPARE
```

Here, I use a backup program called TAPE to back up all the files on drive C:, including files in subdirectories (that's what the /S does). Then the next command runs the TAPE program again, this time using the /COMPARE switch to do a comparison instead of a backup.

Change the Oil Every 5,000 Miles

Like cars, disk drives need periodic maintenance. All versions of DOS come with a command called CHKDSK, which does some of this checking for you. MS-DOS 6.2 (and later versions) comes with an improved disk-maintenance command called ScanDisk. Windows 95 and Windows NT Server also come with ScanDisk.

Chckng yr dsk wth th chkdsk cmmnd

A friend of mine who is an authority on the origins of DOS claims that the CHKDSK command was conceived by a group of biblical scholars, which is why the word CHKDSK has no vowels. (Ancient Hebrew was written without vowels, and I really reached for that one, didn't I? Sorry.)

CHKDSK stands for "check disk," and that's sort of what it does. It checks your disk for problems, but unfortunately, it checks for only a certain class of problems and not all types of disk problems. Hence, the CHKDSK command is flawed: It lulls you into a false sense of security, leaving you thinking that it's checking the reliability of your disk drive, when in fact it is not.

CHKDSK tests for the types of problems that occur when DOS becomes confused about where your files are stored on the disk. These types of problems usually occur when the dog steps on your computer's power cord while you're saving a file. If you run CHKDSK with the /F switch, it happily corrects these problems so that you can go on your merry way.

But CHKDSK does *not* in any way check to see whether your disk is doing a good job of storing data. It won't tell you if part of your disk has gone south for the winter.

  ✔ With MS-DOS 6.2, Microsoft finally realized that the CHKDSK command had outlived its usefulness, so they added a new command called ScanDisk to do more thorough disk checking. If you have MS-DOS 6.2 or a later version, use ScanDisk instead of CHKDSK.

✔ With MS-DOS 6.2, Microsoft also made a dramatic improvement to CHKDSK: It uses commas when it displays big numbers, so now you can tell that 18374368 is 18,374,368 without squinting at the screen while trying to count the digits. Of course, this is a so-what-who-cares improvement because you'll be using ScanDisk from now on.

✔ If you don't have MS-DOS 6.2, don't rely on the CHKDSK command to thoroughly test your disk. Get a utility program like PC Tools or Norton Utilities and use it instead. Or, upgrade to Windows 95.

Scanning your disk with, you guessed it, the ScanDisk command

With MS-DOS 6.2, Microsoft introduced a new command called ScanDisk. ScanDisk does everything the old CHKDSK command does, plus more: It actually checks the reliability of your disk drive by trying to write something into every sector on your disk and then reading it back to see whether it took. (Don't worry — it does this without upsetting any of the existing data on your disk.)

Unlike the other new programs that were introduced with MS-DOS 6.0, the ScanDisk program really is easy to use. Just type **SCANDISK** and let it go. In Windows 95, you get an even better version of ScanDisk in the Start menu under <u>P</u>rograms⇨Accessories⇨System Tools. Figure 14-2 shows the Windows 95 version of ScanDisk.

ScanDisk can do a thorough check of your disk's recording surface to make sure that it can reliably read and write data. It takes a while, but it's worth the wait.

Figure 14-2:
A look
at the
Windows 95
version of
ScanDisk.

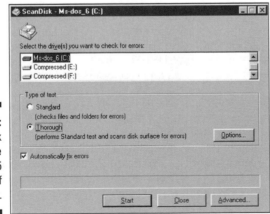

- ✔ If ScanDisk detects a problem, it displays a message that describes the problem and offers to fix it for you. Read the instructions on the screen and select the "More Info" function if you don't understand what's going on.

- ✔ If you want the MS-DOS version of ScanDisk to blast straight through its tests without asking you whether it should do the surface scan or correct errors, add the /SURFACE, /AUTOFIX, and /NOSUMMARY switches so that the command looks like this:

```
scandisk /surface /autofix /nosummary
```

Expecting anyone to type a command like this is totally unreasonable, but you can easily put this command in a one-line batch file named SCAN.BAT. Then you just type SCAN to invoke the command.

- ✔ Aren't you glad (but a little bit surprised) that they didn't name this new command SCNDSK?

- ✔ If you don't have MS-DOS 6.2 or a later version, you can get programs that are similar to ScanDisk, and a bit more exhaustive in their tests, in utility packages such as PC Tools or Norton Utilities.

Defragmenting your disk

Another routine type of service you should perform on your computer periodically is to defragment its disk drives. Defragmenting a drive rearranges all the data that's stored on the drive so that the data can be accessed efficiently. Because normal use causes the data on most drives to become scattered about, defragment your drives on a regular basis.

Windows 95 and Windows 98 both include a program to defragment your hard drives, named appropriately Disk Defragmenter. You can find it on the Start menu under Programs➪Accessories➪System Tools.

Guarding against the Dreaded Computer Virus

Viruses are one of the most misunderstood computer phenomena around these days. What is a virus? How does it work? How does it spread from computer to computer? I'm glad you asked.

What is a virus?

Make no mistake, viruses are real. They're not as widespread as the news media may lead you to believe, but they are very real nonetheless. Every computer user is susceptible to attacks by computer viruses, and using a network increases your vulnerability.

Viruses don't just spontaneously appear out of nowhere. Viruses are computer programs that are created by malicious programmers who've lost a few screws and should be locked up.

What makes a virus a virus is its capability to make copies of itself that can be spread to other computers. These copies, in turn, make still more copies that spread to still more computers, and so on, ad nauseam.

Then on a certain date or when you type a particular command or press a certain key, the virus strikes, sometimes harmlessly displaying a "gotcha" message, sometimes maliciously wiping out all the data on your hard disk. Ouch.

Viruses move from computer to computer mostly by latching themselves onto floppy disks, which are frequently exchanged between computers. But viruses also can travel over the network cables that connect the computers in your network. That's why networked computers are especially vulnerable to virus attack.

Keep in mind that the network can't be infected by a virus unless the virus enters the network through some other means, typically through an infected floppy disk or a file downloaded from the Internet. But after one computer on the network has become infected, it's not unlikely that all the computers on the network will soon be infected, as well.

- ✓ The term *virus* is often used to refer not only to true virus programs (which are able to replicate themselves), but also to any other type of program that's designed to harm your computer. These programs include so-called *trojan horse* programs that usually look like games but are in reality hard disk formatters.

- ✓ Computer virus experts have identified several thousand "strains" of viruses. Many of them have colorful names, such as the Stoned Virus, the Jerusalem Virus, and the Michelangelo Virus.

- ✓ Antivirus programs are able to recognize known viruses and remove them from your system, and they're able to spot the telltale signs of unknown viruses. However, the idiots who write viruses aren't idiots (in the intellectual sense), so they're constantly developing new techniques to evade detection by antivirus programs. New viruses are frequently discovered, and the antivirus programs are periodically updated to detect and remove them.

Using an antivirus program

The best way to protect your network from virus infection is to use an antivirus program. These programs have a catalog of several thousand known viruses that they can detect and remove. In addition, they can spot the types of changes viruses typically make to your computer's files, decreasing the likelihood that some previously unknown virus will go undetected.

MS-DOS 6 came with a basic antivirus program called MSAV. MSAV scans disk drives to determine whether any known viruses are present. How often you use MSAV depends on factors unique to your network (that's a clever way of not telling you that you should do it once a week, which you probably should, but you'd write me off as a paranoid lunatic if I actually said it). Unfortunately, Microsoft decided not to bestow Windows 95 with a similar program.

- ✔ To run MSAV so that it automatically checks all drives, including network server drives, add the /A switch to the command, like this:

```
msav /a
```

   To scan all your local drives but not the network drives, use the /L switch:

```
msav /l
```

   MSAV has a bunch of other command-line switches, all of which are worth ignoring.

- ✔ Several excellent anti-virus programs are out there that you can purchase to purge your server of viruses. One of the best is McAfee's VirusScan. Figure 14-3 shows the Windows 95 version of this program.

- ✔ The good folks who make antivirus programs periodically issue updates that allow them to capture newly discovered viruses. Consult the documentation (ugh!) that came with your antivirus program to find out how you can obtain these updates.

- ✔ DOS 6, as well as antivirus programs, comes with programs that you run to constantly monitor your computer for signs of virus infection. The DOS 6 command for this purpose is VSAFE. Run it and an alert message pops up whenever VSAFE smells a virus sneaking into your computer. To use VSAFE, add this line to your AUTOEXEC.BAT file:

```
\dos\vsafe
```

Safe computing

Besides using an antivirus program, you have a few additional precautions that you can take to ensure virus-free computing. If you haven't talked to your kids about these safe computing practices, you'd better do it soon.

Beware a new kind of virus

Recently, a new kind of virus has begun to appear. It used to be safe to assume that viruses could only be transmitted via program files. In other words, you couldn't catch a virus from a document file such as a word processing document. Unfortunately, this is no longer absolutely true. Most modern word processing and spreadsheet programs (including Word, WordPerfect, WordPro, Excel, and Lotus 1-2-3) have a feature called *autorun macros,* which enables you to attach small programs called *macros* to document files. These macros then automatically run whenever the document is opened.

Unfortunately, unscrupulous people have figured out how to exploit this seemingly innocent feature to infect document files with viruses. So catching a virus from a document file is now possible.

The best protection against this new virus threat is to make sure that you have the most recent version of a good antivirus program such as McAfee's VirusScan 95. The latest versions of these programs should be able to detect document-borne viruses.

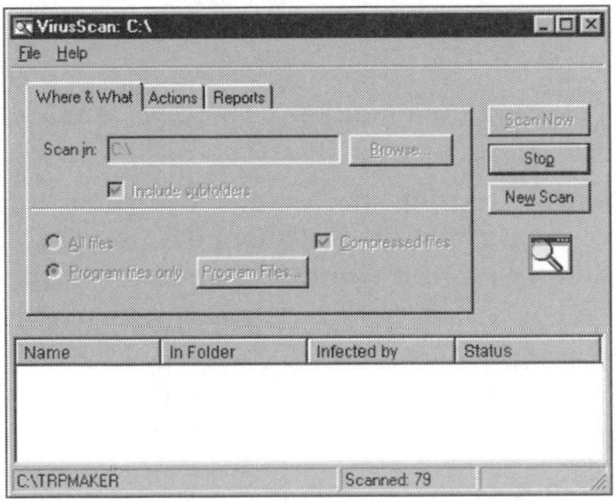

Figure 14-3: McAfee's VirusScan, brave defender against evil computer viruses.

✔ Regularly back up your data. If you do get hit by a virus, you may need the backup to recover your data.

✔ If you buy software from a store and discover that the seal has been broken on the disk package, take the software back. Don't try to install it on your computer. You don't hear about tainted software as often as you hear about tainted beef, but if you buy software that's been opened, it may well be laced with a virus infection.

- Scan your disk for virus infection after your computer has been to a repair shop or worked on by a consultant. These guys don't intend harm, but they occasionally spread viruses accidentally simply because they work on so many strange computers.

- Scan any floppy disk that doesn't belong to you before you access any of its files.

- And above all, don't leave strange disks in your disk drives overnight. The most common way for computer viruses to spread is by starting a computer with an infected disk in drive A.

Chapter 15

How to Stay on Top of Your Network and Keep the Users off Your Back

* *

In This Chapter

▶ Training your users

▶ Organizing a library

▶ Finding sources for help

▶ Coming up with great excuses

* *

*N*etwork managers really have a rotten deal. Users come to you whenever anything goes wrong, regardless of whether the problem has anything to do with the network. They knock on your door if they can't log in, if they've lost a file, or if they can't remember how to use the microwave. They probably even ask you to show them how to program their VCRs.

This chapter brushes over a few basic things you can do to simplify your life as a network manager.

Training Your Users

After you first get your network up and running, invite all the network users to Network Obedience School so that you can train them in how to behave on the network. Teach them the basics of accessing the network, make sure that they understand about sharing files, and explain the rules to them.

A great way to prepare your users for this session is to have each of them read the first five chapters of this book. Remember, those chapters are written with the network user in mind, so they explain the basic facts of network life. If your users read those chapters first, they'll be in a much better position to ask good questions during obedience school.

- ✔ Write up a summary of what your users need to know about the network, on one page if possible. Include everyone's user ID, the names of the servers, network drive assignments and printers, and the procedure for logging in to the network. Make sure that everyone has a copy of this Network Cheat Sheet.

- ✔ Emphasize the etiquette of network life. Make sure that everyone understands that all the free space on the network drive isn't their own personal space. Explain the importance of treating other people's files with respect. Suggest that it may be nice to check with your fellow users before sending a three-hour print job to the network printer.

- ✔ Don't bluff your way through your role as network manager. If you're not a computer genius, don't pretend to be one just because you know a little more than everyone else. Be up front with your users; tell them that you're all in over your collective heads, but that you're in this together, and you're going to do your best to try to solve any problems that may come up.

- ✔ If you have your users read the first five chapters of this book, place special emphasis on Chapter 5, especially the part about bribes. Subtly suggest which ones are your favorites.

Organizing a Library

One of the biggest bummers about being the network manager is that every network user expects you to be an expert at every computer program they use. That's a manageable enough task when you have only two network users and the only program they use is WordPerfect. But if you have a gaggle of users who use a bevy of programs, being an expert at all of them is next to impossible.

The only way around this dilemma is to set up a well-stocked computer library that has all the information you may need to solve problems that come up. When a user bugs you with some previously undiscovered bug, you can say with confidence, "I'll get back to you on that one."

Your library should include:

- ✔ A copy of your (not your original) network binder, containing all the information you need about the configuration of your network.

- ✔ A copy of the manuals for every program that's used on the network. Most users ignore the manuals, so they won't mind if you "borrow" them for the library. If a user won't part with the manual, at least make a note of the manual's location so that you know where to find it.

✔ A DOS manual for every version of DOS that's being used on the network. With luck, all the computers are running the same version, so only one manual is needed. But if you have several DOS versions on your network, you need a copy of the manual for each version.

✔ A copy of the network software manual or manuals.

✔ At least 20 copies of this book (hey, I have bills to pay). Seriously, your library should contain books appropriate to your level of expertise. Of course, ...*For Dummies* books are available on just about every major computer subject. Devoting an entire shelf to these yellow-and-black books isn't a bad idea.

Keeping Up with the Computer Industry

The computer business changes fast, and one of the things that your users probably expect is for you to be abreast of all the latest trends and developments. "Hey, Ward," they'll ask, "what do you think about the new version of SkyWriter? Should we upgrade, or should we stick with version 23?"

"Hey, Ward, we'd like to get into desktop publishing. What's the hottest desktop publishing program nowadays for under $200?"

"Hey, Ward, my kid wants me to buy a sound card. Which one is better, the SoundSmacker Pro or the BlabberMouth 9000?"

The only way to give halfway intelligent answers to questions like these is to read about the industry. Visit your local newsstand and pick out a few computer magazines that appeal to you.

✔ Subscribe to at least one general-interest computer magazine and one magazine specifically written for network users. That way, you can keep abreast of general trends plus the specific stuff that applies just to networks.

✔ Look for magazines that have a mix of good how-to articles and reviews of new products.

✔ Don't overlook the value of the advertisements in many of the larger computer magazines. Some people (myself included) subscribe to certain magazines because of the number of mail-order advertisements the magazines carry.

✔ Keep in mind that most computer magazines are very technical. Try to find magazines that seem to be written to your level. You may discover that after a year or two, you outgrow one magazine and are ready to replace it with one that's more technical.

✔ Subscriptions to some of the most popular computer magazines are available through Publishers Clearinghouse. Who knows, you may win $10,000,000. Then you can quit your job as network manager, and you won't need the computer magazines after all!

The Guru Needs a Guru Too

No matter how much you know about computers, plenty of people know more than you do. This rule seems to apply at every rung of the ladder of computer experience. I'm sure that a top rung exists somewhere, occupied by the world's best computer guru. But I'm not sitting on that rung, and neither are you.

As the local computer guru, one of the most valuable assets you can have is a knowledgeable friend who's a notch or two above you on the geek scale. That way, when you run into a real stumper, you've got a friend you can call for advice.

✔ When it comes to your own guru, don't forget the Computer Geek's Golden Rule: "Do unto your guru as you would have your own users do unto you." Don't pester your guru with simple stuff that you just haven't spent the time to think through. But if you have thought it through and can't come up with a solution, give your guru a call. Most computer experts welcome the opportunity to tackle an unusual computer problem. It's a genetic defect.

✔ If you don't already know someone who knows more about computers than you do, consider joining your local PC users' group. The group may even have a subgroup that specializes in your networking software, or a user group may be devoted entirely to local folks who use the same networking software you do. Odds are, you're sure to make a friend or two at a users' group meeting. And you can probably convince your boss to pay any fees required to join the group.

✔ If you can't find a real-life guru, try to find an on-line guru. Check out the various computing newsgroups on the Internet.

✔ Remember that the bribes listed way back in Chapter 5 can be used on your own guru. The whole point of these bribes is to make your guru feel loved and appreciated.

Network Manager BS

As network manager, sometimes you just won't be able to solve a problem, at least not immediately. You can do two things in this situation. The first is to explain that the problem is particularly difficult and that you'll have a solution as soon as possible. The second is to lie. Here are some of my favorite excuses and phony explanations:

- Blame it on El Niño.
- Blame it on the version of whatever software you're using.
- Blame it on cheap, imported memory chips.
- Blame it on Democrats. Or Republicans. Whatever.
- Hope that the problem wasn't caused by stray static electricity. Those types of problems are very difficult to track down. Did the user discharge him- or herself before using the computer?
- You don't have enough memory to do that.
- You don't have a big enough disk to do that.
- You need a Pentium Pro to do that.
- You can't do that under Windows.
- You can only do that under Windows.
- You're not using disk compression, are you?
- Sounds like a virus.
- It must be because of the year 2000.
- Your mind is fuzzy. You'll have to think about it over a round of golf.

Part IV
Webifying Your Network

The 5th Wave   By Rich Tennant

@RICHTENNANT

"OOPS, I FORGOT TO LOG OFF AGAIN."

In this part . . .

You discover how to meld your network with the Internet. In Chapter 16, you find out how to connect your network users to the Internet so that they can access the exciting World Wide Web. In Chapter 17, you discover how to create your own presence on the Internet by using your network to host your very own Web site. In Chapter 18, you find out how to create an Intranet, which is sort of like a Local Area Internet. With an Intranet, you can set up a Web server which can be accessed only by users on your own network, not by Internet users outside of your network.

Chapter 16
Connecting to the Internet

· ·

In This Chapter

▶ Getting acquainted with the Internet

▶ Connecting your computers to the Internet

▶ Selecting a Browser

· ·

*T*he Internet is a hot topic among computer users. Thousands of new users are jumping on the Internet every day, and the explosion shows no signs of slowing down. Should you link your computer network up with the Internet? This chapter helps you to decide.

What Is the Internet?

The Goliath of all computer networks, the Internet links tens of millions of computer users throughout the world. Strictly speaking, the Internet is a network of networks. It consists of tens of thousands of separate computer networks all interlinked so that a user on any of those networks can reach out and touch a user on any of the other networks. This network of networks connects more than 16 million computers to each other.

The Internet is made up of several distinct types of networks:

- ✔ Government agencies, such as the Library of Congress and the White House
- ✔ Military sites (Did you ever see *War Games*?)
- ✔ Educational institutions, such as universities and colleges (and their libraries)
- ✔ Businesses, such as IBM and Microsoft
- ✔ Internet Service Providers, which enable individuals to access the Internet
- ✔ Commercial on-line services such as CompuServe, America Online, and of course, The Microsoft Network

TECHNICAL STUFF

Just how big is the Internet?

Because the Internet is not owned or controlled by any one organization, no one knows how big the Internet really is. Several organizations do attempt to periodically determine the size of the Internet. One such organization is Network Wizards, which completed its last survey in July 1997. Network Wizards found that 1,301,000 separate computer networks were represented on the Internet in the form of domain names, and more than 19 million host computers existed. The same survey showed a mere 488,000 domains and 16 million hosts in January 1995, so the size of the Internet has grown considerably.

Unfortunately, no one knows how many actual users are on the Internet. Each domain can support a single user or — in the case of domains such as AOL.COM (America Online), COMPUSERVE.COM (CompuServe), or MSN.COM (The Microsoft Network) — hundreds of thousands or perhaps even millions of users. So no one really knows. Still, the indisputable point is that the Internet is big, and it's getting bigger every day.

(If you're already on the Net and are interested, you can check up on the latest Internet statistics from Network Wizards by visiting its Web site at www.nw.com.)

What Does the Internet Have to Offer?

In addition to its massive size, the Internet also boasts a great number of different services for its users. The following sections describe the various services that are available on the Internet.

File Transfer Protocol (FTP)

File Transfer Protocol, or *FTP,* as it's usually called, is the Internet's way of moving files around. Think of FTP as the Internet equivalent to a file server. Hundreds, if not thousands, of computers make their files available for downloading on the Internet. These computers are called FTP sites. You can use FTP to get files from Microsoft and other computer companies, government agencies, and universities. Most of these FTP sites enable anyone to access their treasures, but access to some is restricted to a lucky few.

The newest incarnation of Microsoft Office — known as Office 97 — enables you to access FTP sites from any Office program by using the standard File Open and Save As dialog boxes. Thus, if you want to retrieve a word processing document that's been archived at an FTP site, you can do so directly from Word. Or, if you want to upload an Excel spreadsheet file to an FTP site, you can do it directly from Excel.

Boring Internet History You Can Skip

The Internet has a fascinating history, if such things interest you. There's no particular reason that you should be interested in such things, of course, except that a superficial understanding of how the Internet began may help you understand and cope with the way this massive computer network exists today. So here goes.

The Internet traces its beginnings back to a small network called ARPANET, built by the Department of Defense in 1969 to link defense installations. ARPANET soon expanded to include not only defense installations, but universities as well. In the 1970s, ARPANET was split into two networks, one for military use (which was renamed MILNET) and the original ARPANET for non-military use. The two networks were connected using a networking link called IP, the internet protocol, so called because it allowed communication between two networks.

The good folks who designed IP had the foresight to realize that soon more than two networks would want to be connected. In fact, they left room for tens of thousands of networks to join the game, which is a good thing because it wasn't long before the Internet began to take off.

By the mid 1980s, ARPANET was beginning to reach the limits of what it could do. Enter the National Science Foundation (NSF), which set up a nationwide network designed to provide access to huge supercomputers, those monolithic computers used to discover new prime numbers and calculate the orbits of distant galaxies. The supercomputers themselves were never put to much use, but the network that was put together to support the supercomputers, called NSFNET, did. It replaced ARPANET as the new backbone for the Internet.

Then, out of the blue, it seemed as if the whole world became interested in the Internet. Stories about it appeared in *Time* and *Newsweek*. The Net began to grow so fast that even NSFNET couldn't keep up, so private commercial networks got into the game. The size of the Internet has doubled every year for the past few years, and who knows how long this dizzying rate of growth will continue.

Internet e-mail

E-mail is the main reason most people use the Internet. Internet e-mail is similar to e-mail on your local area network (LAN), except that you aren't limited to exchanging mail with users of your own network. With Internet e-mail, you can send and receive messages to anyone anywhere on the Internet.

Internet Relay Chat (IRC)

Internet Relay Chat, or *IRC*, is the Internet's real-time chat feature. It enables Internet users all across the globe to go online at the same time and exchange messages, kind of like a giant conference call. Discussion topics range from politics to lingerie, though IRC conversations tend to be unfocused.

Mailing lists

A *mailing list* is a list of the e-mail addresses of a group of people who are interested in a particular subject, such as flat tax proposals, *Star Trek* movies, or origami. The mailing list itself has an e-mail address. When you send e-mail to the mailing list address, your message is automatically distributed to everyone else on the list. To get on a mailing list, you subscribe to it by sending an e-mail message to the list's administrator. (The subscription address is almost always different from the mailing list's normal address, so be careful to send your subscription request to the correct address.)

As you read further about other Internet services, you may wonder why anyone would bother with the discussions found on mailing lists. That's a very good question. The main reason that mailing lists continue to thrive is that a large number of people have Internet e-mail as their only Internet service. Other services, such as newsgroups and FTP, aren't available to these users, so mailing lists are a lifesaver. As more and more users gain full access to the Internet, mailing lists continue to fade in popularity.

Telnet

Telnet is a way of connecting to another computer on the Internet and actually running programs on that computer as if your computer were a terminal attached to the other computer. Telnet is one of the many Internet services that's rapidly losing popularity as the World Wide Web (described later in this chapter) becomes more popular. However, many Internet services — such as scanning the card catalogs of many public libraries — are still only available via Telnet.

Usenet newsgroups

Newsgroups are on-line discussion groups. They're places where users with common interests gather to share ideas. Newsgroups exist for just about every topic imaginable — everything from gardening to car repair.

For technical reasons you don't need or want to know, Internet newsgroups are distributed over what is called *Usenet*. As a result, you sometimes see the terms Usenet and newsgroups used together.

Unlike Internet Relay Chat, which was discussed in a previous section, Usenet newsgroups are not real-time discussions. Newsgroups are more like e-mail: You post a message and then check back a day or two later to see if anyone has replied.

What about commercial on-line services?

The Internet isn't the only, or necessarily the best, source of on-line information. One of the great strengths of the Internet is also its downfall: The information on the Internet is not organized in any official manner, so finding the information you're looking for can be difficult, if not sometimes impossible. If, like a good Presbyterian, you prefer a sense of decency and order, you may try one of the commercial on-line services such as America Online, CompuServe, or The Microsoft Network. These services provide an organized approach to on-line information. You can get discussion forums and download libraries organized logically by topic. You may also find that the commercial on-line services are a bit more friendly than the Internet, especially to novices. (Many Internet users don't have much patience for the mistakes made by the millions of new users who have recently flooded their once-private turf.)

The main disadvantage of commercial on-line services is that they're more expensive than the Internet. However, many of the commercial on-line services also offer access to the Internet, so you can get the best of both worlds and compare them.

World Wide Web

The *World Wide Web*, or *WWW*, as it's alliteratively called, is the main method of accessing information on the Internet. Think of it as a graphical interface to Internet information, but with an important twist: The Web is filled with special hypertext links which enable you to jump from one Internet locale to another.

The web is a vast collection of individual *pages* which can be viewed one at a time by a program known as a *web browser*. The two most popular web browsers are Netscape Navigator and Microsoft Internet Explorer. I say something about web browsers later in this chapter, in the section "Choosing a Web Browser."

A home page is a virtual "page" which serves as the entry-point to a company's or individual's collection of Web pages. All the big companies have their own home pages, and many small companies and even some individuals have their own home pages, too. The entire collection of Web pages for a company or an individual is known as a *web site*.

The latest development in the Web is known as *push technology.* Push enables you to subscribe to Web sites which interest you. After you've subscribed to a site, the site automatically sends you information on a regular basis or whenever the information available at the site changes. For example, you can subscribe to a Web site that informs you automatically whenever an update to your Windows software is available. Or you can get sports scores or stock quotes sent to you automatically every hour, on the hour.

Push technology is not necessarily a good thing for users who are connected to the Internet via a LAN connection. With push, network users can create an almost constant stream of information flowing to them from the Internet. Unfortunately, this information must travel across the LAN to get from the Internet to the user, using up valuable bandwidth on the LAN and slowing down the overall speed of the network. If you're a network administrator, you may want to put limits on the use of push subscriptions.

Understanding Internet Addresses

Just as every user of your LAN must have a user-ID, everyone who uses the Internet must have an Internet address. Because the Internet has so many computers and so many users, a single user-ID would not be sufficient. As a result, Internet addresses are constructed using a method called the Domain Name System, or DNS.

An Internet address for an individual user follows this format:

```
username@organization.category
```

As you can see, the address consists of these three parts:

- **Category.** The category is a two- or three-character suffix that indicates the broad category into which the user's computer system falls. The six most commonly used categories are summarized in Table 16-1. The category portion of an Internet address is also known as the *top-level domain*.

- **Organization.** The organization name is, well, the name (or abbreviation of the name) of the organization, institution, or agency. For example, ibm.com is a commercial organization named IBM. The educational institution named MIT has the name mit.edu. And nasa.gov is a government agency named NASA.

- **Username.** This is the name assigned to the user at his or her computer. It's the Internet's equivalent to Microsoft Network's user-ID. If you're an employee of nasa.gov and you log in to NASA's computer as Neil, your full Internet address would be neil@nasa.gov.

Occasionally, some Internet addresses are more complicated. Addresses get complicated when large organizations want to subdivide their networks into two or more groups. For example, a university may break its network down by department. Thus, the address of the history department at a university may be his.gadolphin.edu, whereas the track team may be located at track.gadolphin.edu.

Table 16-1	Categories Used in Internet Addresses
Category	*Explanation*
edu	Education
mil	Military
gov	Government
com	Commercial
net	Network
org	Organizations that don't fit one of the other categories

When pronouncing Internet addresses, the @ symbol is pronounced *at,* and the periods are pronounced *dot.* Thus, the address neil@nasa.gov would be pronounced *Neil at NASA dot gov.*

In addition to e-mail addresses, you also need to know a bit about addresses of places you can visit on the Internet. These addresses are called *URLs,* which stands for *Uniform Resource Locators.* URLs usually consist of three words separated by periods. If the first word is *www,* the site is a page on the World Wide Web. For FTP sites, the first word is usually *ftp.* The second word is typically the name of a company or organization that sponsors the site, and the third is the sponsor's category name (like the category names used in an e-mail address, which are listed in Table 16-1). Thus, `www.ibm.com` is the URL for IBM's Web page, and `www.microsoft.com` is the address for Microsoft's Web page.

You sometimes see Web addresses that begin with `http://`, as in `http://www.microsoft.com`. All WWW addresses use this prefix, but depending on the software you use to access the Internet, you may or may not be able to omit the `http://` prefix when you type in a site's address.

You may also see additional information tacked on to the end of a Web address, as in `http://www.nasa.gov/hqpao/nasacenters.html`. This Web address displays a page that lists the various centers within NASA. Typing in the information following `www.nasa.gov` is required in order to reach the page at NASA that outlines its various centers.

Another type of address that you may encounter is the address of an Internet newsgroup. Newsgroup addresses begin with one of the following words:

✔ alt

✔ comp

- misc
- news
- rec
- sci
- soc
- talk

The rest of the address indicates the topic discussed in the newsgroup. For example, `comp.answers` is a place to get answers to general computer questions. Try `comp.sys.ibm.pc.hardware.networking` for answers to questions about network hardware.

Options for Connecting Your Network to the Internet

If you want to enable the users of your network to access the Internet, you have several options. The following sections describe the most commonly used methods of connecting network users to the Internet.

Connecting with modems

A *modem* is a device that enables your computer to connect to another computer via the telephone. Modems are the most common way to connect to the Internet. Modems are inexpensive — cheap ones can be purchased for as little as $50. Most modems connect to the Internet at a speed of 33.6 Kbps, which means that the modem can send about 33,600 bits of information per second over a standard phone connection. Faster modems, which cost a bit more than 33.6 Kbps modems, operate at 56 Kbps.

To use a modem, you must also have a phone line with a phone jack located near the computer. The modem ties up the phone line whenever you're connected to the Internet, so you can't use the phone for a voice conversation and connect to the Internet at the same time.

The easiest way to connect your network users to the Internet with modems is to give each user who needs Internet access his or her own modem and dedicated phone line. This system enables each user to access the Internet independently of the LAN. After the modems and phone lines are installed, contact a local Internet Service Provider, and they can help you set up your Internet accounts.

Setting up a separate modem and phone line for each user is probably the easiest way to set up your Internet access. However, this system can get pretty expensive when you start to add up the monthly costs of all those phone lines. To cut costs, you can install a modem on a server computer and use software that enables network users to access the modem as a shared device. This process is a little more complicated because it requires extra work to set up the modem so that it can be shared. Neither NetWare, Windows NT Server, Windows 95, nor LANtastic can do this on their own, so you have to purchase additional modem-sharing software to make it work.

If you go this route, only one network user is able to access the Internet at a time. And performance on the server computer is affected whenever the modem is in use. A better way to share modems among your network users is to set up a separate computer to function as a communications server. Then you can install one or more modems in the communications server computer so that the modems can be accessed by your network users. Once again, you have to purchase separate modem sharing software to enable the server to share its modems with the network.

An even better way to share modems is to install a special-purpose device that's designed to connect your network to the Internet via modems. For example, Ramp Networks makes a product called the WebRamp M3 which is a combination of several devices in a single box: A *router* creates a link between your LAN and the Internet, a four-port 10baseT Ethernet hub enables you to connect four computers (or more if you cascade additional hubs), and three serial ports can be connected to modems. The WebRamp M3 enables you to share up to three modems on your network and sells for under $400. (For more information, you can visit Ramp Networks on the Internet at www.rampnct.com.)

ISDN

ISDN, which stands for *Integrated Services Digital Network,* is a digital rather than analog phone line. ISDN allows data to be sent much faster than a conventional phone line — up to 128 Kbps rather than 33.6 Kbps or 56 Kbps. As an added plus, a single ISDN line can be split into two separate channels so that you can carry on a voice conversation while your computer is connected to the Internet. Each channel operates at 56 Kbps.

Sounds great. The only catch is that it's expensive. An ISDN connection doesn't require a modem. Instead, a special ISDN adapter is used, and that can set you back at least $200. In addition, an ISDN line is more expensive to install than a normal phone line, and the monthly fees for ISDN usually amount to $25–$50, depending on your area. On top of that, you may be billed by the minute for usage. For example, in my area, an ISDN line costs $24.95 per month plus a penny per minute.

What about the cable guy?

One of the newest methods of connecting to the Internet is to use the same cable that delivers cable TV to homes and businesses. Cable Internet service uses a technology called *broadband* to enable television and data to travel over the cable at the same time. Cable Internet service has many advantages over a dial-up Internet connection:

✔ With cable, the Internet is always immediately available. You don't have to wait for a phone to dial up a service provider.

✔ A cable Internet connection is much faster than any type of dial-up connection. With cable, you can download information from the Internet at a whopping 10 Mbps, which makes it just about the fastest Internet connection you can get. For technical reasons you don't want to know, uploading information is slower than downloading information. But uploads still run at a brisk 2 Mbps pace.

✔ Cable Internet doesn't tie up a phone line while you're connected to the Internet. It doesn't tie up your television, either: You can watch TV and surf the Web at the same time.

✔ Cable Internet is inexpensive. In fact, a typical TV and Internet subscription costs about $40 per month, which isn't much more than the cost of a basic cable subscription and a dial-up Internet subscription added together. You do have to purchase a special cable modem, but that probably won't cost much more than $100.

✔ Although cable Internet is ideal for home users, most of whom already subscribe to cable TV anyway, it's also great for businesses.

The only drawback to cable Internet access is that it isn't available everywhere yet. In fact, at the time I'm writing this, only a few select cities have cable Internet service. Cable companies are hard at work getting ready for cable Internet access, however. So cable Internet will probably be available in your area soon.

An ISDN line can be shared among network users just as a modem can. You can install an ISDN line in a server computer and use special software to share the line with the network, or you can purchase a device called an *ISDN router* which connects to your network using a standard 10baseT or 10base2 Ethernet connection and connects to the Internet via one or more ISDN connections. ISDN routers cost anywhere from $500 to $2,500 or more.

High speed private lines: T1 and T3

If you're really serious about high-speed Internet connections, contact your local phone company (or companies) about installing a dedicated high-speed digital line. These lines can cost you plenty (on the order of hundreds of dollars per month) so they're best suited for large networks in which 20 or more users are accessing the Internet simultaneously.

A T1 line has more than ten times the capacity of an ISDN connection, with speeds up to 1.544 Mbps — that's *million* bits per second. A T1 line can service as many as 24 users simultaneously, each working at 64 Kbps, roughly equivalent to the speed each user would achieve with a dedicated 56 Kbps modem and phone line or an ISDN connection.

A T3 line is even faster than a T1 line. A T3 line transmits data at an amazing 44.184 Mbps. Each T3 line can be divided into 28 T1 lines. Since each T1 line can handle 24 users at 64 Kbps, that means a T3 line can handle 672 users (24 X 28 = 672). Of course, T3 lines are also considerably more expensive than T1 lines.

If you don't have enough users to justify the expense of an entire T1 or T3 line, you can lease just a portion of the line. With a *fractional T1 line,* you can get connections with speeds of 128 Kbps to 768 Kbps and *fractional T3* enables you to choose speeds ranging from 4.6 Mbps to 32 Mbps.

Setting up a T1 or T3 connection to the Internet is stuff best left to professionals. Getting this type of connection to work is far more complicated than setting up a basic LAN.

Choosing a Web Browser

When you connect your LAN to the Internet, you must provide software known as a *Web browser* for your network's users to use when accessing the network. Although you have many different Web browsers to choose from, most people use one of two popular programs: Netscape Navigator or Microsoft Internet Explorer. Navigator has been around longer than Internet Explorer, so it's used by more people. However, Internet Explorer is gaining popularity fast and may eventually match Navigator's success.

The debate about which browser is better — Navigator or Internet Explorer — is one of the hottest holy wars being fought in computerdom these days. Proponents of each program have a nasty tendency to demonize the other, suggesting either that Navigator is a relic of the Stone Age or that Internet Explorer is nothing more than Microsoft chairman Bill Gates's most recent attempt at world domination.

The truth is that both Navigator and Internet Explorer are excellent programs. Both are so good, in fact, that recommending one over the other on any basis is difficult, other than personal preference. I recommend that you use Internet Explorer, but I base my recommendation solely on the fact that I've written a book about Internet Explorer titled *Internet Explorer 4 For Dummies* (IDG Books Worldwide, Inc., naturally), and I'd like to retire young.

Both Internet Explorer and Navigator come loaded with features that go beyond simple Web browsing. The complete Internet Explorer package includes a bunch of extra goodies, such as:

- ✔ Outlook Express, an e-mail program that can also handle Internet newsgroups.
- ✔ NetMeeting, a conferencing program that enables you to conduct online meetings with other Internet users.
- ✔ Microsoft Chat, an online chatting program that can display chats in normal text mode or in an interesting (but annoying after awhile) comic-strip mode.
- ✔ Microsoft FrontPage Express, a Web page creation tool.

Netscape distributes its Navigator program in a bundle of Internet products called Communicator. Besides Navigator, the Communicator package includes:

- ✔ Netscape Messenger, an e-mail program.
- ✔ Netscape Collabra, a program for accessing Internet newsgroups that also enables you to create private newsgroups on your LAN.
- ✔ Netscape Composer, a tool for creating Web pages.
- ✔ Netscape Netcaster, which enables you to create online channels which users can subscribe to. (Internet Explorer has a similar feature.)
- ✔ Netscape Conference, which enables you to conduct online meetings with other users much like Microsoft's NetMeeting.

The best news about Internet Explorer and Navigator is that both programs are inexpensive. In fact, Internet Explorer is free. It's supplied free of charge along with Windows 95, and you can download it free of charge from the Internet at Microsoft's Web page, `www.microsoft.com/ie`. Netscape charges $49 for its complete Communicator package, but you can download Communicator from Netscape's Web site at `www.netscape.com` and use it for 90 days free of charge.

Whichever browser you choose, it's a good idea to standardize your entire network on one browser or the other. After all, when someone's Internet connection breaks, you're the one who is called in to fix it. If you standardize your Web browser, you become an expert in only one of them. If you don't standardize, you have to be an expert in both Navigator and Internet Explorer.

With the forthcoming new release of Windows 98, Internet Explorer 4 is a built-in part of Windows, so you don't have to install it separately. However, you can still use Navigator if you prefer.

Internet Explorer's legal problems

At the time that I wrote this, the U.S. Department of Justice was going after Microsoft for its practice of requiring that computer manufacturers install Internet Explorer 4 on all Windows 95 computers. At issue is whether Microsoft's bundling of Internet Explorer 4 with Windows 95 is a violation of a "Consent Decree" issued back in 1995 which said that Microsoft could not require that computer manufacturers who license Windows 95 also be forced to license any other Microsoft software product.

The Justice Department contends that Microsoft is violating the consent decree by forcing computer manufacturers to take Internet Explorer as a part of Windows 95. Microsoft contends that this is not a violation of the consent decree because the consent decree also included a clause which allowed Microsoft to incorporate new integrated features into Windows, and Internet Explorer 4 is actually an integrated feature of Windows 95.

No one knows how this will all turn out, but in all likelihood, very few computer manufacturers will choose to leave Internet Explorer 4 off of their systems anyway. After all, Internet Explorer 4 is free and customers want it. Why refuse to give it to them?

With Windows 98, Internet Explorer truly is an integrated feature of Windows, and Microsoft will probably distribute it as such. We'll have to wait and see if the Justice Department continues to push the issue after Windows 98 is released.

Chapter 17

Hosting Your Own Web Site

. . . .

. . . .

*S*ooner or later, you're going to discover that all your competitors have created their own home page on the World Wide Web, and you're going to want to do likewise. Take a deep breath. Setting up your LAN so that your users can access the Internet is difficult enough. Creating your own Internet site is another matter altogether. I'll start by saying outright that this isn't something you should attcmpt on your own. Seek professional help.

If you choose to ignore my sage advice, read on.

Serving Up Your Web

You have two basic approaches to setting up a server to host your Web page on the Internet. The first and simplest approach is to contact a local Internet Service Provider and find out how much setting up shop on their computer will cost. Most ISPs allow their users to store a few megabytes of data on the ISP's computers, so you can easily set up a simple home page, provided that you don't want it to be too fancy. 2MB isn't nearly enough disk space to include complicated graphics, sounds, and video clips — things that make a Web page worth viewing. You'll probably want to pay for additional space.

The second way to create your own home page is to set up your own Web server computer. The Web server computer is connected to the Internet via a high-speed connection such as an ISDN or a T1 or T3 line. The Internet server computer may run Windows NT Server, NetWare, or UNIX; most Internet servers run UNIX, although Windows NT is growing in popularity. In addition, special Internet server software is required.

Life gets more complicated if you want the Internet server computer connected to your LAN. In that case, you must take special precautions to ensure that strangers can't use your Internet server as a back door into your LAN. Hackers love to break into computer systems this way, either to trash files, steal information, or just prove they can do it.

Selecting a Web server

To set up a Web site, you need to dedicate a separate computer to act as a Web server. All the information that's available via your Web site resides on this computer's disk, so plenty of disk storage is a must for your Web server. Plenty of RAM is a must also — consider 32MB to be the minimum.

As for operating systems, you have two basic choices: Windows NT Server or UNIX. Because the Internet got its start in the UNIX world, more Web sites run UNIX than Windows NT. However, Windows NT is gaining ground, especially in Intranets. If you're familiar with Windows, but have never touched a UNIX computer, Windows NT Server is the way to go.

In addition to a server operating system, you also need Web server software. The following sections briefly describe the most popular Web server software choices.

NCSA HTTPd

Far and away the most popular Web server software on the Internet is NCSA HTTPd, often called simply NCSA. *NCSA* stands for the National Center for Supercomputing Applications, located at the University of Illinois in Urbana, Illinois. HTTPd is a UNIX-only Web server, and it requires a certain amount of UNIX expertise to install and operate it.

This Web server is so popular for two reasons:

- NCSA was the first Web server. In fact, NCSA *invented* the Web.
- NCSA is free. You can download it from hoohoo.ncsa.uiuc.edu.

Apache

Apache is another UNIX-only Web server which is available free of charge. Apache is essentially an improved version of NCSA, and is almost as popular on the Internet. You can obtain Apache from the Internet at www.apache.org.

Netscape Web Servers

Netscape, one of the most successful Internet companies, markets several Web servers. Unlike NCSA or Apache, the Netscape servers run on UNIX or Windows NT Server. The bad news is that these servers aren't free: You must pay a one-time fee of $295–$995, depending on which server you choose.

Netscape offers the following server products:

- ✔ **Netscape Enterprise Server.** The latest and greatest version of Netscape's Web server, which includes support for Java, the Web scripting language that everyone's talking about but few people are actually using (at least not yet). This server is also available as a part of a suite of server products called SuiteSpot.

- ✔ **Netscape FastTrack Server.** A user-friendly Web server which includes setup wizards to make installation easier, as well as point-and-click tools for creating Web pages.

Microsoft Internet Information Server

Internet Information Server, or IIS, is Microsoft's answer to Netscape's servers. Unlike Netscape, IIS runs only on Windows NT Server (after all, IIS is from Microsoft). But also unlike Netscape, IIS is free — you can download it from www.microsoft.com. Or, you can get it by purchasing Windows NT Server 4.0.

Protecting Your LAN from the Internet

A *firewall* is a security-conscious router that sits between your network and the rest of the world in an effort to prevent *them* from getting to *us*. The firewall acts as a security guard between the Internet and your LAN. All network traffic into and out of the LAN must pass through the firewall, which runs special software that prevents unauthorized users from accessing the LAN.

Firewalls are Pat Buchanan's favorite computer component.

Some type of firewall is a must if you're going to host a Web site on a server computer that's connected to your LAN. Without a firewall, anyone who visits your Web site can potentially break into your LAN and steal your top-secret files, read your private e-mail, or worse yet, format your hard drive.

Choosing Tools for Creating Web Pages

Back when the Web was young, the easiest way to crank out Web pages was to fire up your trusty text editor and start typing. Your text had to include complicated formatting commands, called *HTML tags,* which resembled a rudimentary programming language and therefore required a graduate degree in computer science to comprehend.

Those days are gone. Now, point-and-click tools are available to help you create Web pages without worrying about the details of HTML tags. There are basically four categories of development tools for creating the pages that make up your Web site:

- ✔ **Web-Enhanced Office Suites.** All three of the major Office suites — Microsoft Office, Lotus SmartSuite, and Corel Office — are now Internet enabled. That means, for example, that you can create a document in Microsoft Word and save it in HTML format, suitable for publishing on the Web. These applications are ideal when your Intranet exists primarily as a means of making corporate publications (policy manuals, for example) available.

- ✔ **HTML Editors.** The better HTML editors offer a WYSIWYG (What You See Is What You Get) approach to creating HTML documents. One of the best known is SoftQuad's HoTMetaL, which earns the coveted "gOofiEst UsE oF CapiTallZation iN a ProDUct naME" award. HoTMetaL gives you a WYSIWYG view of your HTML document, but also lets you roll up your sleeves and dig into the HTML codes.

- ✔ **Home Page Editors.** These are easy to use programs which are designed to enable individuals or small businesses to create their own home pages. The best known is Microsoft's FrontPage. Internet Explorer 4 comes with a free, scaled-down version of FrontPage called FrontPage Express. Although these programs are easy to use, they're also limited in their HTML capabilities.

- ✔ **Hard-core Development Tools.** Serious Web developers should look into the new breed of Java development tools which are just becoming available, such as Symantec's Visual Café and Microsoft's Visual J++.

Dealing with CGI

The earliest forms of HTML allowed only static information to be displayed on Web pages. Users could request certain pages to be displayed, but the flow of information was in one direction only: from the server to the client.

Then along came an HTML feature called *forms,* which enable Web developers to put simple data entry fields on their Web pages. Form fields were limited to simple text boxes, radio buttons, checkboxes, and just two types of command buttons: one to send data to the server, the other to clear data entered on the form. This limited repertoire of controls allowed only simple interactions, but forms took off. The best Web sites utilized forms to create simple interactive applications.

Probably the best known examples of Web sites that use forms are the search sites like Yahoo and Alta Vista. In a search site, you type a keyword into a text box and then click a command button. The search site then displays a list of Web sites which are related to the keyword you entered.

To use HTML forms, you have to contend with a feature called *CGI,* which stands for *Common Gateway Interface.* Here's how a form-based interaction using CGI works:

1. The client (that is, the Web browser) requests a page that contains a form. The server sends the requested page to the client, which displays the page along with its form fields.

2. The user types information into the form fields and then clicks the Submit button. The Web browser gathers the information entered by the user and sends it back to the server.

3. The server receives the information sent from the client, realizes that it's data from a form, and runs a program that's specially designed to handle the data from the form. This program is called a *CGI program.* You have to create the CGI program yourself, which means you have to understand the CGI scripting language if you want to use forms in your Web site.

4. The CGI program examines the data that was entered on the form and does something worthwhile with it. In most cases, the CGI program retrieves information from a database.

5. The CGI program generates an HTML document that contains the results of the processing done in Step 4. For example, if the CGI program performed a database query, the HTML document will contain the results of the query.

6. The server sends the HTML document generated by the CGI program to the client.

7. The client displays the HTML document.

The key thing to note about CGI is that the CGI program itself always runs on the server. So although CGI enables you to create interactive applications on the Web, it isn't very flexible or efficient.

Wake Up and Smell the Java

The latest rage in the Web world is to use slick new products that are named after various types of coffee. The whole thing started when Sun Microsystems released a revolutionary programming language for Web pages called *Java*. Everyone soon jumped on the bandwagon. Now you have JavaScript, Visual Café, Latte, Mocha, Hot Java (as if you want your Java cold), Star Buck, and Java Beans. It all sounds like a scene from *L.A. Story*. ("I'll have a double decaf Java Bean Latte with a twist.")

So what exactly is Java? Java is a programming language that's used to create programs that run on an Internet user's computer rather than on the server computer. Java Web programs are called *applets* because they're not stand-alone programs. An applet must be run within a Java-enabled Web browser such as Navigator or Internet Explorer.

Java solves many of the problems inherent in the form-based CGI approach to building interactive Web applications. For starters, form-based applications can use only a limited range of controls: text boxes, radio buttons, checkboxes, and Submit and Reset buttons. In contrast, a Java applet can be built to display any type of custom control that you want on a Web page. With Java, you can build interactive Web applications that sport fancy slider boxes, spin buttons, draggable objects, and any other type of control you can imagine.

But even better than the ability to use fancy controls is the simple fact that Java programs are run within the Internet user's Web browser. In contrast, CGI programs run on the Web server computer. This results in huge improvements in performance.

Of course, Microsoft isn't about to concede defeat in the coffee wars. Microsoft has countered with its own equivalent to the whole Java phenomenon: ActiveX and VBScript. And just to hedge its bet, Microsoft also supports Java in Internet Explorer.

One of the most difficult choices you must make when you set out to create a Web site is whether you'll use Java-based tools or Microsoft's ActiveX and VBScript tools. Both lead to the same results: Web pages that are flashy and fun to use. The only question is, which will last longer?

I don't have a crystal ball, so I can't predict with any accuracy whether Java or ActiveX will rule the Web roost five years from now. So you may as well flip a coin.

Chapter 18

Creating an Intranet

. . . .

In This Chapter

▶ Getting acquainted with Intranets

▶ Finding good uses for Intranets

▶ Setting up an Intranet with Personal Web Server

. . . .

*N*o, I'm not mispronouncing the word *Internet*. *Intranet* is a term that's gained in popularity in recent years. It's similar to the Internet, but with a twist: Instead of connecting your computer to millions of other computers around the world, an Intranet connects your computer to other computers in your company or organization. How is an Intranet different from your ordinary, run-of-the-mill network? Read on and I'll explain.

What Is an Intranet?

Everyone knows that the Internet, and especially the World Wide Web, has become a phenomenon. Millions of computer users worldwide are using the Web, and thousands are joining the bandwagon every day.

Recently, ingenious network managers at large companies figured out that although the Web is interesting for distributing public information to the world, it's even better for distributing private information within a company. Thus, the idea of Intranets was born. An Intranet is a network that's built using the same tools and protocols that are used by the global Internet, but applied to a company or other organization's internal network.

You can think of an Intranet as a small, private version of the World Wide Web. Anyone who is connected to your local area network (LAN) can access your Intranet. The Intranet is accessed via a Web browser program such as Netscape or Microsoft's Internet Explorer. However, no dial-up connection or Internet Service Provider is required because the information on the Intranet is stored on the company's server computers rather than on a computer that must be accessed via the Internet.

The Intranet is analogous to a closed-circuit television system, which can only be viewed by those within the organization that owns the system. In contrast, the Internet is more like cable television in that anyone who's willing to pay $20 or so per month can watch.

 ✔ According to some computer industry pundits, the Intranet is actually more popular than the Internet. For example, Netscape, one of the biggest and best-known Internet browser companies, actually makes more money selling software used for Intranets than for the Internet. And Novell is so keen on the idea of Intranets that it changed the name of its flagship product from NetWare to IntranetWare.

 ✔ On the other hand, some industry pundits think the Intranet phenomenon is merely a fad, and that it will be replaced by some other promising new technology such as pet rocks or hula hoops in a few years. Only time will tell.

What Are Intranets Used For?

Intranets can distribute just about any type of information within a company. You have two basic types of Intranet applications:

 ✔ **Publishing applications.** Information is posted in the form of pages which can be viewed from any computer with access to the Intranet. This type of Intranet application is commonly used for company newsletters, policy manuals, price lists, and so on.

 ✔ **Transaction applications.** Information is gathered from users of the Intranet. Examples include filing on-line expense reports, sales, help-desk problem reporting, and so on.

The key difference between these two types of Intranet applications is that in a publishing application, the flow of information is one way: from the Intranet to the user. The user requests some information and the Intranet system delivers it. In a transaction application, information flows in both directions — not only does the user request information from the Intranet system, but the Intranet system itself requests information from the user.

Publishing applications are simple to set up. In fact, you may be able to set one up yourself without a lot of outside help from highly paid computer consultants. Transaction applications are much more complicated, however. Expect to spend big bucks on computer consulting to get an Intranet transaction application set up.

What You Need to Set Up an Intranet

An Intranet is fairly simple to set up. Here's a list of the various requirements:

✓ A LAN. An Intranet doesn't require its own cabling; it can operate on an existing Ethernet LAN using twisted pair or coax wiring.

✓ A server computer that's dedicated to the Intranet. Make sure that this computer has plenty of RAM (at least 16MB) and gigabytes (at least 2GB) of disk space. Of course, the more users your network has and the more information you intend to place on the server, the more RAM and disk storage you'll need.

✓ The server computer should run either Windows NT Server or a UNIX operating system, which is required by the Web server software.

✓ Web server software for the server computer. You can find more information about Web server software in the section "Serving up Your Web" in Chapter 17.

✓ Programs to help you create Web pages. If you're the type who dreams in binary, you can create Web pages by typing HTML codes directly into text files. In that case, the only program you need is Notepad. Alternatively, you can choose one of the many Web authoring programs described in the section "Creating Web Pages" in Chapter 17.

✓ Make sure that each client computer that accesses the Intranet has a 486 or better processor, at least 8MB of RAM, 20MB or more of free disk space, and a connection to the LAN.

✓ A Web browser such as Netscape or Internet Explorer must be installed on each client computer.

Creating a Small Intranet with Personal Web Server

One of the easiest ways to create a small Intranet is to use a free Microsoft program called Personal Web Server. This program is included with Microsoft's Internet Explorer 4, and you can also find it buried on the Microsoft Office 97 CD-ROM.

Personal Web Server works only with Windows 95, and it isn't nearly as slick as a real Web server such as Microsoft's Internet Information Server or Netscape's Enterprise Server. But it is an ideal way to set up an Intranet on a small LAN which can be accessed by just a few users.

Although Personal Web Server is distributed with Internet Explorer 4 and is designed to work with Internet Explorer 4, it also works with other Web browsers including Netscape's Navigator.

The following sections show you step-by-step how to set up and use Personal Web Server.

Starting Personal Web Server

To start Personal Web Server, follow these steps:

1. **Click the Start button in the Windows 95 taskbar and then click Settings⇨Control Panel.**

   The Control Panel folder appears.

2. **Double-click the Personal Web Server icon in the Control Panel folder.**

   This launches the Personal Web Server Properties dialog box, shown in Figure 18-1.

   If you can't find the Personal Web Server icon in the Control Panel folder, you didn't install Personal Web Server when you installed Internet Explorer. Jump on the Internet and hop over to www.microsoft.com/ie/ie40/download to download and install Personal Web Server. With a 28.8 Kbps modem, this process takes less than five minutes.

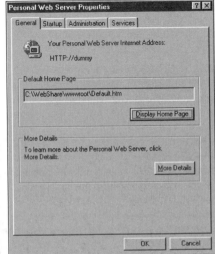

Figure 18-1:
The Personal Web Server Properties dialog box.

3. **Click the Startup tab at the top of the Personal Web Server Properties dialog box.**

   The Startup options appears, as shown in Figure 18-2.

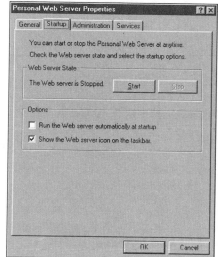

Figure 18-2: Personal Web Server's Startup options.

4. **Click the Start button.**

   The Personal Web Server responds.

    If you want Personal Web Server to start automatically every time you start your computer, check the Run the Web Server Automatically at Startup option.

5. **Click OK.**

   The Personal Web Server Properties dialog box is dismissed.

    After Personal Web Server starts, the icon shown in the margin appears in the Windows taskbar. You can double-click this icon at any time to summon the Personal Web Server Properties dialog box.

    Personal Web Server comes with a set of Web pages that serve as help files to give you an overview of how the Web Server works and how you can manage it. To access these help files, call up the Personal Web Server Properties dialog box and click the More Details button, which launches Internet Explorer for a view of the help files.

Posting a Web page to Personal Web Server

Posting your HTML files to Personal Web Server so that you can view them using a Web browser from your computer or from another computer connected to your local area network is easy. Personal Web Server uses a folder named C:\WebShare\wwwroot as the root directory for your Web pages. To post an HTML file to Personal Web Server, all you have to do is save the file in the C:\WebShare\wwwroot folder.

Accessing a Web page on Personal Web Server

To access a page stored in Personal Web Server, you need to know the Internet address for your Personal Web Server root directory. To find out, double-click the Personal Web Server icon in the Windows 95 taskbar or the Personal Web Server icon in Control Panel. The Personal Web Server Properties dialog box appears. Click the General tab (if it's not already selected). The Internet address of your Web server is shown.

To check out an example, refer to Figure 18-1. Here, the Internet Address for my Personal Web Server is HTTP://dummy.

The default Web page for Personal Web Server is default.html. Thus, if you've created a file named default.html in C:\WebShare\wwwroot, you can display that page simply by entering your Personal Web Server address in Internet Explorer's Address box. For example, if your Web Server address is dummy, just type **dummy** in the Address box to display your home page.

To display a different HTML file, type the filename after the Internet address, separated by a slash. For example, to display a page named softball.html, you type **dummy\softball.html**.

The Internet address used by Personal Web Server is based on your Windows 95 computer name, which you created when you first installed Windows 95 on your computer. If you want to change this name, open Control Panel and double-click the Network icon. This reveals the Network dialog box. Click the Identification tab and then type a new computer name in the Computer Name field. When you click OK, your computer restarts and then you can use the new name for your Personal Web Server Internet address.

Part V
More Cool Things You Can Do with Your Network

The 5th Wave   By Rich Tennant

"PREDICT SECURITY EMISSIONS ON YOUR NETWORK? NO PROBLEM. WHAT ARE YOU RUNNING? TWISTED PAIR CABLING ON A LAN? HOW ABOUT YOUR OPERATING SYSTEM,..."

In this part . . .

After you've got the basics down, this part helps you do some of the more advanced stuff, which includes sharing devices such as CD-ROM drives and fax modems, setting up a network at your home, creating a dial-up connection so that you can access your network while you're at home or on the road, and incorporating Macintosh computers into your network.

Chapter 19

More Things You Can Share on Your Network

*T*his chapter shows you how to share a variety of oddball devices and programs on your network. Everything I describe in this chapter is strictly optional. Most networks can live for years without setting up a voice mail system or playing multi-user Quake.

Sharing CD-ROM Drives

CD-ROM drives are popular additions to computers, and if yours is the only computer in the office with a CD-ROM drive, you may have users waiting in line to borrow time on your computer so that they can use your CD drive.

Fortunately, all the network operating systems described in this book enable you to set up a CD-ROM drive as a shared network drive so that users throughout the network can access it. In fact, sharing a CD-ROM drive is no different than sharing a regular disk drive.

But an annoying problem crops up when you share a desktop computer's CD-ROM drive with other network users. Imagine that you're using your CD-ROM drive for important work, such as browsing the latest edition of Microsoft's Cinemania to figure out what movie you should rent tonight, when some clown down in sales wants to access the master price list CD just sent from corporate headquarters. You get an annoying message that says something like `Please Insert the Master Price List CD in Drive D`. And that won't be the last of it, either. You're pestered by annoying interruptions like this all day long.

If you're going to share a CD-ROM drive, make sure that it's located on a dedicated server computer, and the drive is dedicated to a particular disk. For example, if corporate headquarters really does send you a CD disc containing the master price list, and network users need to access this CD frequently, dedicate an entire CD-ROM drive just for this disk. Then you won't have to contend with annoying messages about changing the disks.

If you have more than one CD to be shared, just install more than one CD-ROM drive in the server computer. With the cost of CD-ROM drives being so low — good ones cost under $100 — this solution isn't unrealistic. If you share more than a few CDs, you can even buy CD-ROM servers with stacks of CD-ROM drives built in. For example, a recent advertisement from a mail-order supplier of network components listed a "CD-ROM Tower" with seven 12x-speed CD-ROM drives for $2,399. These towers are self-contained servers with network software built in, so you can connect them directly to your network.

An alternative to a CD-ROM tower is a *jukebox*. A jukebox is a single CD-ROM drive that can hold several discs and automatically swaps discs as they are accessed. Jukeboxes are less expensive than towers, but they're slower; whenever a user accesses a disc that isn't currently in the CD-ROM drive, the jukebox must switch discs. If two users are accessing two discs simultaneously, the jukebox spends a lot of time shuttling discs back and forth. (To avoid this problem, you can get jukeboxes that have more than one CD reader built in — for more money, of course.)

Setting Up a Voice Mail System

If you have a small office — say, five or fewer employees — you can set up a voice mail system on your LAN that can rival even the biggest company's annoying phone systems. Upon calling, your loyal customers are greeted by a message such as, "Welcome to The Wannabies! If you would like to place an order, press 1! For service or support, press 2! To leave a message for Bob, press 3! To leave a message for Martha, press 4! To talk to a real person, hang up now and call someone else!"

The whole idea of mixing telephones and computers is called *computer telephony*.

One way to set up a computer voice mail system is to install a special type of modem called a *voice modem* at each user's computer and connect the voice modem to a separate phone line. A voice modem is like an answering machine, speakerphone, fax machine, and modem all in one box. Voice modems come with special software that enables you to set up a voice mail system with one or more mailboxes that store your phone messages on disk.

Because each minute of voice mail consumes about half a megabyte of disk space, you need to have plenty of free disk space available on the computer to store voice mail messages.

The problem with creating a telephony system using voice modems is that voice modems are designed to work with a single incoming phone line, and the software that comes with most voice modems isn't designed to operate over a network. Setting up a computer voice system that supports multiple lines and works on the LAN is not a do-it-yourself project; you need the help of an expert.

To set up a network-aware computer telephony system, you need to get specialized hardware and software from a company that specializes in computer telephony. It won't be cheap, but then again, good phone systems are never cheap. A good computer telephony system requires a dedicated server running Windows NT Server, NetWare, or UNIX.

For information about setting up a computer telephony system based on Windows NT Server, check out the Microsoft telephony page on the Internet at `www.microsoft.com/communications/telephony.htm`. For information about Netware telephony, see the Novell telephony page at `www.novell.com/products/telephony`.

One of the best uses for computer telephony is to set up a fax back system. A fax back system navigates a caller through a series of voice menus ("Press 3 now!") to have a particular document faxed to a fax number the caller provides. This function can be handled by a dedicated computer which doesn't even have to be connected to the network, although you probably want to connect the fax server to the network so that you can access the fax back documents from any computer on the network.

Sharing a Fax

If you have a modem that's capable of sending and receiving faxes, you can configure this modem as a shared network resource so that other network users can use it. If your company sends out a constant stream of faxes day in and day out, invest in a specialized fax server system. But for occasional faxing, you can use the built-in fax serving capability of Windows 95 to turn any Windows 95 computer on the network into a fax server.

To set up a Windows 95 computer as a fax server, you must first install a fax modem in the computer and connect the modem to a phone line. Then follow these steps:

1. **Call up Control Panel and double-click the Mail and Fax icon.**

   A dialog box called Exchange Settings Properties appears, as shown in Figure 19-1.

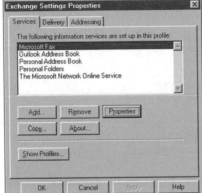

Figure 19-1:
The
Exchange
Settings
Properties
dialog box.

2. **Double-click Microsoft Fax in the list of information services.**

   This summons the Microsoft Fax Properties dialog box.

3. **Click the Modem tab at the top of the Microsoft Fax Properties dialog box.**

   The modem properties appear, as shown in Figure 19-2.

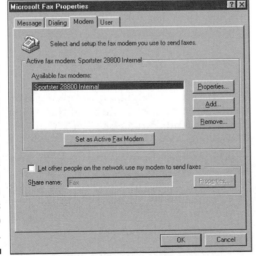

Figure 19-2:
The
Microsoft
Fax
Properties
dialog box
with the
modem
Properties
tab
activated.

4. **Check the "Let other people on the network use my modem to send faxes" checkbox.**

   A dialog box asking which drive and folder you want to use for the fax service appears.

5. **Change the drive and folder that you want to use for the fax service if you want and then click OK.**

6. **Click the Properties button.**

   This brings up the share properties for the Fax sharing folder you created in Step 5, as shown in Figure 19-3.

Figure 19-3:
Setting the
share
properties
for a
shared fax
folder.

7. **Click the Properties button next to the Fax share name and then assign access rights for the fax sharing folder.**

   How you assign access rights for the fax sharing folder depends on how you configured Windows 95 security. If you set up Windows 95 for user-level security, you have to grant full access rights to each user who should be allowed to use the fax. If you set up Windows 95 for share-level security, just give full access rights to the fax sharing folder.

8. **Click OK.**

9. **Keep clicking OK until the Microsoft Exchange Properties dialog box is finally gone.**

That's all there is to it. You've just created your first fax server and you didn't have to pay $100 per hour for a consultant to do it for you!

Sharing Network Games

The following section contains information that may cost you your job.

Admit it. One of the main reasons computers are so appealing is because of the games. In recent years, computer games have become very intense. In the early days of computer games, an exciting play was when you typed in "Kill the troll with the sword," and the game would respond, "You miss! The troll hacks your arm off with his sword." ("It's just a flesh wound!" you replied.)

In today's games, you actually see the troll on the screen, and the entire playing area is covered with vivid 32-bit blood when he cuts off your arm.

New game-playing possibilities arise when you install a network, because many of today's best games can be played in multi-player mode over a network. For example, ID Software's Quake can be played by up to four players on a network. Quake can be played in Cooperative Mode that enables the players to work together to annihilate computer-generated bad guys, or in DeathMatch mode, where players attempt to eliminate each other.

Of course, more peaceful network games are available. The best known example is Hearts, which comes with Windows for Workgroups and Windows 95. If you can find three other network users who don't have anything else to do, you can enjoy a friendly game of Hearts without leaving the comfort of your own office. Figure 19-4 shows a friendly game of Hearts in action.

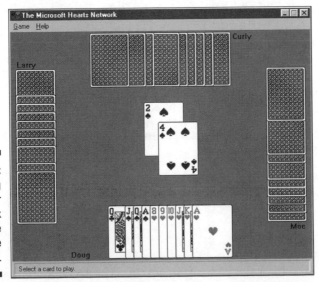

Figure 19-4:
Playing Hearts over the network is a sure way to lose your job.

Chapter 20

Networking Your Home

• •

In This Chapter

▶ A seven-step program for setting up a simple network for two or three computers in your home

▶ Some things to worry about with a home network

• •

*T*hese days, more and more people have more than one computer in the home. Some families have several generations of hand-me-down computers: an old clunker 386, a workable 486, and a Pentium — or maybe even two.

In this chapter, I show you a simple, step-by-step procedure that you can follow to network two computers in your home so that you can share a printer, disk drive, or CD-ROM drive. Nothing fancy here, just the bare necessities you need to get a network up and running.

To keep things simple, this chapter assumes that all the computers you want to network are already running Windows 95. If you want to add Macintosh computers to your network, refer to Chapter 22.

Step 1: Go Shopping

First, make a shopping list of things you need to buy when you go to your local computer warehouse store. Here's what to include on your shopping list:

✔ **An Ethernet network card for each computer.** You have no need to spend big money on the networking cards. If you can find them for $25 each, buy them.

Make sure that the cards say "Plug and Play" on the box. If they don't, you have to fuss around with configuring the cards' IRQ settings and port addresses. With Plug and Play cards, all the configuration settings are made automatically so you don't have to worry about such details.

Also, make sure that you get a card that will fit one of the available expansion slots inside your computer. You'll need to know what type of available expansion slots your computer has. Most newer computers have two types of slots: ISA and PCI. If you have an older computer, you may have a different type of slot, most likely VESA or EISA. You'll have to check the manual that came with your computer to find out for sure.

Ethernet network cards come in two flavors: *coax,* which uses connectors called BNC connectors, and *twisted-pair,* which uses RJ-45 connectors. Some Ethernet cards have both connectors. You can keep costs down by building your home network with coax cable, so make sure that the cards you get have BNC connectors. If you can find cards with both styles of connectors for just a few dollars more than cards with BNC connectors only, get the cards with both connector types.

Each card comes with a T connector and a terminator. If yours doesn't, you have to purchase these items separately.

✔ **A coax cable with BNC connectors on each end.** A 25-foot length of coax cable costs about $10. If that isn't long enough, you can string together two or more cables end-to-end. You need a special connector called a *barrel connector* to connect the cables together.

Do *not* buy TV cable. The coax cable used by cable TV looks like Ethernet coax cable, but it isn't the same. Make sure that the cable you purchase is RG58 Ethernet cable.

Step 2: Install the Cards

Follow the instructions that come with the cards to install them into your computers. The only tools you need are a flathead and a Phillips screwdriver.

Make sure that you shut down Windows 95, turn off your computer, and unplug the power cord before you remove the computer's case and start working inside.

Step 3: Connect the Cable

Connect one of the T connectors to the connector on the back of each card. Then connect one end of the cable to each of the T connectors. Connect a terminator to the other end of each of the T connectors.

Step 4: Restart the Computers

After you restart each computer, Windows 95 notices that you've installed a new card into your computer and automatically configures it. If for some reason Windows 95 doesn't notice the card, double-click on the Add New Hardware icon in the Control panel. Then instruct the Add Hardware Wizard to automatically sniff out your new networking cards and install them for you.

Step 5: Check the Network Settings

Double-click the Network icon in the Control Panel to summon the Network dialog box, shown in Figure 20-1. Then check to make sure that the following items appear in the list of installed network components:

- ✓ "Client for Microsoft Networks."

- ✓ Your network card, which may appear as "NE2000 Compatible" or may be specific to the brand of network card you purchased.

- ✓ "NetBEUI -> NE2000 Compatible." (If your network card is other than "NE2000 Compatible," the name of your network card appears here instead.)

- ✓ "File and printer sharing for Microsoft networks."

If any of these items are missing, click the Add button to add them.

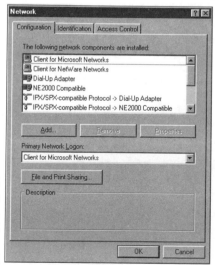

Figure 20-1:
Checking
the network
settings.

Now click the Identification tab in the Network. This brings up the computer identification settings shown in Figure 20-2. Type a different name and description for each computer, but make sure that both computers use the same Workgroup Name.

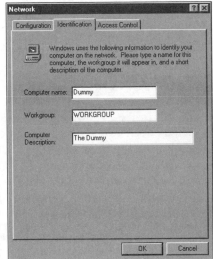

Figure 20-2:
Eliminating
your
computer's
identity
crisis.

Step 6: Share Your Disk Drives

The next step is to set up each computer's disk drive so that the other computer can access it. To do so, follow these steps:

1. **Double-click on My Computer**.

   The My Computer window appears.

2. **Click the disk drive you want to share.**

   Ordinarily, this is the C drive.

3. **Choose the File⇨Sharing command.**

   The Sharing properties dialog box appears, as shown in Figure 20-3. (The figure shows how the dialog box appears after the settings in Steps 4 and 5 have been made.)

4. **Click Shared As.**

   If you wish, you can change the Share Name and Comment fields.

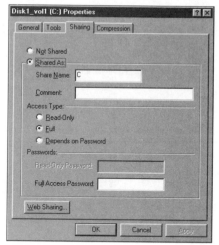

Figure 20-3:
The Sharing
properties.

5. Click Full for the Access type.

This enables you to do anything you want to the shared drive from the other computer — including creating, deleting, or renaming files or folders.

6. Click OK.

The Properties dialog box disappears.

Be sure to perform the procedure on both computers.

To access another computer's shared disk drive, double-click the Network Neighborhood icon. The Network Neighborhood window lists the name of the workgroup you specified for both computers. Double-click the workgroup name to see a list of all the computers that belong to that workgroup. Then double-click the computer whose disk you want to access to see a list of shared disks and folders for that computer.

Step 7: Share Your Printers

If you have a printer that you want to share on the network, you can do so by following these steps:

1. On the computer with the printer you want to share, double-click My Computer.

2. **Double-click Printers in the My Computer window.**

   The Printers folder appears, listing all the printers that are available on your computer.

3. **Click the printer you want to share and then choose the File⇨Sharing command.**

   The Sharing properties for the printer appears.

4. **Click Share As.**

   This enables the sharing options, so the Properties dialog box now resembles Figure 20-4.

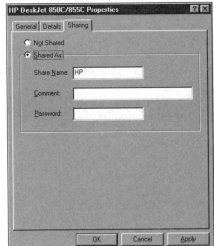

Figure 20-4:
Sharing a
printer.

5. **Type a name for the printer if you wish.**

6. **Click OK.**

7. **On the other computer, double-click My Computer and then double-click Printers.**

   The Printers folder appears.

8. **Double-click the Add Printer icon.**

   The Add Printer Wizard appears, as shown in Figure 20-5.

9. **Follow the Add Printer Wizard steps to add the printer you shared in Steps 1-6.**

   The Add Printer Wizard asks if you're installing a local or network printer and enables you to browse the network to locate the printer you want to access. You also have to indicate to the Wizard the make and model of the printer that you're adding. If the exact make and model of your printer doesn't appear in the list provided by the Wizard, you have to insert the disk that came with the printer to complete the installation.

10. You're done!

You're now able to print to the network printer by choosing the network printer from the normal File⇨Print command in any Windows 95 program.

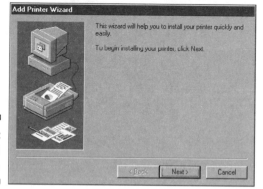

Figure 20-5:
Adding a
printer.

Managing Your Home Network

After you network the computers in your home, you — or whoever has the most computer savvy in your household — must become the home network manager. Unfortunately, all the concerns that arise when using a network in a business situation apply to home networks as well. In particular, the following list highlights some of the things to stay on top of with your home network:

✓ **Make sure that everyone knows how to access the network and use the shared drives and printers.** Hold a family meeting to go over the do's and don'ts of the network.

✓ **Think about whether or not you really want to grant full access to the C drive over the network.** What if your teenager gets mad at you because you won't let him borrow the car, so he decides to delete a bunch of your important files from the privacy of his bedroom? Maybe you should think about security, giving each user a user ID and password, sharing only certain folders on each drive rather than the entire drive, and password protecting folders that contain private information.

✔ **Make sure that everyone knows that back up is their own responsibility.** Don't let your kid blame you when he or she loses a 30-page term paper because of the "stupid network." The epitome of '90s parenting would be to add backing up the network to the list of Saturday chores the kids have to do, right after mowing the lawn and cleaning the bathrooms.

✔ **Keep an eye on disk space.** With the whole family using the network, you'll be amazed at how quickly the gigabytes can fill up.

Chapter 21

Dialing In to Your Network

. . . .

In This Chapter

▶ Creating a dial-up connection with Windows 95

▶ Finding other ways to connect

. . . .

*W*ith portable computers and home computers becoming more and more popular, many computer users are taking work home with them, working on it in the evening or over the weekend, and bringing their work back to the office the following morning. This arrangement works reasonably well, except that exchanging information between a portable or home computer and your office computer is far from easy.

One way to exchange files is by copying them from one computer to a diskette and then copying the files from the diskette to the other computer. However, this approach has its drawbacks. What if the files you want to exchange won't fit on a single diskette? And what if, in the rush to get out of the house the following morning, you forget to put the diskette in your pocket?

If you use a portable laptop or notebook computer, you can use a software program such as LapLink to connect the portable computer to your office computer by using a cable connected to both computers' serial or parallel ports. After you connect the computers, you can then transfer files over the cable. This process is much more efficient than copying the files using diskettes, but it still has drawbacks. What if you get home and discover that you forgot to copy one important file?

If you must work from home, the best way to get your work to work is to create a dial-up connection that uses modems to connect your home computer directly to your office network. Using this setup, you can access any shared disk drives that are available on the network from your home computer, just as if your home computer were a part of the office network.

This chapter shows you how to create a remote connection using a feature of Windows 95 called Dial-Up Networking. This feature provides a simple but limited modem link between a remote computer and a networked computer. Dial-Up Networking then points out some advantages of using a more sophisticated approach to remote access, such as Windows NT Remote Access Service or IntranetWare Connect.

Security is a major concern whenever you enable dial-up networking. If you can dial in to your office computer and access your files, so can anybody else. Passwords offer some measure of protection, but serious computer hackers can get past simple password protection as easy as experienced car thieves can hotwire a car. If security is a concern, use Windows NT Server or IntranetWare Connect access rather than Windows 95 Dial-Up Networking. Both programs provide tighter security controls than Windows 95.

Throughout this chapter, I assume that you're using remote access to call in to your work computer from a home computer. Of course, this isn't the only way to use dial-up connections. You can do it the other way around: Call up your home computer from the office. Or, you can call your office computer from a hotel room to connect with a laptop computer. The point is that I refer to the computer that you're using to call in to another computer as the *home computer,* and I refer to the other computer — the one that you're calling in to — as the *office computer.*

Windows 95 Dial-Up Networking

If both your computer at work and your computer at home use Windows 95, you can easily set up a dial-up connection between the two which enables you to connect to your office computer while you're at home. After you're connected to your office computer, you can use its disk drives and printers. In addition, you're able to use any network disks or printers that are accessible to your office computer. In short, any resource — disk drive or printer — that's available to your office computer becomes available to your home computer when you establish the dial-up connection.

The Windows 95 feature that enables you to create a dial-up connection is called *Dial-Up Networking,* sometimes known as *DUN* because computer geeks love to confuse us with three-letter acronyms. I promise not to use the term *DUN* again in this chapter.

To use DUN — oops, I mean Dial-Up Networking — to connect from home to office, both your home and office computers must have a modem, and they must both be connected to a phone line. In addition, you must install a program called Microsoft Plus! on the computer at the office. If you don't already have Microsoft Plus! installed on your computer, you can purchase it at just about any computer store for around $50.

You can tell if Microsoft Plus! has already been installed on your computer by watching the *splash screen* display whenever you start up Windows 95. If the words "Microsoft Plus!" appear beneath the Windows 95 logo on the splash screen, Microsoft Plus! is installed. Another way to tell is to go to the Control Panel and double-click the Add/Remove Programs icon. If "Microsoft Plus! for Windows 95" appears in the list of programs, Microsoft Plus! is installed. If not, you need to install it before you can configure your office computer as a dial-up server.

The Plus! features needed to create a dial-up host for Windows 95 have been incorporated into the soon-to-be-released Windows 98. So, if you're lucky enough to have Windows 98, you don't have to worry about getting Microsoft Plus! because you already have what you need.

Before you can use a dial-up connection, you must configure both your home and office computers for Dial-Up Networking. First, you must configure your computer at work to work as a *dial-up server.* Then you must configure your computer at home to function as a *dial-up client.* After both computers are configured, you can use the dial-up client computer at home to call in to the dial-up server computer at work. The steps for configuring the dial-up server and client are described in the following sections.

Configuring a dial-up server

The following procedure explains how to configure your office computer so that it can function as a dial-up server:

1. **Choose the Start⇨Programs⇨Accessories⇨Dial-Up Networking command.**

   The Dial-Up Networking window appears, as shown in Figure 21-1. Note that if you've previously used Dial-Up Networking to create a connection to an Internet Service Provider or some other dial-up network, other icons besides the Make a New Connection icon appear in the Dial-Up Networking window.

2. **Choose the Connections⇨Dial-Up Server command.**

   The Dial-Up Server dialog box appears, as shown in Figure 21-2.

3. **Click Allow caller access.**

   This allows other computers to call into the Office computer. After you click Allow caller access, the Change Password button is enabled.

4. **Click the Change Password button.**

   A dialog box appears asking you to enter a password.

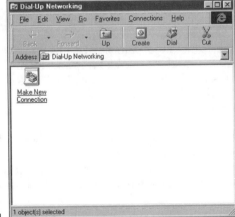

Figure 21-1:
The Dial-Up
Networking
window.

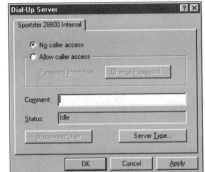

Figure 21-2:
The Dial-Up
Server
dialog box.

5. **Type a password and then click OK.**

Choose a password that you'll use when you call in to your office computer. Write it down somewhere so that you won't forget it.

Creating a password when you set up a dial-up server is very important. If you don't create a password, anyone who knows the phone number can call up your computer and access not only your computer, but also your entire network.

6. **Click OK.**

The computer is now set up as a dial-up server. All that remains is to share any disk drives or printers you want to be able to access from home.

7. **To share a disk drive so that you can access it from home, double-click My Computer. Then click the drive you want to share and choose the File⊃Sharing command. Click Share As and then click OK.**

8. **To share a printer, double-click the Printers icon in the My Computer window, select the printer in a My Computer window, choose File⊃Sharing, click Share As, and then click OK.**

Now you're all set.

Here are a few additional points to ponder when you use a dial-up server:

✔ After you click OK in Step 6, a Dial-Up Server icon appears in your taskbar. This icon indicates that the computer is monitoring the phone line, waiting to pick up an incoming call to establish a dial-up connection.

✔ To disable the dial-up server, double-click the Dial-Up Server icon in the taskbar. This summons the Dial-Up Server dialog box. Click No Caller Access and then click OK. The Dial-Up Server dialog box is dismissed and the Dial-Up Server icon vanishes from the taskbar. To reinstate the Dial-Up Server, you have to repeat the entire procedure.

✔ If you shut down your computer while it's in Dial-Up Server mode, the Dial-Up Server is automatically restarted after you restart your computer.

✔ If the Dial-Up Networking window doesn't have a Connections⊃ Dial-Up Server command, you haven't installed Microsoft Plus! You have to install Microsoft Plus! before you can set up a Dial-Up Server.

✔ If Dial-Up Networking isn't installed on your computer, you can install it from the Windows 95 CD-ROM. Call up Control Panel and then double-click the Add/Remove Programs icon. In the Add/Remove Programs dialog box, click the Windows Setup tab. Double-click the Communications icon in the list of optional Windows components and then click Dial-Up Networking. Click OK and then insert the Windows 95 CD-ROM to complete the installation.

✔ Don't under any circumstances set up a Dial-Up Server without a password! Yes, I know I already warned you about this, but it's worth a second warning.

✔ If you're a network administrator, the thought of users creating Dial-Up Servers to gain remote access to your network may give you the willies. If so, you can ban the Dial-Up Server function by using a Windows 95 program called the System Policy Editor.

Configuring your home computer for Dial-Up Networking

To configure your home computer to call in to your office computer, you must create a new dial-up connection by following these steps:

1. **Choose the Start⇨Programs⇨Accessories⇨Dial-Up Networking command.**

   The Dial-Up Networking window appears. It was shown in Figure 21-1.

2. **Double-click the Make New Connection icon.**

   The Make New Connection Wizard comes to life. This Wizard asks you a few simple questions. Then it creates an icon for the connection to your office computer.

3. **Type a name for the connection to your office computer.**

   Use a simple name, such as "Office."

4. **Click Next.**

   The Wizard asks for your office computer's phone number.

5. **Type the phone number for the phone line that's connected to your office computer's modem and then click Next.**

   The Wizard displays a confirmation dialog box saying that it's ready to create the connection.

6. **Click Finish.**

   The Wizard creates the new connection, which appears as an icon in the Dial-Up Networking window.

Here are a few tidbits to consider when setting up your home computer for Dial-Up Networking:

- ✔ The Make New Connection Wizard may ask for additional information if it discovers that your modem hasn't yet been configured for Dial-Up Networking. If this happens, just follow the bouncing ball and answer whatever questions it asks as best you can. If you become confused, just act like you know what you're doing, and the Wizard won't notice.

- ✔ If you can't find Dial-Up Networking anywhere on your computer, you may not have installed it. Find your Windows 95 CD and then double-click the Add/Remove Programs icon in Control Panel. Click the Windows Setup tab in the Add/Remove Programs dialog box and then double-click the Communications icon and make sure that Dial-Up Networking is selected. Click OK and then insert your Windows 95 CD in your CD-ROM drive to install Dial-Up Networking.

✔ If you plan on calling up your office computer often, drag the office computer connection icon from the Dial-Up Networking window on to your desktop. Then you won't have to wade through Start➪Programs➪ Accessories➪Dial-Up Networking every time you want to connect.

Making the connection

Okay, now that you've configured your office and home computers for Dial-Up Networking, it's time to actually call up your office computer and put Dial-Up Networking to work. Here's how:

1. **On your home computer, choose the Start➪Programs➪ Accessories➪Dial-Up Networking and then double-click the icon for the office computer's connection.**

   Or, if you dragged a copy of the icon to your desktop, just double-click the icon on your desktop. Either way, the Connect To dialog box appears, as shown in Figure 21-3.

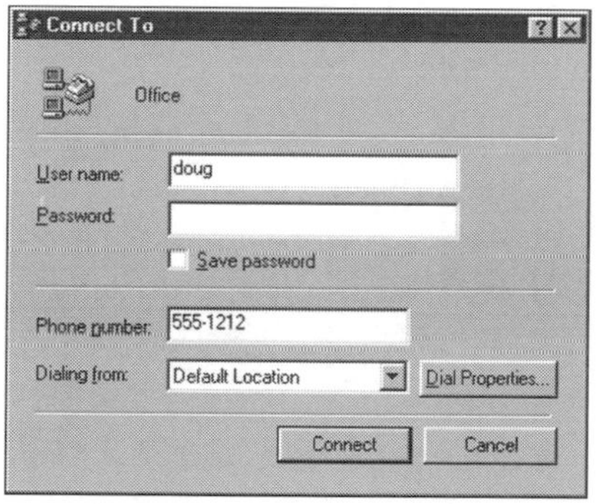

Figure 21-3:
The
Connect To
dialog box.

Connect To

Office

User name: doug

Password:

☐ Save password

Phone number: 555-1212

Dialing from: Default Location ▾ Dial Properties...

Connect   Cancel

2. **Make sure that the phone number, user name, and passwords are correct. Then click Connect.**

   Windows 95 calls in to your office computer and establishes a connection. This may take a minute or so, so be patient. You see various messages on the screen while the connection is being made, such as "Dialing," "Verifying User Name and Password," "Waiting for Godot," "Twiddling Thumbs," and so on. Eventually the message says "Connected," at which point you're officially connected to your office computer.

After you're connected, you can access your office computer's disk drives and printers. However, you can't use the Network Neighborhood icon to access your office computer's resources. Windows 95 automatically disables Network Neighborhood for dial-up connections because the dial-up connection is so slow compared to a normal Ethernet connection. Instead, follow these steps to access your office computer's resources when connected over the phone:

1. **Choose the Start⇨Run command.**

2. **Type two slashes followed by the name of your office computer.**

   For example, **//Office**.

3. **Click OK.**

   Your home computer takes a while to access your office computer over the phone. Eventually, though, a window such as the one shown in Figure 21-4 is displayed.

You can access your office computer's shared disk drives and printers from your home computer.

To disconnect from the office computer, double-click the modem icon that appears in the taskbar and then click Disconnect.

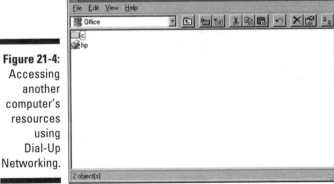

Figure 21-4:
Accessing
another
computer's
resources
using
Dial-Up
Networking.

Other Ways to Let Users Dial In

If you're concerned about the security of your remote network connection, or if you want to enable several network users to dial in from home, abandon Windows 95 Dial-Up Server altogether and use a more sophisticated program to enable users to dial in to your network. You have two basic approaches to doing this. One is to use software such as Windows NT Server's Remote Access Service or Novell's IntranetWare Connect. The other way is to add special remote-access hardware to your network.

Software for remote access

Windows NT Server includes built-in support for remote access, using a program called Remote Access Service, also known as RAS. With RAS, you equip a server computer with one or more modems (standard modems or ISDN) and dedicate it as a remote access server. Remote users can then dial in to the network and, once connected, use the network as if they were connected with an Ethernet cable. Of course, the connection is much slower because it operates over phone lines rather than real Ethernet cable.

The advantage of Remote Access Service over a simple dial-up server using Windows 95 is that you have more control over security when you use RAS. RAS enables you to use all the basic security features of Windows NT Server, plus it has a few extra security features that are designed just for dial-up users. For example, you can use call-back security, which works like this:

1. A user dials in to the RAS server from a home computer.
2. The RAS server verifies the user's name and password.
3. The RAS server hangs up on the user.
4. The RAS server then calls the user back, using a prearranged phone number.
5. The user's computer answers the phone and re-verifies the connection.
6. The user can then use the network.

Novell offers a similar remote access program called IntranetWare Connect. Connect enables you to create a modem pool so that network users can share modems for outbound calls (for example, to connect to the Internet or send a fax) as well as for remote access.

Hardware for remote access

An alternative to creating a dedicated communication server running Windows NT Server or IntranetWare is to use specialized remote access hardware. That way, you don't have to contend with setting up and maintaining Windows NT Server or IntranetWare, and you don't have to dedicate an entire PC to the task of sharing modems for remote access.

The best known remote access hardware is LanRover, made by Shiva. The LanRover is a self-contained remote access server that includes an Ethernet port so you can connect it to your network, and either four or eight serial ports which can be connected to modems. Or you can get the LanRover Plus, which includes built-in modems. LanRover can use normal modem connections, or you can use high-speed ISDN connections for faster connections.

For more information about LanRover, check out Shiva's home page on the Internet, at www.shiva.com.

Chapter 22

Networking Macintosh Computers

● ●

In This Chapter

▶ Hooking up a Macintosh Network

▶ Using a Macintosh Network

▶ Mixing Macs and PCs

● ●

*T*his book has dwelt on networking PCs as if IBM were the only game in town. To be politically correct, I should at least acknowledge the existence of an altogether different breed of computer: The Apple Macintosh computers.

Apple prides itself on its ability to include stuff in its Macintosh operating system that Windows users have to purchase separately. In fact, Windows is the classic example of that; Macintosh users don't have to purchase a graphical user interface separately because the Macintosh operating system is a graphical user interface. Network support is another example. Every Macintosh ever manufactured has come with built-in networking support. All you have to do to network your Macintosh computers is buy network cable.

Well, there's actually a lot more to it than that. This chapter presents what you need to know to hook up a Macintosh network, what you need to know to use a Macintosh network, and what you need to know to mix Macintoshes and PCs on the same network. This is not a comprehensive tome on networking Macintoshes, but if you want more information, you can pick up the humongoid book, *Macworld Networking Bible,* 2nd Edition, by Dave Kosiur, Ph.D., and Joel M. Snyder, Ph.D. (IDG Books Worldwide, Inc.).

What You Need to Know to Hook Up a Macintosh Network

Hooking up a small Macintosh network is easy: There's not much more to it than buying cables and plugging them in.

AppleTalk and Open Transport

As I said, every Macintosh ever built has included networking support. The built-in networking features are similar to those of Windows 95: Not as powerful as IntranetWare or Windows NT Server, but more than enough to set up a basic network so that several users can share files and printers.

The Macintosh's built-in network feature is called AppleTalk. One of the advantages of having AppleTalk built in is that it has become an inarguable networking standard among Macintosh users. You don't have to worry about the differences between different network operating systems, because all Macintosh networking is based on AppleTalk.

In 1996, with the release of MacOS System 7.5.3, Apple folded AppleTalk into a grander networking scheme known as Open Transport. The idea behind Open Transport is to bring all the different communications software used on Macintoshes under a common umbrella and make them easy to configure and use. Currently, two types of networking are handled by Open Transport.

- Open Transport/AppleTalk handles local area networks based on the AppleTalk protocols. Open Transport/AppleTalk is a beefed-up version of AppleTalk that's more efficient and flexible.

- OpenTransport/TCP handles TCP/IP communications, such as Internet connections.

- Open Transport is standard fare on all new Macintosh computers, and old Macintosh computers can be upgraded to Open Transport provided that they're powerful enough. (The minimum system requirements for Open Transport are a 68030 processor, 5MB RAM, and MacOS System 7.5.3.)

- AppleTalk enables you to subdivide a network into *zones,* which are similar to workgroups in Windows for Workgroups. Each zone consists of the network users who regularly share information.

- Although basic support for networking is built into every Macintosh, you still have to purchase cables to connect the computers to one another. You have several types of cables to choose from. AppleTalk can be used with two different cabling schemes that connect to the Macintosh's printer port, or it can be used with faster Ethernet interface cards.

Who's winning in the AFP West?

AFP is not a division of the NFL, but an acronym for "AppleTalk Filing Protocol." It's the part of AppleTalk that governs how files are stored and accessed on the network. AFP is designed to allow files to be shared with computers that run DOS. Macintoshes can be integrated into any network operating system that recognizes AFP. NetWare and Windows NT, and Windows 95 use AFP to support

Macintoshes in their networks. Unfortunately, Windows for Workgroups doesn't support AFP, so you can't use Macintoshes in a Windows for Workgroups network.

In case you're interested (and you shouldn't be), AFP is a presentation-layer protocol. See Chapter 27 if you don't have a clue as to what I'm talking about.

LocalTalk: The cheap way to network

LocalTalk is Apple's low-speed cabling scheme for AppleTalk networks. To connect a Macintosh to a LocalTalk network, you plug a LocalTalk connector into each Macintosh computer's printer port. Then you connect the LocalTalk connectors together with LocalTalk cable.

- ✔ LocalTalk connectors are self-terminating, which means that separate terminators are not required on both ends of the cable segment.

- ✔ Each LocalTalk connector comes with a 2-meter-long LocalTalk cable (that's about 6 ½ feet). You can also purchase 10-meter cables if your computers aren't that close together.

- ✔ LocalTalk uses shielded twisted-pair cable. The shielding protects the cable from electrical interference but limits the total length of cable used in a network segment to 300 feet.

- ✔ No more than 32 computers and printers can be connected to a single segment.

- ✔ A popular alternative to LocalTalk is PhoneNET, made by Farallon Computing. PhoneNET uses inexpensive telephone cable rather than the shielded twisted-pair cable used by LocalTalk.

Using Ethernet with Macintosh computers

LocalTalk is popular because it's cheap. But LocalTalk has one major problem: It's unbearably slow. LocalTalk uses the Macintosh serial printer ports, so it transmits data over the network at a paltry 230,400 bits per second. This transmission rate is acceptable for casual use of a network printer and occasionally copying a small file to or from another computer, but it's not sufficient for serious networking.

Fortunately, AppleTalk also supports Ethernet network adapters and cables. With Ethernet, data is sent at 10 million bits per second. Much more suitable for real-life networking.

When you use Ethernet, you have access to all the cabling options described elsewhere in this book: 10base5 (yellow cable), 10base2 (thinnet), and 10baseT (twisted pair). Fast (100 Mbps) Ethernet works as well.

- An AppleTalk network that uses Ethernet is sometimes called an *EtherTalk network.*

- Ethernet interface cards for Macintoshes are a bit more expensive than their PC counterparts, mostly because they aren't as widely used. However, most Macs built within the last few years have Ethernet built in, so if your Macs are new, you probably don't need cards.

- The current batch of Power Macintosh computers use the same PCI expansion slots that PCs do, which means that you can use any PCI Ethernet card in a PCI-equipped Macintosh. (Well, almost any. The manufacturer of the card must supply a Macintosh driver for the card, and some manufacturers don't.)

- When you opt for an Ethernet network, you have to contend with a device driver to support the network card. You use the Installer program to set up the driver.

- Apple has also developed a specialized interface for Ethernet cards called the Ethernet cabling system. When the Ethernet cabling system is used, the network cards themselves don't have coax or 10baseT connectors. Instead, they have a special type of connector called an Apple Attachment Unit Interface (AAUI). You must plug a device called a transceiver into the AAUI connector so that you can attach the computer to a coax or twisted-pair cable. Many of Apple's Macintosh computers which come with a built-in Ethernet port use this AAUI interface.

- You can use a router to connect a LocalTalk network to an Ethernet network. This arrangement is often used to connect a small group of Macintosh users to a larger network or to connect an existing LocalTalk network to an Ethernet network.

AppleShare

AppleShare turns a Macintosh computer into a dedicated file server. It's the Macintosh equivalent to Windows NT Server or IntranetWare.

The current version of AppleShare, called AppleShare IP 5.0, offers the following features:

- ✔ File server using AppleTalk's standard file protocol, ATP
- ✔ Print server
- ✔ Mail server
- ✔ Web server
- ✔ FTP server
- ✔ Supports both AppleTalk and TCP/IP protocols so that it can connect to your AppleTalk network and to the Internet

What You Need to Know to Use a Macintosh Network

Here are some of the most common questions that come up after you've installed the network cable. Note that the following sections assume that you are working with AppleTalk networking. The procedures may vary somewhat if you're using Open Transport networking.

How to configure a Mac for networking

Before you can access the network from your Mac, you must configure it for networking by activating AppleTalk and assigning your network name and password.

Activating AppleTalk

After all the cable is in place, you have to activate AppleTalk. Here's how:

1. **Choose the Chooser desk accessory from the Apple menu.**
2. **Click the Active button.**
3. **Close the Chooser.**

That's all there is to it.

Assigning your name and password

Next, assign an owner name, a password, and a name for your computer. This process allows other network users to access your Mac. To do that:

1. **Choose the Sharing Setup control panels from the Apple menu.**

2. **Type your name in the Owner Name field.**

3. **Type a password in the Owner Password field. Don't forget what the password is.**

4. **Type a descriptive name for your computer in the Macintosh Name field. This is the name that other network users will know your computer by.**

5. **Close Sharing Setup.**

Piece of cake, eh?

How to access a network printer

Accessing a network printer with AppleTalk is no different than accessing a printer when you don't have a network. If more than one printer is available on the network, you use the Chooser to select the printer you want to use. Chooser displays all the available network printers; just pick the one you want to use:

✔ Be sure to enable Background Printing for the network printer. If you don't, your Mac is tied up until the printer finishes your job — that can be a long time if someone else sent a 500-page report to the printer just before you. When Background Printing is enabled, your printer output is captured to a disk file and then sent to the printer later while you continue with other work.

To enable Background Printing, choose the printer you want to use from the Chooser and click the Background Printing On button.

✔ Rescind that last order if a dedicated print server has been set up. In that case, print data is automatically spooled to the print server's disk, so that your Mac doesn't have to wait for the printer to become available.

How to share files with other users

To share files on your Mac with other network users, you must set up a shared resource. You can share an entire disk, or you can share just individual folders. And you can restrict access to certain users if you want.

Activating file sharing

Before you can share files with other users, you must activate the AppleTalk file sharing feature. Here's how:

1. **Choose the Sharing Setup control panel from the Apple Menu.**
2. **Click the Start button in the File Sharing section of the control panel.**
3. **Close Sharing Setup.**

Sharing a folder or disk

To set up a folder or an entire disk so that other network users can access it, follow this procedure:

1. **Select the folder or disk that you want to share.**
2. **Choose Sharing from the File menu.**
3. **Click the Share This Item and Its Contents box.**
4. **Close the window and click the Save button in the dialog box that appears.**

You can reverse this procedure if you decide later that you don't want the folder or disk to be shared.

Restricting access to certain users

If you want, you can restrict access to your shared resources to certain users or groups. First, you must create a list of registered users:

1. **Choose the Users & Groups control panel from the Apple menu.**
2. **Choose New User from the File menu.**
3. **Type the name of the user.**
4. **If you want to specify a password for the new user, double-click the user's icon and type the password.**

If you want to grant access to a particular folder or disk to more than one user, you must create a group that contains each of those users. To create a group:

1. **Choose the Users & Groups control panel from the Apple menu.**
2. **Choose New Group from the File menu.**
3. **Type a name for the group.**
4. **Drag the icon for each user you want in the group from the Users & Groups window to the New Group window.**

Now that you've set up users and groups, here's how to restrict access for a folder or drive:

1. **Choose the folder or disk you want to share.**

2. **Choose Sharing from the File menu.**

3. **Use the User/Group pop-up menu to choose an individual user or group for the folder or drive.**

4. **Uncheck the checkboxes next to Everyone so that other users have no access to the folder or disk.**

5. **Close the window and click the Save button in the dialog box that appears.**

Preventing guests from accessing your system

Even if you set up a list of registered users, anyone can access your Mac if you leave the Guest user enabled. To disable the Guest user, do this:

1. **Choose the Users & Groups control panel from the Apple menu.**

2. **Double-click the Guest icon.**

3. **Uncheck the Allow Guests to Connect box.**

4. **Close the Guest window and click the Save button in the dialog box that appears. Then close the Users & Groups window.**

How to access other users' files

To access files on another Macintosh, follow this procedure:

1. **Choose the Chooser from the Apple menu.**

2. **Click the AppleShare icon from the Chooser window.**

3. **Click the name of the computer you want to access. (If your network has zones, you must first click the zone you want to access.)**

4. **Click OK.**

5. **A login screen appears. If you're a registered user on the computer, click the Registered User button and enter your user name and password. Otherwise, click the Guest button. Then click OK.**

6. **A list of shared folders and disks appears. Click the ones you want to access and then click OK.**

A checkbox appears next to each item on this list. If you check this box, you'll be connected to the folder or disk automatically each time you start your computer.

Mixing Macintoshes and PCs on a Network

Life would be too boring if Macs lived on one side of the tracks and PCs lived on the other. If your organization has a mix of both Macs and PCs, odds are you'll eventually want to network them together. Fortunately, you have several ways to do so:

✔ If your network has an AppleShare server, you can use the Windows client software that comes with AppleShare to connect any version of Windows to the AppleShare server. This enables Windows users to access the files and printers on the AppleShare server.

✔ If you have Windows NT Server, you can use a feature called Services for Macintosh to allow Macintosh computers to access files and printers managed by the Windows NT Server using the AppleTalk protocol. This feature doesn't require that you install special client software on the Macintosh computers.

✔ If you use NetWare, you must purchase separate NetWare client software for your Macintosh computers from Novell. After you install this client software, the Macs are able to access files and printers managed by your NetWare servers.

The biggest complication that occurs when you mix Macintosh and Windows 95 computers on the same network is that the MacOS and Windows have slightly different rules for naming files. For example, Macintosh file names are limited to 31 characters, but Windows 95 filenames can be up to 255 characters. And while a Macintosh filename can include any characters other than a colon, Windows 95 filenames can't include backslashes, greater than or less than sign, and a few other oddball characters.

These filename conflicts are resolved by translating any filenames that violate the rules of the system being used into a form that is acceptable to both Windows and the Macintosh. Unfortunately, this sometimes leads to cryptic or ambiguous filenames. To avoid filename problems, try to stick with short names (under 31 characters) and limit your filenames to letters, numbers, and common symbols such as the hyphen or pound sign.

Part VI
The Part of Tens

The 5th Wave   By Rich Tennant

WE'RE HERE TO SERVICE YOUR LOCAL-AREA-NETWORK.

In this part . . .

*I*f you keep this book in the bathroom, the chapters in this section are the ones that you'll read most. Each of these chapters consists of ten (more or less) things that are worth knowing about various aspects of networking. Without further ado, here they are, direct from the home office in Fresno, California.

Chapter 23

Ten Big Network Mistakes

*J*ust about the time you figure out how to avoid the most embarrassing computer mistakes, such as folding a 5 ¼" disk in half to make it fit in a 3 ½" drive, the network lands on your computer. Now you have a whole new list of dumb things you can do, mistakes that can give your average computer geek a belly laugh because they seem so basic to him. Well, that's because he's a computer geek. Nobody had to tell him not to fold the disk — he was born with an extra gene that gave him an instinctive knowledge of such things.

Here's a list of some of the most common mistakes made by network novices. Avoid these mistakes and you'll deprive your local computer geek of the pleasure of a good laugh at your expense.

Turning Off or Restarting a Server Computer While Users Are Logged On

The fastest way to blow your network users to kingdom come is to turn off a server computer while users are logged on. Restarting it by pressing its reset button or giving it the three-finger salute (Ctrl+Alt+Del) can have the same disastrous effect.

If your network is set up with a dedicated file server, you probably won't be tempted to turn it off or restart it. But if your network is set up as a true peer-to-peer network, where each of the workstation computers — including your own — also doubles as a server computer, be careful about the impulsive urge to turn your computer off or restart it. Someone may be accessing a file or printer on your computer at that very moment.

Before turning off or restarting a server computer, find out whether anyone is logged on. If so, politely ask him or her to log off.

Deleting Important Files on the Server

Without a network, you can do anything you want to your computer, and the only person you can hurt is yourself. Kind of like the old "victimless crime" debate. Put your computer on a network, though, and you take on a certain amount of responsibility. You must find out how to live like a responsible member of the network society.

That means you can't capriciously delete files from a network server just because you don't need them. They may not be yours. You wouldn't want someone deleting your files, would you?

Be especially careful about files that are required to keep the network running. For example, every LANtastic server has a directory named LANTASTI.NET. Delete the files in this directory and poof! — the server is history.

Copying a File from the Server, Changing It, and Then Copying It Back

Sometimes working on a network file is easier if you first copy the file to your local disk. Then you can access it from your application program more efficiently because you don't have to use the network. This is especially true for large database files that have to be sorted to print reports.

You're asking for trouble, though, if you copy the file to your PC's local hard disk, make changes to the file, and then copy the updated version of the file back to the server. Why? Because there's no guarantee somebody else didn't try the same thing at the same time. If that happens, the updates made by one of you — the one who copies the file back to the server first — are lost.

Copying a file to a local drive is an okay thing to do, but not if you plan on updating the file and copying it back.

Sending Something to the Printer Again Just Because It Didn't Print the First Time

What do you do if you send something to the printer and nothing happens? Right answer: Find out why nothing happened and fix it. Wrong answer: Send it again and see whether it works this time. Some users keep sending it over and over again, hoping that one of these days, it will take. The result is rather embarrassing when someone finally clears the paper jam and then watches 30 copies of the same letter print.

Unplugging a Cable While the Computer Is On

Bad idea! If for any reason you need to unplug a cable from behind your computer, turn your computer off first. You don't want to fry any of the delicate electronic parts inside your computer, do you?

If you need to unplug the network cable, it's a good idea to do it when all the computers on the network are off. This is especially true if your network is wired with thinnet coax cable; it's not such a big deal with twisted-pair cable.

Note: With thinnet cable, it's okay to disconnect the T connector from your computer as long as you don't disconnect the cable itself from the T connector.

Assuming That the Server Is Safely Backed Up

Some users make the unfortunate assumption that the network somehow represents an efficient and organized bureaucracy worthy of their trust. Far from the truth. Never assume that the network jocks are doing their jobs backing up the network data every day. Check up on them. Conduct a surprise inspection one day: Burst into the computer room wearing white gloves and demand to see the backup tapes. Check the tape rotation to make sure that more than one day's worth of backups are available.

If you're not impressed with your network's backup procedures, take it upon yourself to make sure that you never lose any of your data. Back up your most valued files to floppy disks frequently.

Thinking You Can't Work Just Because the Network Is Down

A few years back, I realized that I can't do my job without electricity. Should a power failure occur and I find myself without electricity, I can't even light a candle and work with pencil and paper because the only pencil sharpener I have is electric.

Some people have the same attitude about the network: They figure that if the network goes down, they may as well go home. That's not always the case. Just because your computer is attached to a network doesn't mean that it won't work when the network is down. If the wind flies out of the network sails, it's true that you can't access any network devices. You can't get files from network drives, and you can't print on network printers. But you can still use your computer for local work: accessing files and programs on your local hard disk and printing on your local printer (if you're lucky enough to have one).

Always Blaming the Network

Some people treat the network kind of like the village idiot who can be blamed whenever anything goes wrong. Networks do cause problems of their own, but they aren't the root of all evil.

If your monitor displays only capital letters, it's probably because you pressed the Caps Lock key. Don't blame the network.

If you spill coffee on the keyboard, well, that's your fault. Don't blame the network.

Your three-year-old sticks Play Doh in the floppy drive — hey, kids will be kids. Don't blame the network.

Get the point?

Chapter 24

Ten Networking Commandments

"*B*lessed is the network manager who walks not in the council of the ignorant, nor stands in the way of the oblivious, nor sits in the seat of the greenhorn, but delights in the Law of the Network, and meditates on this Law day and night."

— Networks 1:1

And so it came to pass that these Ten Networking Commandments were passed down from generation to generation, to be worn as frontlets between the computer geeks' eyes and written upon their doorposts. Obey these commandments and it shall go well with you, with your children, and with your children's children.

I. Thou shalt back up thy hard disk religiously

Prayer is a wonderful thing, but when it comes to protecting the data on your network, nothing beats a well-thought-out schedule of backups followed religiously.

II. Thou shalt not drop thy guard against the unholy viri

Remember Col. Flagg from *M*A*S*H*, who hid in trash cans looking for commies? You don't exactly want to become him, but on the other hand, you don't want to ignore the possibility of getting zapped by a virus. Start by making sure that every user realizes that any floppy disk from the outside can be infected, and after one computer on the network is infected, the entire network is in trouble. Then show the users how easily they can scan suspicious disks before using them.

III. Remember thy network disk, to keep it clean of old files

Don't wait until your 2GB network drive is down to just one cluster of free space before thinking about cleaning it up. Set up a routine schedule for disk housekeeping, where you wade through the files and directories on the network disk to remove old junk.

IV. Thou shalt not tinker with thine network configuration files unless thou knowest what thou art doing

Networks are finicky things. After yours is up and running, don't mess around with it unless you know what you're doing. And be especially careful if you think you know what you're doing. It's people who think they know what they're doing who get themselves into trouble!

V. Thou shalt not covet thy neighbor's network

Network envy is a common malady among network managers. If your network uses LANtastic and it works, nothing can be gained by coveting someone else's NetWare network. If you run NetWare 3.12, resist the urge to upgrade to 4.1 unless you have a really good reason. And if you run NetWare 4.1, fantasizing about Windows NT Server is a venial sin.

You're especially susceptible to network envy if you're a gadget freak. There's always a better hub to be had or some fancy network protocol gizmo to lust after. Don't give in to these base urges! Resist the devil, and he will flee!

VI. Thou shalt schedule downtime before working upon thy network

As a courtesy, try to give your users plenty of advance notice when you intend to take down the network to work on it. Obviously, you can't predict when random problems will strike. But if you know you're going to add a new computer to the network on Thursday morning, you'll earn points if you tell everyone about the inconvenience two days before rather than two minutes before.

VII. Thou shalt keep an adequate supply of spare parts

There's no reason that your network should be down for two days just because a cable breaks. Always make sure that you have at least a minimal supply of network spare parts on hand. As luck would have it, Chapter 25 suggests ten things you should keep in your closet.

VIII. Thou shalt not steal thy neighbor's program without license

How would you like it if Inspector Clouseau barged into your office, looked over your shoulder as you ran Lotus 1-2-3 from a network server, and asked, "Do you have a liesaunce?"

"A liesaunce?" you reply, puzzled.

"Yes of course, liesaunce, that is what I said. The law specifically prohibits the playing of a computer program on a network without a proper liesaunce."

You don't want to go against the law, do you?

IX. Thou shalt train thy users in the way in which they should go

Don't blame the users if they don't know how to use the network. It's not their fault. If you're the network administrator, it's your job to provide training so that the network users know how to use the network.

X. Thou shalt write down thy network configuration upon tablets of stone

If you cross the river Jordan, who else will know diddly-squat about the network if you don't write it down somewhere? The back of a napkin won't cut it. Write down everything and put it in an official binder labeled "Network Bible" and protect the binder as if it were sacred.

Your hope should be that 2,000 years from now, when archaeologists are exploring caves in your area, they find your network documentation hidden in a jar and marvel at how meticulously the people of our time recorded their network configurations.

They'll probably draw ridiculous conclusions such as we offered sacrifices of burnt data packets to a deity named NOS, but that makes it all the more fun.

Chapter 25

Ten Things You Should Keep in the Closet

*W*hen you first networkize your office computers, you need to find a closet where you can stash some network goodies. If you can't find a whole closet, shoot for a shelf, a drawer, or at least a sturdy cardboard box.

Here's a list of what stuff to keep on hand.

Tools

Make sure that you have at least a basic computer tool kit, the kind you can pick up for $15 from just about any office supply store. You also should have wire cutters, strippers, and cable crimpers that work for your network cable type.

Extra Cable

When you buy network cable, never buy exactly the amount you need. In fact, buying at least twice as much cable as you need isn't a bad idea, so that half the cable is left over in case you need it later. You will. Something will go wrong and you'll suspect a cable problem, so you'll need extra cable to replace the bad cable. Or you may add a computer or two to the network and need extra cable.

If you glue your entire network together with preassembled 25' lengths of thinnet coax cable, having at least one 25' segment lying around in the closet is a good idea.

Extra Connectors

Don't run out of connectors, either. If you use twisted-pair cabling, you'll find that connectors go bad more often than you'd like. Buy the connectors 25, 50, or 100 at a time so that you'll have plenty of spares lying around.

If you use thinnet cable, keep a few spare BNC connectors handy, plus a few T connectors and a few terminators. Terminators have been known to mysteriously disappear. Rumor has it that they are sucked through some kind of time vortex into the 21st century, where they're refabricated and returned to our time in the form of Arnold Schwarzenegger.

Preassembled Patch Cables

If you wired your network the professional way, with wall jacks in each office, keep a few preassembled patch cables of various lengths in the closet. That way, you won't have to pull out the cable crimpers every time you need to change a patch cable.

Twinkies

If left sealed in their little individually wrapped packages, Twinkies will keep for years. In fact, they'll probably outlast the network itself. You can give 'em to future network geeks, ensuring continued network support for generations to come.

An Extra Network Card

Ideally, you want to use identical network cards in all your computers. But if the boss's computer is down, you'll probably settle for whatever network card the corner network street vendor is selling today. That's why you should always keep at least one spare network card in the closet. You'll rest easy knowing that if a network card fails, you have an identical replacement card sitting on the shelf, just waiting to be installed — and you won't have to buy one from someone who also sells imitation Persian rugs.

Obviously, if you have only two computers on your network, justifying spending the money for a spare network adapter card is hard. With larger networks, it's easier to justify.

Complete Documentation of the Network on Tablets of Stone

I've mentioned several times in this book the importance of documenting your network. Don't spend hours documenting your network and then hide the documentation under a pile of old magazines behind your desk. Put the binder in the closet with the other network supplies so that you and everyone else always know where to find it.

Don't you dare chisel passwords into the network documentation, though. Shame on you for even thinking about it!

If you do decide to chisel the network documentation in stone tablets, consider using sandstone. It's attractive, inexpensive, and easy to update (just rub out the old info and chisel in the new). Keep in mind, however, that sandstone is subject to erosion from spilled Jolt Cola or Snapple. Oh, and make sure that you store it on a reinforced shelf.

The Network Manuals and Disks

In the land of Oz, a common lament of the Network Scarecrow is "If I only had the manual." True, the manual probably isn't a Pulitzer prize candidate, but that doesn't mean you should toss it in a landfill, either. Put the manual where it belongs: in the closet with all the other network tools and artifacts.

Likewise the disks. You may need them someday, so keep them with the other network stuff.

Ten Copies of This Book

Obviously, you'll want to keep an adequate supply of this book on hand to distribute to all your network users. The more they know, the more they'll stay off your back. Sheesh, 10 copies may not be enough — 20 may be closer to what you need.

Chapter 26

Ten Network Gizmos Only Big Networks Need

*P*eople who compile statistics on things, such as the ratio of chickens to humans in Arkansas and the likelihood of the Mets losing when the other team shows up, report that more than 40 percent of all networks have fewer than ten computers and that this percentage is expected to increase in coming years. A Ross Perot-style pie chart would be good here, but my editor tells me I'm running long, so we'll have to pass on that.

The point is that if you're one of the lucky 40 percent with fewer than ten computers on your network, you can skip this chapter altogether. It's a brief description of various network gizmos to find out whether your network is really big. How big is big? There's no hard-and-fast rule, but the soft-and-slow rule is that you should look into this stuff when your network grows to about 25 computers.

The exceptions to the soft-and-slow rule are: (1) Your company has two or more networks that you want to hook together, and these networks were designed by different people who refused to talk to each other until it was too late; (2) your network needs to connect computers that are more than a few hundred yards apart, perhaps in different buildings.

Repeaters

A repeater is a gizmo that's designed to give your network signals a boost so that they can travel farther. It's kind of like the Gatorade stations in a marathon. As they travel past the repeater, the network signals pick up a cup of Gatorade, take a sip, splash the rest of it on their heads, toss the cup, and hop in a cab when they're sure that no one is looking.

You need a repeater when the total length of a single span of network cable is larger than the maximum allowed for your cable type:

Cable	*Maximum Length*
Thick coax (Yellow Stuff)	500 meters, or 1,640 feet
Thin coax (Cheapernet)	185 meters, or 606 feet
10baseT (Twisted Sister)	100 meters, or 328 feet

For coax cable (thick and thin), the preceding cable lengths apply to cable segments, not individual lengths of cable. A segment is the entire run of cable from one terminator to another and may include more than one computer. In other words, if you have ten computers and you connect them all with 25-foot lengths of thin coax cable, the total length of the segment is 225 feet. (Made you look! Only nine cables are required to connect ten computers — that's why it's not 250 feet.)

For 10baseT cable, the 100-meter length limit applies to the cable that connects a computer to the hub or the cable that connects hubs to each other when hubs are daisy-chained using twisted-pair cable. In other words, each computer can be connected to the hub with no more than 100 meters of cable, and hubs can be connected to each other with no more than 100 meters of cable.

Figure 25-1 shows how a repeater may be used to connect two groups of computers that are too far apart to be strung on a single segment. When you use a repeater like this, the repeater divides the cable into two segments. The cable length limit still applies to the cable on each side of the repeater.

✔ Repeaters are used only with Ethernet networks wired with coax cable. 10baseT networks don't use repeaters.

✔ Actually, that's not quite true: 10baseT does use repeaters. It's just that the repeater isn't a separate device. In a 10baseT network, the hub is actually a multiport repeater. That's why the cable used to attach each computer to the hub is considered to be a separate segment.

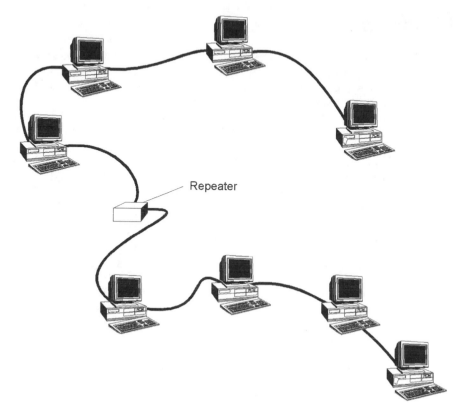

Figure 26-1:
Using a
repeater.

Repeater

- Most 10baseT hubs have a BNC connector on the back. This BNC connector is a thinnet repeater that enables you to attach a full 185-meter thinnet segment. The segment can attach other computers, 10baseT hubs, or a combination of both. (Some cheaper 10baseT hubs don't have this extra connector, which means that you can't connect them to a thinnet segment.)

- A basic rule of Ethernet life is that a signal cannot pass through more than three repeaters on its way from one node to another. That doesn't mean you can't have more than three repeaters or hubs, but if you do, you have to carefully plan the network cabling so that the three-repeater rule isn't violated.

- Two-port thinnet repeaters can be had for about $200 from mail-order suppliers.

- Repeaters are legitimate components of a by-the-book Ethernet network. They don't extend the maximum length of a single segment; they just enable you to tie two segments together. Beware of the little black boxes that claim to extend the segment limit beyond the standard 185-meter limit for thinnet or 500-meter limit for the yellow stuff. These products usually work, but it's better to play by the rules.

Bridges

A *bridge* is a device that's used to connect two networks so that they act as if they're one network. Bridges are used to partition one large network into two smaller networks for performance reasons. You can think of a bridge as a kind of smart repeater. Repeaters listen to signals coming down one network cable, amplify them, and send them down the other cable. They do this blindly, paying no attention to the content of the messages they repeat.

In contrast, a bridge is a little smarter about the messages that come down the pike. For starters, most bridges have the capability to listen to the network and automatically figure out the address of each computer on both sides of the bridge. Then the bridge can inspect each message that comes from one side of the bridge and broadcast it on the other side of the bridge only if the message is intended for a computer that's on the other side.

This key feature enables bridges to partition a large network into two smaller, more efficient networks. Bridges work best in networks that are highly segregated. For example (humor me here — I'm a Dr. Seuss fan), suppose that the Sneetches networked all their computers and discovered that, although the Star-Bellied Sneetches' computers talked to each other frequently and the Plain-Bellied Sneetches' computers also talked to each other frequently, it was a rare occasion that a Star-Bellied Sneetch computer talked to a Plain-Bellied Sneetch computer.

A bridge can be used to partition the Sneetchnet into two networks: the Star-Bellied network and the Plain-Bellied network. The bridge automatically learns which computers were on the Star-Bellied network and which were on the Plain-Bellied network. The bridge forwards messages from the Star-Bellied side to the Plain-Bellied side (and vice versa) only when necessary. The overall performance of both networks is improved, although the performance of any network operation that had to travel over the bridge is slowed down a bit.

- As I mentioned, some bridges also have the capability to translate the messages from one format to another. For example, if the Star-Bellied Sneetches build their network with Ethernet and the Plain-Bellied Sneetches use Token Ring, a bridge can be used to tie the two together.

- You can get a basic bridge to partition two Ethernet networks for about $500 from mail-order suppliers. More sophisticated bridges can cost as much as $5,000 or more.

- If you've never read Dr. Seuss's classic story of the Sneetches, you should.

- If you're not confused yet, don't worry. Read on.

Switches

A *switch* is similar to a bridge but provides much better performance. The difference between a switch and a bridge is that a switch can create a separate internal connection (called a *segment*) between any two of the switch's ports. Each of these connections operates at a full 10 MHz, or in the case of a 100 MHz switch, at 100 MHz.

The best switches are able to constantly monitor the traffic that comes across them and reroute its internal connections automatically to provide the most efficient operation for the network. This technique is called *load balancing*.

Switches have become so popular that they have all but replaced bridges except for unusual applications. You can get an inexpensive 2-port switch for under $300, and 16-port switches can be had for about $1,500. Switches with all the bells and whistles are naturally more expensive.

Routers

A *router* is like a bridge or a switch, but with a key difference. Bridges and switches can tell the address of the network node to which each message is sent, and can forward the message to the appropriate segment. But *routers* have the extra ability to actually peek inside the message to see what type of information is being sent. In contrast, bridges and switches are completely ignorant of the content of network messages.

You can think of a router as a super-intelligent bridge. Bridges know the addresses of all the computers on each side of the bridge and can forward messages accordingly. But routers know even more about the network. A router knows not only the addresses of all the computers but also other routers on the network and can decide the most efficient path to send each network message. In fact, the router knows everything about you and your little network.

One key difference between a bridge and a router is that a bridge is essentially transparent to the network. In contrast, a router is itself a node on the network, with its own address. That means that messages can be directed to a router, which can then examine the contents of the message to determine how the message should be handled.

A network can be configured with several routers which can work cooperatively together. For example, some routers are able to monitor the network to determine the most efficient path for sending a message to its ultimate destination. If a part of the network is extremely busy, a router can automatically route messages along a less-busy route. In this respect, the router is kind of like a traffic reporter up in a helicopter. The router knows that 101 is bumper-to-bumper all the way through Sunnyvale, so it sends the message on 280 instead.

- Routers aren't cheap. But for big networks, they're worth it.

- The functional distinctions between bridges, switches, and routers get blurrier all the time. As bridges and switches become more sophisticated, they're able to take on some of the chores that used to require a router, thus putting many routers out of work. (Ross Perot blames this situation on NAFTA.)

- Some routers are nothing more than computers with several network interface cards and special software to perform the router functions. In fact, NetWare comes with a router program that lets a NetWare server act as a router.

- Routers can also be used to connect networks that are geographically distant from one another via a phone line (using modems) or ISDN. You can't do that with a bridge.

- If you're confused about the distinction between bridges, switches, and routers, join the club. The technical distinction has to do with the OSI Reference Model network layer where the devices operate. Bridges operate at the MAC layer (MAC stands for "Media Access Control"), whereas routers operate at the next level up: the network layer.

Gateways

No, not the Bill Gates way. This kind of gateway is a super-intelligent router, which is a super-intelligent bridge, which is a super-intelligent repeater. Notice a pattern here?

Gateways are designed to connect radically different types of networks together. They do this by translating messages from one network's format to another's format, much like the Universal Translator that got Kirk and Spock out of so many jams. (Ever notice how all those planets with gorgeous females never seem to have a word for "kiss," so Kirk has to demonstrate?)

Gateways usually are used to connect a network to a mainframe or minicomputer. If you don't have a mainframe or minicomputer, you probably don't need a gateway.

> ✔ Gateways are necessary only because of the mess that computer manufacturers got us into by insisting on using their own proprietary designs for networks. If computer manufacturers had talked to each other 20 years ago, we wouldn't have to use gates to make their networks talk to each other today.

> ✔ Gateways come in several varieties. My favorite is ornamental wrought iron.

Superservers

A funny thing happened to personal computers when networks became popular. They turned into mainframe computers.

As networks grew and grew, some organizations found that they had to have dozens of PCs functioning as dedicated file servers. Some networks had 50 or 100 dedicated servers! You can imagine the network management nightmares you'd have to contend with on a network that large.

To ease the burdens of managing a gaggle of file servers, some network managers are turning to superservers, unbelievably high-powered computers that can single-handedly take on the duties of half a dozen or more mere mortal computers. These superservers have huge cabinets that can hold stacks of disk drives, specialized high-speed disk controllers, room for more memory than Colonel Hathi, and — get this — more than one CPU.

Superservers aren't cheap — they sell for tens of thousands of dollars. But they're often less expensive than an equivalent number of ordinary computers, they're more efficient, and they're easier to manage.

One common argument against the use of superservers is the old "don't put all your eggs in one basket" line. What if the superserver breaks? The counter to this argument is that superservers are loaded with state-of-the-art fault-tolerance gizmos that make it unlikely that they'll ever break. In contrast, if you use ten separate file servers, you actually increase the likelihood that one of them will fail, probably sooner than you'd like.

It's RAID!

In most small networks, it's a hassle if a disk drive goes south and has to be sent to the shop for repairs. In some large networks, a failed disk drive is more than a hassle: It's an outright disaster. Big companies don't know how to do anything when the computer goes down. Everyone just sits around, looking at the floor, silently keeping vigil 'til the computers come back up.

A *RAID system* is a fancy type of disk storage that hardly ever fails. It works by lumping several disk drives together and treating them as if they were one humongous drive. RAID uses some fancy techniques devised by computer nerds at Berkeley. These computer nerds guarantee that if one of the disk drives in the RAID system fails, no data is lost. The disk drive that failed can be removed and repaired, and the data that was on it can be reconstructed from the other drives.

- RAID stands for "Redundant Array of Inexpensive Disks," but that doesn't matter. You don't have to remember that for the test.

- A RAID system is usually housed in a separate cabinet that includes its own RAID disk controller. It's sometimes called a disk subsystem.

- In the coolest RAID systems, the disk drives themselves are hot swappable. That means that you can shut down and remove one of the disk drives while the RAID system continues to operate. Network users won't even know that one of the disks has been removed because the RAID system reconstructs the data that was on the removed disk using data from the other disks. When the failed disk has been replaced, the new disk is brought on-line without a hitch.

Firewalls

A *firewall* is a security-conscious router that sits between your network and the rest of the world in an effort to prevent "them" from getting to "us."

It's also Pat Buchanan's favorite computer component.

Firewalls are normally used when you're creating a World Wide Web (WWW) site, which enables Internet users all around the world to access files on your network. Naturally, you want to limit the files that Internet users can access. A firewall is the best way to do that.

If your network doesn't host a WWW site, it doesn't need a firewall. If your network does host a Web site, you need to hire a firewall consultant.

Fast Ethernet

Most small networks operate just fine with standard Ethernet connections. However, if your network is large enough to merit a high-speed backbone connection, or if your users are constantly sharing huge amounts of data such as video files, you may want to look into Fast Ethernet. Fast Ethernet is a relatively new version of Ethernet, which is ten times as fast: 100 Mbps instead of 10 Mbps.

The most common form of Fast Ethernet is called 100baseT. As its name suggests, 100baseT uses twisted-pair cable like 10baseT. In some cases, you can use existing 10baseT cable, but only if you use top-quality Category 5 cable and keep the cable lengths under 100 meters. Another popular form of Fast Ethernet is called 100VG AnyLAN. It too can use standard Category 5 twisted pair cable with 100 meter cable-length limits. Unfortunately, neither Fast Ethernet variety can operate on coax cable.

If you're willing to spend the money, you can connect all your computers using Fast Ethernet rather than normal Ethernet. It costs you about $100 extra per computer to purchase Fast Ethernet adapters instead of normal Ethernet adapters, plus you have to buy Fast Ethernet hubs. The hubs are still pretty expensive. When I wrote this, the cheapest 8-port 100baseT hubs were about $500. That's about eight times the cost of the cheapest 8-port 10baseT hubs. However, the prices of Fast Ethernet components (like all other computer components) are coming down as we speak.

Chapter 27

Ten (or Fewer) Layers of the OSI Model

● ●

● ●

*O*SI sounds like the name of a top-secret government agency you hear about only in Tom Clancy novels. What it really stands for, as far as this book is concerned, is "Open System Interconnection," as in the "Open System Interconnection Reference Model," affectionately known as the OSI model.

The OSI model breaks the various aspects of a computer network into seven distinct layers. These layers are kind of like the layers of an onion: Each successive layer envelopes the layer beneath it, hiding its details from the levels above. The OSI model is also like an onion in that if you start to peel it apart to have a look inside, you're bound to shed a few tears.

The OSI model is not itself a networking standard in the same sense that Ethernet and Token Ring are. Rather, the OSI model is a framework into which the various networking standards can fit. The OSI model specifies what aspects of a network's operation can be addressed by various network standards. So, in a sense, the OSI model is sort of a standard's standard.

Although the OSI model contains seven layers, the bottom two are the layers that have the most practical impact on smaller networks. Networking standards like Ethernet and Token Ring are layer-1 and layer-2 standards. The higher layers of the OSI model have not resulted in widespread standards.

Don't read this if you're dyslexic

The OSI standard was developed by a group known as ISO, for "International Standards Organization." So technically, it can be called the ISO OSI standard. Hold that up to a mirror and see what happens.

ISO develops standards for all sorts of stuff, like the size of sprinkler pipes and machine screws. Other ISO standards include SOI, SIO, OIS, and IOS.

Layer 1: The Physical Layer

The bottom layer of the OSI model is the physical layer. It addresses the physical characteristics of the network: the types of cables used to connect devices, the types of connectors used, how long the cables can be, and so on. For example, the Ethernet standard for 10baseT cable specifies the electrical characteristics of the twisted-pair cables, the size and shape of the connectors, the maximum length of the cables, and so on.

Another aspect of the physical layer is the electrical characteristics of the signals used to transmit data over the cables from one network node to another. The physical layer doesn't define any meaning to those signals other than the basic binary values 0 and 1. It's up to higher levels of the OSI model to assign meanings to the bits that are transmitted at the physical layer.

Layer 2: The Data Link Layer

The data link layer is the layer at which meaning is assigned to the bits that are transmitted over the network. A standard for the data link layer must address things such as the size of each packet of data to be sent, a means of addressing each packet so that it's delivered to the intended recipient, and a way to ensure that two or more nodes don't try to transmit data on the network at the same time.

The data link layer also provides basic error detection and correction to ensure that the data sent is the same as the data received. If an uncorrectable error occurs, the data link standard must specify how the node is to be informed of the error so that it can retransmit the data.

You don't really care how Ethernet fits into the OSI model, do you?

Ethernet is a standard published by the IEEE (if you pronounce this term eye-triple-ee, people will think you know what you're talking about). It's official title is 802.3, pronounced eight-oh-two-dot-three. The 802.3 standard addresses both the physical layer of the OSI model and the data link layer.

You can blame the portion of the 802.3 that addresses the physical layer for the need to attach terminators to each end of a segment of thinnet coax, for the fact that BNC connectors are a pain in the rumpus to attach, and for the limit on the number of hubs that can be daisy-chained together when twisted-pair cabling is used. The physical-layer portion of the 802.3 standard is also responsible for the colorful terms 10base5, 10base2, and 10baseT.

The portion of 802.3 that deals with the data link layer actually deals only with one portion of the data link layer, called the "Media Access Control Sublayer," or MAC sublayer. The MAC portion of 802.3 spells out how the CSMA/CD operation of Ethernet works — how Ethernet listens for network traffic, sends data if the network appears to be free of traffic, and then listens for collisions and resends the information if necessary.

The other portion of the data link layer of the OSI model is called the "Logical Link Control Sublayer," or (you guessed it) the LLC sublayer. The LLC sublayer spells out the basics of sending and receiving packets of information over the network and correcting errors. The LLC standard used by Ethernet is called 802.2.

None of this stuff really matters unless you plan on building network interface cards in your garage.

Layer 3: The Network Layer

The network layer addresses the interconnection of networks by routing packets from one network to another. The network layer is most important when you use a router to link two different types of networks, such as an Ethernet network and a Token Ring network. Because the network layer is one step above the data link layer, it doesn't matter whether the two networks use different standards at the data link and physical layers.

Layer 4: The Transport Layer

The transport layer is the basic layer at which one network computer communicates with another network computer. The transport layer identifies each node on the computer with a unique address and manages connections between nodes. The transport layer also breaks large messages into smaller messages and reassembles the messages at the receiving node.

The transport layer and the OSI layers above it are implemented differently by various network operating systems. You can thank the OSI model for the capability to run NetWare, LANtastic, Windows for Workgroups, or just about any other network operating system on a standard Ethernet network. Ethernet addresses the lower layers of the OSI model. As long as the network operating system's transport layer is able to interface with Ethernet, you're in business.

Layer 4a: The Lemon-Pudding Layer

The lemon-pudding layer is squeezed in between the rather dry and taste-less transport and session layers to add flavor and moisture.

Layer 5: The Session Layer

The session layer establishes "sessions" between network nodes. A session must be established before data can be transmitted over the network. The session layer makes sure that these sessions are properly established and maintained.

Layer 6: The Presentation Layer

The presentation layer is responsible for converting the data sent over the network from one type of representation to another. For example, the presentation layer can apply sophisticated compression techniques so that fewer bytes of data are required to represent the information when it's sent over the network. At the other end of the transmission, the transport layer then uncompresses the data.

The presentation layer also can scramble the data before it's transmitted and unscramble it at the other end, using a sophisticated encryption technique that even Sherlock Holmes would have trouble breaking.

Layer 7: The Application Layer

The highest layer of the OSI model, the application layer deals with the techniques that application programs use to communicate with the network. The name of this layer is a little confusing. Application programs like Lotus 1-2-3 and WordPerfect aren't a part of the application layer. Rather, it's the network operating system itself that works within the application layer.

Chapter 28

Ten Tips for Networking Windows 3.1

*T*hroughout this book, I emphasize networking with Windows 95 and 98. However, millions of Windows 3.1 users are still out there, most of them happy campers just waiting to be connected to a network. Many of these users are working with computers which can barely run Windows 3.1, so upgrading to Windows 95 or 98 is out of the question. For those users, I dedicate these tips for networking Windows 3.1.

The mother of all Windows 3.1 networking tips is this: Throw away the Windows 3.1 computers, buy everyone a brand new 266 MHz Pentium II computer with 32MB of RAM, a 5G disk, and — of course — Windows 95 or, better yet, Windows 98. (Well, don't actually throw away the old computers. Donate them to a school. They're a huge step up from the Apple II's that they're probably using now.)

Consider Installing a Shared Version of Windows

If you use Windows on a network — especially a NetWare network — you must make a basic decision: Do you install a separate copy of Windows on each user's local hard disk, or do you install a shared copy of Windows on the network server? You have advantages and disadvantages to each approach.

The advantage of installing a separate copy of Windows for each user is that the user has more control over his or her Windows setup, and you won't have to contend with many of the special Windows setup options for installing a shared copy. The disadvantage of separate Windows installations is that you have to support each user's customized setup. And if you need to make a change to the way Windows is set up, you have to repeat the change for each user's copy of Windows.

The advantage of installing a shared copy of Windows on the server is that you save about 10MB of disk space on each client, and you have to maintain just one copy of Windows rather than a separate copy for each client. The disadvantage is that Windows won't perform as efficiently.

If you opt to install a shared version of Windows on the server, here's the general procedure:

1. **Insert the Windows Setup disk #1 into a floppy drive, log onto that drive, and type this command:**

```
SETUP /A
```

   This command copies all the files from the Windows setup disks to a network directory. When Setup asks for the drive and directory to copy the files to, specify a network drive.

2. **To install a shared copy of Windows for a client, log onto the network for that client, log onto the network drive that contains the Windows files, and type this command:**

```
SETUP /N
```

   This command installs just the files that are required to configure Windows for this client. When Setup asks for the drive and directory to copy these files to, specify either a local drive or a private network directory. Don't copy these files to a shared network directory!

If you decide to install a shared copy of Windows on a server, you still must have a separate license for each client that runs Windows. You can't legally buy just one copy of Windows and use it for every computer on the network!

Consider Windows 95

Windows 95 (or Windows 98 if it is available) is a great network choice for small networks on which all of the computers are capable of running it. With Windows 95 or 98, all the networking support you could ever dream of is built right into Windows. No need to install a separate program, read two manuals, or get on a conference call with Microsoft and your network software vendor to decide whether you have discovered a Windows bug or a network bug.

For a Peer-to-Peer Network with a Dedicated Server, Don't Run Windows on the Server

If you run LANtastic or some other peer-to-peer network (other than Windows for Workgroups) and you have set up a computer to run as a dedicated server, don't run Windows on that computer. You'll just tie up a hefty portion of that computer's memory and CPU cycles displaying the pretty Windows user interface. Because no one is using the dedicated server computer to run application programs, the memory can be better used for a larger disk cache, and the CPU cycles can be put to better use servicing network I/O requests.

Create a Permanent Swap File on Each User's Local Disk

One of the most important things you can do to improve the performance of Windows on a network is to make sure that every user is set up with a permanent swap file on a local disk.

Windows uses the swap file to make up for not having enough memory. Basically, the swap file acts as an extension to your computer's RAM so that Windows can pretend that your computer has more RAM than it really does.

Window's normal configuration is to use a temporary swap file, and if that temporary swap file is set up on a network disk, Windows slows to a crawl. A permanent swap file allows Windows to access this RAM-extension area more efficiently. Here's the procedure to switch to a more efficient permanent swap file on a local drive:

1. **Double-click the Control Panel icon in the Main Program Manager group.**

2. **In the Control Panel window, double-click the 386 Enhanced icon.**

3. **Click the Virtual Memory button.**

4. **Click the Change button.**

5. **Change the Type field to Permanent and the Drive field to a local drive (usually C:). If you want, you can specify a size for the swap file. The bigger the better, as long as you remember that the swap file uses disk space. I usually set up a 4,096K or 8,192K swap file.**

6. **Click OK to change the settings and then restart Windows so that they take effect.**

Set Up Your Network Connections before Starting Windows

As much as humanly possible, set up your login script or STARTNET.BAT file so that your network drive and printer assignments are set up before Windows is started.

Depending on your networking software, you may be able to specify that any changes you make to your network configuration while running Windows remain in effect when you quit Windows. Although this feature sounds attractive, I usually disable it. That's because I prefer to rely on the login script or STARTNET.BAT file to set up my standard network assignments. Then any changes I make during a Windows session are temporary; I can easily return to my standard network setup at any time just by restarting Windows.

Disable Print Manager

All networks employ some form of print spooling. Windows' own Print
Manager is also a form of print spooling. Using both the network's print
spooling and Windows' print spooling wastes time and leads to errors.

Here's the procedure for disabling Print Manager:

1. **Double-click the Printers icon in the Main Program Manager group.**

2. **In the Printers window, click the Use Print Manager checkbox to
   uncheck it.**

3. **Click the Close button to activate the change.**

Create a Shared Program Manager Group for Shared Network Applications

Here's a tricky technique that makes maintaining programs that are shared
on a network easier: Create a Program Manager group that can be shared by
all network users. Then put your shared programs in this group. Any
changes you make to this group — adding a program, changing an icon, and
so on — automatically appear on each client.

Here's the procedure:

1. **In Program Manager, choose the New command from the File menu.**

2. **When Program Manager asks whether you want to create a group or
   a program item, choose Program Group.**

3. **Type a description for the group, such as Network Applications. Then
   in the Group File field, specify a file on a network drive, such as
   H:\NETAPPS.GRP.**

4. **On each client, edit the user's PROGMAN.INI file (in the \WINDOWS
   directory) and add a line similar to this one to the [groups] section:**

   Group9=H:\NETAPPS.GRP

The group number depends on the groups that already exist in
PROGMAN.INI. The drive letter (H: in this case) specifies a network drive so
that all users access the same copy of the program group file.

Buy the Windows Resource Kit

That last one was a little tricky, wasn't it? That's why you may want to buy the Microsoft Windows Resource Kit, a $20 book, which has exhaustive documentation of Windows details (like what goes in the PROGMAN.INI file) and a disk that contains a few interesting utility programs. If you get the Resource Kit, you'll know how to edit PROGMAN.INI.

Most Windows users don't need the Windows Resource Kit. But if you're responsible for setting up and maintaining Windows on a network, you'd better get it. You can get it at most software stores, or you can order it directly from Microsoft.

Chapter 29

Ten Hot Network Buzzwords
Guaranteed to Enliven
a Cocktail Party

*T*ired of boring cocktail parties where everyone talks about the latest Oliver Stone movie or who's winning the late-night talk-show wars? Here are some conversation topics guaranteed to liven things up a bit or get you thrown out. Either way, they work. Try 'em.

Intranet

What it means: I've grown weary of the Internet and now I want to create my own little private Internet on my LAN. An Intranet uses the tools of the Internet: TCP/IP, HTTP, HTML, and Web server software, but isn't connected to the Internet. Intranets are used to create "internal" home pages which can be accessed from the company LAN but not from outside the company.

Used in a sentence: I won't be home for supper tonight, honey. I've got to finish uploading the third quarter results to the company Intranet!

Client/Server

What it means: A computer system in which part of the work happens on a client computer and part of it happens on a server computer. To be a true client/server application, real work must be done on the server. Any server-based network can be loosely called client/server, but in a true client/server system, at least part of the real work — not just file access — is done on the server. For example, in a true client/server database, a database query is processed on the server computer, and just the results of the query are sent back to the client computer. If you want to know more, get a copy of my very own book, *Client/Server Computing For Dummies,* 2nd Edition, (IDG Books Worldwide, Inc.).

Used in a sentence: I heard that it took your company five years to replace your old mainframe invoicing system to client/server! You should have got a copy of *Client/Server Computing For Dummies,* 2nd Edition.

Enterprise Computing

What it means: The complete computing needs of a business enterprise. In the past, computing was too often focused on individual needs of small departments or workgroups. The result was a hodgepodge of incompatible systems: Marketing had a minicomputer, sales had a NetWare network, and accounting had an abacus. Enterprise computing views the computing needs of the organization as a whole. Very smart.

Used in a sentence: Our enterprise computing effort is sailing along at warp 9; I hear you guys are still stuck at one-quarter impulse. Fascinating.

Interoperability

What it means: Fitting round pegs into square holes. Literally, linking estranged networks together so that they work well together. This one is so hot that a whole trade show called Interop is devoted to making different networks work together.

Used in a sentence: We've finally solved our interoperability problems — we fired the guy who bought the stuff that wasn't interoperable.

Fiber Optics

What it means: The fastest form of network cable, where signals are transmitted by light rather than by electricity. Fiber optics are typically used to form the backbone of large networks or to link networks in separate buildings, where the 500-meter limit of yellow cable just won't do. Fiber-optic cables hum along at a cool 100 Mbps (Megabits per second), ten times faster than pokey little Ethernet.

Used in a sentence: What am I going to do now that I've linked three buildings on the campus using a fiber optic backbone? I'm going to Disneyland.

SNA

What it means: IBM's grand scheme of old to dominate the networking business. SNA is found wherever IBM mainframes are found. SNA stands for "Systems Network Architecture" and is pronounced *snaw* by mainframers.

Used in a sentence: After we get the link between SNA and Ethernet worked out, our mainframe users will be able to access the advanced computing power of our PCs.

Groupware

What it means: Software that's designed to take advantage of network capabilities to facilitate collaborative work. For example, a word processor with groupware features enables several network users to add comments or revisions to a document and keep track of who made what change and when.

Used in a sentence: Our productivity has shot up so much since we switched to groupware that we've decided to retire and move to Vail. I hear you're still using WordStar.

TCP/IP

What it means: TCP/IP is the protocol for Internet. It stands for "Transmission Control Protocol/Internet Protocol."

Used in a sentence: Don't worry, after you get TCP/IP up and running, you'll be on the Internet soon enough.

Broadband

What it means: Broadband is a new Cable TV system that can send more than just TV: It can also handle your phone lines and an Internet connection. And it's lightning fast. In fact, an Internet connection over broadband cable is just as fast as an Ethernet connection on a local area network.

Used in a sentence: No, uh, I don't have broadband yet. Boy, weird weather we've been having lately, don't you think?

Part VII
References for
Real People

The 5th Wave   By Rich Tennant

ON A BET, HOWIE LENDELMAN, THE OFFICE TINKERER, TRIES LINKING
HIS T.I. CALCULATOR INTO THE WORKGROUP'S DESKPRO 386/25
NETWORK FILE SERVER.

HE'S GETTING FILES!
HE'S GETTING FILES!

In this part . . .

This section summarizes the most commonly used commands for two popular network operating systems: NetWare and Windows.

Why fuss with network commands in the days of Windows? Because many times, working from a command-prompt is more efficient than clicking through layer upon layer of icons and menus. And besides, some of us long for the day when true computer jockeys rode keyboards instead of mice.

Chapter 30

NetWare Commands You'll Use

● ●

In This Chapter

▶ A summary of various NetWare commands

▶ The Sin Tax

▶ Examples

▶ A little BS about most of the commands

● ●

*I*n case you're a command-line junkie and want to get a feel for NetWare's commands, this chapter presents the ones you're most likely to want to use, along with a few you may not want to use but may have to, plus a few that are good to know about even if you never use them.

ATTACH

What it does:	Connects you to another file server. Used only when your network has more than one server.
Syntax:	ATTACH server/user ID
Example:	ATTACH SERVER2/BEAVER
Who can use it:	Anyone.
BS:	If your account requires a password, you'll be prompted for it. ATTACH is often used in login scripts.

BROADCAST

What it does:	Displays a message to all users who are logged in to a server.
Syntax:	BROADCAST message
Example:	BROADCAST This network will self-destruct in five minutes!
Who can use it:	Console operators.
BS:	BROADCAST is commonly used as a courtesy shortly before downing a server.

CAPTURE

What it does:	Sets up network print spooling.
Syntax:	CAPTURE L=port Q=queue TI=seconds
	CAPTURE L=port EC
Example:	CAPTURE L=2 Q=LASER TI=10
Who can use it:	Anyone.
BS:	If you omit L=port, LPT1 is captured. CAPTURE has a bunch of other options for customizing print jobs. The EC variant replaces the older ENDCAP command.

CHKVOL

What it does:	Displays information about a server volume.
Syntax:	CHKVOL
	CHKVOL drive:
	CHKVOL [server\]volume:
Examples:	CHKVOL F:
	CHKVOL WARD\SYS:

Who can use it: Anyone.

BS: Displays the size of the volume, the number of files on it, the disk space in use, the free disk space, and the number of directory entries available for new files.

CLAP ON

What it does: Enables you to down the server by clapping your hands loudly once or twice.

Syntax: CLAP ON [1 | 2]

Who can use it: Console operators.

BS: Yes.

CLEAR STATION

What it does: Cleans up after a workstation that has crashed.

Syntax: CLEAR STATION n

Who can use it: Console operators.

CONFIG

What it does: Displays information about your server's network configuration.

Syntax: CONFIG

Who can use it: Console operators.

BS: The configuration info displayed by CONFIG includes the network drivers, the server's network address, network driver settings, and the server's disk configuration.

DISABLE LOGIN

What it does: Prevents users from logging in to a file server.

Syntax: DISABLE LOGIN

Who can use it: Console operators.

BS: DISABLE LOGIN doesn't force anybody off the system, but it does prevent users who aren't logged in from logging in. It's usually used before a DOWN command. You can restore logins later by typing ENABLE LOGIN.

DISMOUNT

What it does: Takes a volume off the network so that you can perform maintenance tasks.

Syntax: DISMOUNT volume

Example: DISMOUNT SYS2:

Who can use it: Console operators.

BS: It would be polite to broadcast a message first (see the BROADCAST command).

DOWN

What it does: Shuts down a file server.

Syntax: DOWN

Who can use it: Console operators.

BS: Always use DOWN before turning off a server. It shuts down the server in an orderly fashion so that files that happen to be open won't be trashed in the process. It's polite to warn users with a BROADCAST command before downing a server.

DSPACE

What it does:	Limits the amount of space a user can use.
Syntax:	DSPACE
Who can use it:	Supervisors.
BS:	This is a menu-driven utility, so no command-line options are used.

ENABLE LOGIN

What it does:	Enables logins after a DISABLE LOGIN command has been used.
Syntax:	ENABLE LOGIN
Who can use it:	Console operators.
BS:	You don't have to use this command if you down a server and then restart it; logins are automatically enabled when the server starts.

ENDCAP

What it does:	Stops capturing printer output for network printing.
Syntax:	ENDCAP [L-port]
	ENDCAP ALL
	ENDCAP C=port
	ENDCAP CANCEL ALL
Example:	ENDCAP L=1
Who can use it:	Anyone.

BS: If you type just ENDCAP with no options, print capture for LPT1 is stopped. ENDCAP ALL stops printer capture for all ports. ENDCAP C=port stops capture for the specified port and discards any output already captured; ENDCAP CANCEL ALL discards output for all ports. In NetWare 4.1, the ENDCAP command has been superceded by the CAPTURE EC command.

ENGAGE

What it does: Nothing, but it makes you feel like the Captain.

Syntax: ENGAGE

Who can use it: Picard.

BS: Yes.

EXIT

What it does: After a server has been downed, returns to the DOS prompt.

Syntax: EXIT

Who can use it: Console operators.

BS: EXIT is sometimes used to restart a server with new parameters. First run DOWN and then EXIT. This returns you to a DOS prompt, where you can run SERVER to restart the server with new parameters.

FCONSOLE

What it does: Displays information about the file server.

Syntax: FCONSOLE

Who can use it: Console operators.

BS: FCONSOLE provides a menu interface for some of the other NetWare console commands, such as BROADCAST and DOWN. These functions are only used by wimps, though. Real network geeks use FCONSOLE to peek at dirty cache buffers.

FILER

What it does: Creates and manages directories.

Syntax: FILER

Who can use it: Anyone.

BS: FILER is a menu-driven program with lots of options to enable you to look at directories and subdirectories and the files they contain. FILER also enables you to delete files, rename files, and copy or move files or entire subdirectories to another drive or directory.

For NetWare 4.0, the FILER command has been expanded to include the functions of the SALVAGE, PURGE, and VOLINFO commands.

FLAG

What it does: Displays or sets file attributes.

Syntax: FLAG [directory/]filename [flags]

Flags can be any of the following:

A   Archive needed

C   Copy inhibit (3.x only)

D   Delete inhibit (3.x only)

E   Execute only

H   Hidden

I	Indexed
P	Purge (3.x only)
RO	Read only
RW	Writable
R	Rename inhibit (3.x only)
S	Shareable
SY	System file
T	Transactional

Example: FLAG *.EXE SRO

Who can use it: Supervisors.

BS: FLAG is often used after installing software to make program files shareable and read-only.

FLAGDIR

What it does: Displays or changes directory attributes.

Syntax: FLAGDIR [directory] [flags]

Flags can be any of the following:

D	Delete inhibit (3.x only)
H	Hidden
N	Normal
P	Private (2.x only)
P	Purge (3.x only)
R	Rename inhibit (3.x only)
SY	System

Example: FLAGDIR DOCS DR

Who can use it: Supervisors. In NetWare 4.1, use FLAG instead.

GRANT

What it does: Grants rights to users for a file or directory.

Syntax: GRANT rights FOR path TO USER/GROUP name [/F or /S]

Example: GRANT S FOR SYS:DOCS TO USER BEAVER /S

Who can use it: Supervisors.

BS: /F grants rights for files, /S for subdirectories. Rights can
                    also be granted by the FILER command. After being
                    granted, rights can be revoked by the REVOKE command.
                    Replaced by NETADMIN in 4.0.

LISTDIR

What it does: Lists the directory structure of a volume.

Syntax: LISTDIR [/A]

                    LISTDIR [server\]volume:directory[/A]

                    LISTDIR drive: [/A]

Examples: LISTDIR WARD\SYS:

                    LISTDIR F: /A

Who can use it: Anyone.

BS: The /A switch displays additional information about the
                    directories besides just the directory name.

LOAD (3.x only)

What it does:	Loads an NLM (NetWare Loadable Module).
Syntax:	LOAD name
Who can use it:	Console operator.

LOGIN

What it does:	Logs you in to the network.
Syntax:	LOGIN [user /ID]
Example:	LOGIN BEAVER
Who can use it:	Anyone and everyone.
BS:	LOGIN prompts you for your password and for your user ID if you don't include it as a command-line option. Before using LOGIN, switch to the network drive (typically F). Most of the time, the LOGIN command is added to your AUTOEXEC.BAT file.

LOGOUT

What it does:	Logs you off the network.
Syntax:	LOGOUT
Who can use it:	Anyone.

MAKEUSER

What it does:	Creates user accounts in batch mode by reading a script file that contains account definitions.
Syntax:	MAKEUSER script file

Who can use it:	Supervisors.
BS:	The script language used by MAKEUSER is complex, but can save you time if you have a lot of user accounts to define. USERDEF can help. If you have only a few accounts to create, you can probably do it faster by using SYSCON. Replaced by NETADMIN in 4.0.

MAP

What it does:	Assigns drive letters to network drives.
Syntax:	MAP [ROOT] drive:=vol:directory
Example:	MAP M:=SYS:DOCS
Who can use it:	Anyone.
BS:	Drive can be a drive letter or a search drive letter (S1 through S16). If you include ROOT, NetWare treats the directory as the root directory of the mapped drive so that directories higher in the directory structure are inaccessible. MAP commands are usually included in the login script.

MEMORY

What it does:	Displays the amount of memory available to the server.
Syntax:	MEMORY
Who can use it:	Console operators.

MENU

What it does:	Displays a menu of program choices for insecure users.
Syntax:	MENU

Who can use it:	Anyone.
BS:	MENU uses a menu definition file that contains a scripted description of the menu that's displayed.

MODULES

What it does:	Displays the various modules that are loaded in the server's memory.
Syntax:	MODULES
Who can use it:	Console operators.

MONITOR

What it does:	Displays the NetWare console monitor screen.
Syntax:	MONITOR
Who can use it:	Console operators.
BS:	MONITOR can be used to password-protect the console.

MOUNT

What it does:	Mounts server volumes so that they can be accessed by network users.
Syntax:	MOUNT volume
	MOUNT ALL
Who can use it:	Console operators.
BS:	MOUNT commands are usually kept in the AUTOEXEC.NCF file.

NCOPY

What it does: Copies files from one location on a server to another location on the same server without sending the contents of the files over the network.

Syntax: NCOPY source target [options]

Example: NCOPY M:MAY94*.* M:JUNE94*.*

Who can use it: Anyone.

BS: NCOPY works much like COPY, but is more efficient when both the source and destination are on the same server.

NDIR

What it does: Displays directory listings for network drives, much like the DOS DIR command.

Syntax: NDIR path [/options]

Example: NDIR SYS:*.EXE

Who can use it: Anyone.

BS: NDIR has way too many options to list here. Sorry.

NETADMIN (4.0 only)

What it does: Manages the server.

Syntax: NETADMIN

Who can use it: Supervisors.

BS: NETADMIN is a menu-driven command, so no command-line options are used. NETADMIN combines the functions of the SYSCON, DSPACE, USERDEF, and SECURITY commands.

NPRINT

What it does:	Prints a file on a network printer.
Syntax:	NPRINT file
Example:	NPRINT CONFIG.SYS
Who can use it:	Anyone.
BS:	NPRINT is the network equivalent of the DOS PRINT command.

PCONSOLE

What it does:	Controls the network printer.
Syntax:	PCONSOLE
Who can use it:	Console operators.
BS:	PCONSOLE is menu driven, so it's a complicated command even though it doesn't have elaborate command-line options.

PRINTCON

What it does:	Configures printer jobs so that you don't have to type scads of options on CAPTURE and NPRINT commands.
Syntax:	PRINTCON
Who can use it:	Anyone.
BS:	PRINTCON is menu-driven, so no command-line options exist. Sniff.

PRINTDEF

What it does:	Defines special printer forms and print devices.
Syntax:	PRINTDEF
Who can use it:	Anyone.
BS:	PRINTDEF is menu-driven, no command-line options exist.

PSC

What it does:	The command-line junkie's version of PCONSOLE.
Syntax:	PSC [options-ad-nauseum]
Who can use it:	Command-line junkies.

PURGE

What it does:	Wipes files off the face of your disk.
Syntax:	PURGE
Who can use it:	Anyone.
BS:	When you delete a file, the file isn't really deleted until you run PURGE.

RENDIR

What it does:	Renames a directory.
Syntax:	RENDIR directory TO new name
Example:	RENDIR SYS:APPLES TO ORANGES
Who can use it:	Anyone.
BS:	DOS should have had this command years ago.

REVOKE

What it does:	Removes rights granted by GRANT.
Syntax:	REVOKE rights FOR path FROM USER/GROUP name [/F or /S]
Example:	REVOKE S FOR SYS:DOCS FROM USER BEAVER /S
Who can use it:	Supervisors.
BS:	This can also be done via the FILER command. Replaced by the NETADMIN command in 4.0.

RIGHTS

What it does:	Views your rights for a directory.
Syntax:	RIGHTS directory
	RIGHTS drive
Example:	RIGHTS SYS:ORANGES
	RIGHTS L:
Who can use it:	Anyone.

SALVAGE

What it does:	Recovers a deleted file.
Syntax:	SALVAGE
Who can use it:	Anyone.
BS:	SALVAGE is a menu-driven program that prompts you through the process of recovering deleted files. It won't do you any good if you've purged your files with the PURGE command.

SECURE CONSOLE

What it does:	Locks the file server up and throws away the key.
Syntax:	SECURE CONSOLE
Who can use it:	Console operator.
BS:	SECURE CONSOLE is a good way to secure a file server. Among other things, it removes DOS from the server's memory.

SECURITY

What it does:	Checks your system's security for possible leaks, like users without passwords.
Syntax:	SECURITY
Who can use it:	Paranoid supervisors.

SEND

What it does:	Sends a message to a specific user or users.
Syntax:	SEND "message" TO user [,user...]
Example:	SEND "Pizza after work?" TO WALLY, BEAVER
Who can use it:	Console operators.

SET

What it does:	Sets various server parameters.
Syntax:	SET parameter=value
Examples:	SET MAXIMUM PACKET RECEIVE BUFFERS = 200
	SET DIRECTORY CACHED BUFFER NONREFERENCED DELAY = 10

Who can use it:	Console operators.
BS:	Loads and loads of parameters exist for this command. SET commands are usually included in the STARTUP.NCF file, so they're executed automatically whenever the server starts.

SET TIME

What it does:	Sets the date or time.
Syntax:	SET [mm/dd/yy] [hh:mm:ss]
Example:	SET 05/16/94
	SET 11:15:00
Who can use it:	Console operators.

SETPASS

What it does:	Enables you to change your password.
Syntax:	SETPASS [server]
Who can use it:	Anyone.
BS:	SETPASS prompts you for your old password and then prompts you for a new password. The new password isn't displayed as you type it, but you are asked to type the new password twice. That's a precaution — NetWare assumes that if you type the password the same way twice, you've typed it correctly.

SLIST

What it does:	Lists all the file servers on the network.
Syntax:	SLIST
Who can use it:	Anyone.

SYSCON

What it does: SYSCON is the all-around console program for NetWare. You can do just about anything from it.

Syntax: SYSCON

Who can use it: Console operators. Users can access some of its functions.

BS: Try it. You'll like it.

TRACK OFF

What it does: Stops displaying messages sent to or from a workstation or server.

Syntax: TRACK OFF

Who can use it: Console operators.

TRACK ON

What it does: Displays network messages sent to or from a workstation or server.

Syntax: TRACK ON

Who can use it: Console operators.

BS: TRACK ON has lots of other parameters. Check your NetWare manuals for more details.

UNLOAD (3.x only)

What it does: Unloads an NLM.

Syntax: UNLOAD name

Who can use it: Console operators.

USERDEF

What it does:	Makes the MAKEUSER command easier to swallow.
Syntax:	USERDEF
Who can use it:	Supervisors who don't have time for MAKEUSER.
BS:	USERDEF is a menu-driven version of MAKEDEF.

USERLIST

What it does:	Lists all the users who are currently logged in.
Syntax:	USERLIST [/A]
Who can use it:	Anyone.
BS:	/A causes USERLIST to include the address of each user.

VERSION

What it does:	Displays the version number for NetWare commands.
Syntax:	VERSION [command]
Example:	VERSION
	VERSION MAP
Who can use it:	Anyone.

VOLINFO

What it does:	Displays information about network volumes.
Syntax:	VOLINFO

Who can use it:	Anyone.
BS:	VOLINFO displays a list of all volumes on the default server along with the size of the volume and the amount of free space. The list is updated every five seconds.

VOLUMES

What it does:	Lists the currently available volumes.
Syntax:	VOLUMES
Who can use it:	Console operators.

VREPAIR

What it does:	Repairs damage to a network volume.
Syntax:	LOAD VREPAIR
Who can use it:	Console operators.

WHOAMI

What it does:	Tells you who you are. Sung by Jean Valjean in the first act of *Les Miserables*.
Syntax:	WHOAMI
Who can use it:	Anyone.
BS:	WHOAMI tells you your user ID, the address of the workstation you're logged into, and your directory rights. WHOAMI? 24601!

Chapter 31

Windows NET Commands You'll Use

All three of the networking versions of Windows — Windows for Workgroups, Windows 95, and Window NT — sport a similar set of commands which can be used from a command prompt. Most of these commands provide functions which can be performed easier using Windows-based programs, but if you want to put the commands in a batch file, or if you just like commands, this chapter presents the ones that you're likely to use.

Annoyingly, although the three networking versions of Windows use similar commands, just enough differences in the syntax from version to version exist to drive you crazy. In this chapter, I focus on the syntax that's used for Windows for Workgroups and Windows 95 (which are almost identical), pointing out the Windows NT Server variations when they're important.

Note that you use these commands on a client computer running Windows for Workgroups, Windows 95, or Windows NT. Also a few additional NET commands exist that you can run at the command prompt in Windows NT Server, but I don't cover them in this chapter.

Many of the commands presented in this chapter have additional parameters that aren't shown here. This chapter just shows the most commonly used forms of these commands.

NET CONFIG

What it does: Displays your current workgroup settings.

Syntax: NET CONFIG [/YES]

Example: NET CONFIG

BS: /YES processes the NET CONFIG command without asking any questions. Note the different syntax required for Windows NT.

NET DIAG

What it does: Runs the Microsoft Network Diagnostics program to make sure that two computers can communicate and to display information about your computer.

Syntax: NET DIAG [/NAMES | /STATUS]

Example: NET DIAG /STATUS

BS: Use /STATUS to test the communication between two computers.

NET HELP

What it does: Displays help information about NET commands.

Syntax: NET HELP command

NET HELP error number

Example: NET HELP USE

BS: Very helpful indeed. Type NET HELP to get a list of all NET commands. The NET HELP error number variant doesn't work for Windows NT.

NET LOGOFF

What it does: Logs you off the network.

Syntax: NET LOGOFF [/YES]

Example: NET LOGOFF

BS: Use /YES to avoid answering questions. In Windows 95, this command works only when booted into MS-DOS mode; you can't use it from a normal MS-DOS prompt.

NET PASSWORD

What it does: Changes your logon password.

Syntax: NET PASSWORD [oldpassword [newpassword]]

Example: NET PASSWORD WHATEVER FERSHER

BS: If you change your password, don't forget the new one! Also, this command doesn't work for Windows NT.

NET PRINT

What it does: Displays information about the print queue on a shared printer, or controls your print jobs.

Syntax: NET PRINT \\computer[\printer] | port [/YES]

NET PRINT \\computer | port [job# [/PAUSE | /RESUME | / DELETE]] [/YES]

NET PRINT \\computer\printer job# [/HOLD | /RELEASE | / DELETE] (NT Only)

Example: NET PRINT \\WALLY\LASER

BS: You can do all sorts of stuff with this command: pause printing, resume printing you've paused, or delete a print job.

NET TIME

What it does: Displays the time or synchronizes your computer's clock with the network's clock.

Syntax: NET TIME [\\computer] [/SET] [/YES]

Example: NET TIME /SET

BS: Use /SET to synchronize your clock with the network's central clock.

NET USE

What it does: Sets up network drive and printer connections.

Syntax: NET USE drive: \\computer\directory

NET USE printer \\computer\printer

Examples: NET USE G: \\WALLY\DRIVE-C

NET USE LPT2: \\WALLY\LASER

BS: Use NET USE with no parameters to list your current connections.

NET VER

What it does: Displays the version number of your network redirector.

Syntax: NET VER

Example: NET VER

BS: When you need to know, you need to know.

NET VIEW

What it does: Displays a list of computers available on the network.

Syntax: NET VIEW [\\computer]

Example: NET VIEW

Glossary

· ·

10base2 The type of coax cable most often used for Ethernet networks. A.k.a. *thinnet, cheapernet.* The maximum length of a single segment is 185 meters (600 feet).

10base5 The original Ethernet coax cable, now used mostly as the backbone for larger networks. A.k.a. *yellow cable, thick cable.* The maximum length of a single segment is 500 meters (1,640 feet).

10baseT Twisted-pair cable, commonly used for Ethernet networks. A.k.a. *UTP, twisted pair,* or *twisted sister.* The maximum length of a single segment is 100 meters (330 feet). Of the three Ethernet cable types, this one is the easiest to work with.

100baseT The leading standard for 100 Mbps Ethernet. 100baseT uses the same twisted-pair cable in 10baseT. Variations of the 100 Mbps Ethernet standard include 100baseT4 and 100baseTX.

100VG AnyLAN A standard for 100 Mbps Ethernet which isn't as popular as 100BaseT. Like 100baseT, 100VG AnyLAN uses twisted-pair cable.

802.2 The forgotten IEEE standard. The more glamorous 802.3 standard relies upon 802.2 for moral support.

802.3 The IEEE standard known in the vernacular as "Ethernet."

8088 processor The microprocessor chip around which IBM's original PC was designed, marking the transition from the bronze age to the iron age.

80286 processor *Computo-habilis,* an ancient ancestor of today's modern computers; still used by far too many people.

80386 processor The first 32-bit microprocessor chip used in personal computers, now replaced by the 486 chip. 386 computers are slower than their 486 counterparts, but they get the job done.

80486 processor The most popular CPU chip for PCs until the introduction of the Pentium processor.

AAUI *Apple Attachment Unit Interface,* a type of connector used in some Apple Ethernet networks.

access rights A list of rights that tell you what you can and cannot do with network files or directories.

account You can't get into the network without one of these. The network knows who you are and what rights you have on the network by virtue of your account.

acronym An abbreviation made up of the first letters of a series of words.

adapter card An electronic card that can be plugged into one of your computer's adapter slots to give it some new and fabulous capability, such as displaying 16 million colors, talking to other computers over the phone, or accessing a network.

address book In an e-mail system, a list of users with whom you regularly correspond.

administrator The big network cheese who is responsible for setting things up and keeping them running. Pray that it's not you. Also known as the network manager.

AFP *Apple Filing Protocol,* a protocol for filing used by Apple. (That helps a lot, doesn't it?)

allocation unit DOS allocates space to files one allocation unit at a time; the allocation unit is typically 2,048 or 4,096 bytes, depending on the size of the disk. A.k.a., *cluster.* NetWare, Windows NT Server, DriveSpace, and FAT32 use different allocation schemes that are more efficient.

antivirus program A program that sniffs out viruses on your network and sends them into exile.

AppleTalk Apple's networking system for Macintoshes.

application layer The highest layer of the OSI reference model, which governs how software communicates with the network.

archive bit A flag that's kept for each file to indicate whether the file has been modified since it was last backed up.

ARCnet A slow but steady network topology developed originally by Datapoint. ARCnet uses a token-passing scheme similar to Token Ring.

Artisoft The company that makes LANtastic.

attributes Characteristics that are assigned to files. DOS alone provides four attributes: system, hidden, read-only, and archive. Networks generally expand the list of file attributes.

AUI *Attachment Unit Interface,* the big connector found on many network cards and 10baseT hubs that's used to attach yellow cable via a transceiver.

AUTOEXEC.BAT A batch file that DOS executes automatically every time you start your computer.

AUTOEXEC.NCF A batch file that NetWare executes automatically every time you load the server software.

backbone A trunk cable used to tie sections of a network together. The backbone is often 10base5, fiber-optic (FDDI), or 100 Mbps Fast Ethernet.

BackOffice A suite of Microsoft programs designed to be run on server computers based on Windows NT Server.

backup A copy of your important files made for safekeeping in case something happens to the original files; something you should make every day.

banner A fancy page that's printed between each print job so that you can easily separate jobs from one another.

batch file In DOS, a file that contains one or more commands that are executed together as a set. You create the batch file by using a text editor (like the DOS EDIT command) and run the file by typing its name at the command prompt.

benchmark A repeatable test you use to judge the performance of your network. The best benchmarks are the ones that closely duplicate the type of work you routinely do on your network.

bindery The big database where user accounts and other related info are stored on a NetWare server.

BNC connector The connector that's used with 10base2 cable.

bottleneck The slowest link in your network, which causes work to get jammed up. The first step in improving network performance is identifying the bottlenecks.

bridge Not the popular card game, but a device that enables you to link two networks together. Bridges are smart enough to know which computers are on which side of the bridge, so they only allow those messages that need to get to the other side to cross the bridge. This device improves performance on both sides of the bridge.

Btrieve An indexed file access method commonly used on NetWare networks.

buffer An area of memory that's used to hold data enroute to somewhere else. For example, a disk buffer holds data as it travels between your computer and the disk drive.

BUFFERS A line in CONFIG.SYS that sets up buffers used for disk I/O. If a disk cache is used, specify a low number for BUFFERS, like 2 or 3.

bus A type of network topology in which network nodes are strung out along a single run of cable called a *segment*. 10base2 and LocalTalk networks use a bus topology. *Bus* also refers to the row of expansion slots within your computer.

cache A sophisticated form of buffering in which a large amount of memory is set aside to hold data so that it can be accessed quickly.

CAPTURE The NetWare command used to redirect printer output to a network printer. CAPTURE is usually run in a batch file or login script.

cc:Mail A popular electronic mail program.

CD-ROM A high-capacity disc that uses optical technology to store data in a form that can be read but not written over.

Certified NetWare Engineer Someone who has studied hard and passed the official exam offered by Novell. A.k.a. *CNE*.

Certified Network Dummy Someone who knows nothing about networks but nevertheless gets the honor of installing one. A.k.a. *CND*.

CGA A crude type of graphics display used on early IBM computers. CGA stands for *Crayon Graphics Adapter*.

chat What you do on the network when you talk *live* with another network user.

Chaucer A dead English dude.

cheapernet See *10base2*.

CHKDSK A DOS command that checks the record-keeping structures of a DOS disk for errors.

click What you do in Windows to get things done.

client A computer that has access to the network but doesn't share any of its own resources with the network. See *server*.

client/server A vague term meaning roughly that the work load is split between a client and server computer.

Clouseau The most dangerous man in all of France. Some people say he only plays the fool.

cluster See *allocation unit*.

coaxial cable A type of cable that contains two conductors. The center conductor is surrounded by a layer of insulation, which is then wrapped by a braided-metal conductor and an outer layer of insulation.

COM1 The first serial port on a computer.

CompuServe An on-line information network you can access to talk with other users about issues such as NetWare, Windows NT, politics, and El Niño.

computer name A unique name assigned to each computer on a network.

CONFIG.SYS A file on every DOS computer that contains configuration information. CONFIG.SYS is processed every time you start your computer.

console In NetWare, the file server's keyboard and monitor. Console commands can be entered only at the server console.

console operator In NetWare, a user working at the file server's console.

Control Panel In Windows, an application that enables you to configure various aspects of the Windows operation.

conventional memory The first 640K of memory on a DOS-based computer.

CPU The *central processing unit,* or brains, of the computer.

crimp tool A special tool used to attach connectors to cables. No network manager should be without one.

CSMA/CD An acronym for *Carrier Sense Multiple Access with Collision Detection*. The traffic management technique used by Ethernet.

daisy chain A way of connecting computer components in which the first component is connected to the second, which is connected to the third, and so on. In 10baseT Ethernet, hubs can be daisy chained together.

DAT *Digital audiotape,* a type of tape often used for network backup.

data link layer The second layer of the OSI model, responsible for transmitting bits of data over the network cable.

dedicated server A computer used exclusively as a network server.

delayed write A disk-caching technique in which data written to disk is placed in cache memory and actually written to disk later.

differential backup A type of backup in which only the files that have changed since the last full backup are backed up.

digitized sound A file containing a sound that can be played if the computer is equipped with a sound card. See *Clouseau.*

DIP switch A bank of switches used to configure an old-fashioned adapter card. Modern cards configure themselves automatically, so DIP switches aren't required. See *jumper block*.

directory hash A popular breakfast food enjoyed by NetWare managers.

disk A device that stores information magnetically on a disk. A hard disk is

permanently sealed in an enclosure and has a capacity usually measured in thousands of megabytes, A.k.a. gigabytes. A *floppy disk* is removable and can have a capacity of 360K, 720K, 1.2MB, 1.44MB, or 2.88MB.

DMA channel A direct pipeline for I/O that's faster than normal I/O. Network cards use DMA for fast network access.

DOS *Disk Operating System,* the original operating system for IBM and IBM-compatible computers. DOS isn't used as much now that Windows 95 has taken over.

dot-matrix printer A prehistoric type of printer that works by applying various colored pigments to the walls of caves. Once the mainstay printer for PCs, dot-matrix printers are giving way to laser printers and ink-jet printers. High-speed matrix printers still have their place on the network, though, and matrix printers have the advantage of being able to print multipart forms.

DriveSpace The disk compression feature of Windows 95 and MS-DOS 6.2. DriveSpace compresses file data so that files require less disk space. This compression increases the effective capacity of the disk, often by a factor of 2:1 or more.

DVD Drive A new type of CD-ROM drive with much higher storage capacity than standard CD — as much as 17GB on a single disc compared to the 600MB capacity of a standard CD.

dumb terminal Back in the heyday of mainframe computers, a monitor and keyboard attached to the central mainframe. All the computing work occurred at the mainframe; the terminal only displayed the results and sent input typed at the keyboard back to the mainframe.

e-mail An application that enables you to exchange notes with other network users.

Eddie Haskel The kid who's always sneaking around, poking his nose into other people's business, and generally causing trouble. Every network has one.

editor A program for creating and changing text files. DOS 5.0 and later versions come with a basic editor called EDIT. Other editors are available, but EDIT is good enough for most network needs.

EDLIN A primitive editor that came with DOS 1.0 and was not improved upon until DOS 5.0. EDLIN has a distinct mainframe feel to it, which is why network geeks like it.

EGA The color monitor that was standard with IBM AT computers, based on 80286 processors. Now obsolete, but plenty of them are still in use.

EISA bus *Extended Industry Standard Architecture.* An improved I/O bus that is compatible with the standard ISA bus but provides advanced features. Computers with an EISA bus were often used as file servers until the PCI bus became more popular. See *ISA bus*, *Micro Channel bus*, and *PCI bus*.

ENDCAP The NetWare command you use to stop network printer redirection.

enterprise computing A trendy term that refers to a view of an organization's complete computing needs, rather than just a single department's or group's needs.

ESDI An older style of disk drive that's not often used nowadays.

Ethernet The World's Most Popular Network Standard.

EtherTalk What you call Ethernet when you use it on a Macintosh.

ETLA *Extended Three-Letter Acronym.* An acronym with four letters. See *TLA*.

expanded memory An ancient technique for blasting past the 640K limit. Unlike extended memory, expanded memory can be used with 8088 computers.

extended memory Memory beyond the first 640K in a DOS computer. Available only on 80286 or better computers. The term isn't used with Windows 95 or Windows NT; memory is just memory.

Farallon The company that popularized PhoneNET as a cheaper and more flexible alternative to LocalTalk, Apple's cabling scheme for networking Macintoshes.

Fast Ethernet A new Ethernet standard which operates at 100 Mbps rather than 10 Mbps.

FAT The *file allocation table,* a record-keeping structure that DOS uses to keep track of the location of every file on a disk.

FAT32 An improved way of keeping track of disk files that can be used with Windows 98.

FDDI *Fiber Distributed Data Inferface,* a 100 Mbps network standard used with fiber-optic backbone. When FDDI is used, FDDI FDDI/Ethernet bridges are used to connect Ethernet segments to the backbone.

ferrule The outer metal tube that you crimp on to attach a BNC connector to the cable.

fiber optic cable A blazingly fast network cable that transmits data using light rather than electricity. Fiber optic cable is often used as the backbone in large networks, especially where great distances are involved.

file server A network computer containing disk drives that are available to network users.

File Transfer Protocol (FTP) A method for retrieving files from the Internet.

FTP See *File Transfer Protocol*.

full backup A backup of all the files on a disk, whether or not the files have been modified since the last backup. See *differential backup*.

fulminic acid An unstable acid (CNOH) that forms explosive salts of some metals, especially mercury.

Used to punish users who write their passwords on stick-on notes stuck on their monitors.

gateway A device that connects dissimilar networks. Gateways are often used to connect Ethernet networks to mainframe computers or to the Internet.

GB Gigabyte, roughly a billion bytes of disk storage (1,024MB to be precise). See *K, MB,* and *TB*.

generation backup A backup strategy in which several sets of backup disks or tapes are retained, sometimes called grandfather-father-son.

generation gap What happens when you skip one of your backups.

glass house The room where the mainframe computer is kept. Symbolic of the mainframe mentality, which stresses bureaucracy, inflexibility, and heavy iron.

group account A grouping of user accounts that share common access rights.

groupware A relatively new category of application programs that are designed with networks in mind to enable and even promote collaborative work.

guru Anyone who knows more about computers than you do.

HTML The language used to compose pages which can be displayed via the World Wide Web.

HTTP A protocol used by the World Wide Web for sending HTML pages from a server computer to a client computer.

hub In Ethernet, a device that is used with 10baseT and 100baseT cabling to connect computers to the network. Most hubs have from 8 to 24 ports.

IACI International Association of the Computer Impaired.

IDE The most common type of disk interface in use today, popular because of its low cost and flexibility. *IDE* stands for *Integrated Drive Electronics*. For server computers, SCSI is the preferred drive interface. See **SCSI**.

IEEE *Institute of Electrical and Electronic Engineers*. Where they send computer geeks who've had a few too many parity errors.

incremental backup A type of backup in which only the files that have changed since the last backup are backed up. Unlike a differential backup, an incremental backup resets each file's archive bit as it backs it up. See **archive bit**, **differential backup**, and **full backup**.

ink-jet printer A type of printer that creates full-color pages by spraying tiny jets of ink onto paper.

Internet A humongous network of networks that spans the globe and gives you access to just about anything you could ever hope for, provided that you can figure out how to work it.

Internet Explorer Microsoft's popular Web browser.

Internet Service Provider (ISP) A company that provides access to the Internet for a fee.

interoperability Providing a level playing field for incompatible networks to work together, kind of like NAFTA.

Intranet A network that resembles the Internet but is accessible only within a company or organization. Most Intranets use the familiar World Wide Web interface to distribute information to company employees.

IntranetWare The latest and greatest version of the network operating system formerly known as NetWare. IntranetWare is essentially NetWare 4.01 plus a bunch of added programs designed to make NetWare the ideal server for Internet and Intranet applications.

I/O port address Every I/O device in a computer — including network interface cards — must be assigned a unique address. In the old days, you had to configure the port address using DIP switches or jumpers. Newer network cards automatically configure their own port addresses so that you don't have to mess with switches or jumper blocks.

IPX The transport protocol used by NetWare.

IPX.COM The program file that implements IPX.

IRQ *Interrupt ReQuest*. Network interface cards must be configured for the proper IRQ in order to work. In olden times, you had to use DIP switches or jumper blocks to set the IRQ. Nowadays, network cards configure themselves.

ISA bus The most popular type of expansion bus for accommodating adapter cards. *ISA* stands for *Industry Standard Architecture*. See **EISA bus**, **Micro Channel bus**, and **PCI bus**.

ISO *International Standards Organization,* whom we can thank for OSI.

ISP See **Internet Service Provider**.

JetDirect A device made by Hewlett-Packard which enables printers to connect directly to the network without the need for a separate print server computer.

jumper block A device used to configure an old-fashioned adapter card. To change the setting of a jumper block, you remove the jumper from one set of pins and replace it on another.

K Kilobytes, roughly one thousand bytes (1,024 to be precise). See **GB**, **MB**, and **TB**.

LAN *Local-area network;* what this book is all about.

LAN Manager An obsolete network operating system that Microsoft used to sell. Microsoft long ago put all its networking eggs in the Windows NT basket, so LAN Manager exists only on isolated islands along with soldiers who are still fighting World War II.

LAN Server IBM's version of LAN Manager.

LANcache The disk caching program that comes with LANtastic.

LANtastic A peer-to-peer network operating system that was once the most popular choice for small networks, before the built-in Windows for Workgroups and Windows 95 came along.

laser printer A high-quality printer that uses lasers and photon torpedoes to produce beautiful output.

LASTDRIVE A line in CONFIG.SYS that tells DOS how many drive letters to set aside for itself. NetWare uses this setting to determine which drive letter to map to the server's login directory.

lemon-pudding layer A layer near the middle of the OSI reference model that provides flavor and moisture to an otherwise dry and tasteless fruitcake.

LLC sublayer The *logical link sublayer* of layer 2 of the OSI model. The LLC is addressed by the IEEE 802.2 standard.

local bus A fast expansion bus found on 486 and Pentium computers that operates at a higher speed than the old ISA bus and allows 32-bit data transfers. Two types are commonly found: VESA and PCI. Many 486 computers include several VESA local bus slots, but newer Pentium computers use PCI slots. For best network performance, all servers should have VESA or PCI disk I/O and network interface cards.

local resources Disk drives, printers, and other devices that are attached directly to a workstation rather than accessed via the network.

local-area network See *LAN*.

LocalTalk Apple's scheme for cabling Macintosh networks by using the Mac's printer ports. PhoneNET is a cabling scheme that's compatible with LocalTalk but less expensive.

login The process of identifying oneself to the network (or a specific network server) and gaining access to network resources.

LOGIN The NetWare command used to log in to a NetWare network.

LOGIN directory In NetWare, a network directory that's mapped to the workstation before the user has logged in. The LOGIN directory contains commands and programs that are accessible to every computer on the network, whether or not a user has logged in. Chief among these commands is the LOGIN command.

login name In a Windows network, the name that identifies a user uniquely to the network. Same as *username* or *user ID*.

login script A file of NetWare commands that is executed when a user logs in.

logon Same as *login*.

logout The process of leaving the network. When you log out, any network drives or printers you were connected to become unavailable to you.

LOGOUT In NetWare, the command you use to log out.

LPT1 The first printer port on a PC. If a computer has a local printer, it will more than likely be attached to this port. That's why it's a good idea to set up printer redirections using LPT2 and LPT3.

Mac OS 8 The latest and greatest operating system for Macintoshes.

MAC sublayer The *media access control* sublayer of layer 2 of the OSI model. The MAC is addressed by the IEEE 802.3 standard.

Macintosh A cute little computer that draws great pictures and comes with built-in networking.

mail server The server computer on which e-mail messages are stored. This same computer also may be used as a file and print server, or it may be dedicated as a mail server.

mainframe A huge computer housed in a glass house on raised floors and cooled with liquid nitrogen. The cable that connects the disk drives to the CPU weighs more than most PCs.

mapping Assigning unused drive letters to network drives or unused printer ports to network printers. See *redirection*.

MB Megabytes, roughly one million bytes (1,024K to be precise). See *GB*, *K*, and *TB*.

MEM The DOS command that displays information about memory.

MEMMAKER The DOS 6.0 and 6.2 command that optimizes your memory use. Pray you don't have to use this command.

memory The electronic storage where your computer stores data that's being manipulated and programs that are running. See *RAM*.

menu program A program that makes a network user's life easier by hiding the DOS prompt behind a list of choices the user can choose by pressing a number or letter. Before Windows took over, menu programs were popular to soften the hard edge of the DOS user interface. You'll still find menu programs on network computers that don't run Windows.

metaphor A literary construction suitable for Shakespeare and Steinbeck but a bit overused by computer writers.

Micro Channel bus The bus standard used in certain IBM PS/2 computers. The Microsoft Channel bus was a good idea that never caught on.

modem A device that converts signals the computer understands into signals that can be accurately transmitted over the phone to another modem, which converts the signals back into their original form. Computers use modems to talk to each other. *Modem* is a combination of modulator-demodulator.

monochrome Monitors that display only one color, usually green or amber against a dark background. Monochrome monitors are often used on NetWare server computers, where flashy color displays would be wasted on an empty closet.

mouse The obligatory way to use Windows. When you grab it and move it around, the cursor moves on the screen. After you get the hand-eye coordination down, using it is a snap. *Hint:* Don't pick it up and talk into it like Scotty did in *Star Trek 4*. Very embarrassing, especially if you've traveled millions of miles to get here.

Mr. McFeeley The nerdy-looking mailman on *Mr. Rogers' Neighborhood*. He'd make a great computer geek. Speedy delivery!

MSAV The DOS 6.0 and 6.2 command that scans your computer for virus infection. Okay for local computer use, but a more powerful program is best for the network. And it doesn't do Windows.

MSBACKUP The DOS 6.0 and 6.2 command for backing up data to floppy disks. Because it doesn't support tape drives, it's not suitable for network backups. It doesn't work in Windows, but Windows 95 comes with a built-in backup program.

MSD *Microsoft Diagnostics,* a program that comes with DOS 6.0 and 6.2 and Windows 3.1. MSD gathers and displays useful information about your computer's configuration. In Windows 95, you can get similar information from a program called Microsoft System Information, which comes free with Microsoft Office 97.

MSN *The Microsoft Network,* an online service similar to CompuServe or America Online.

NE2000 The standard by which network interface cards are judged. If your card is NE2000 compatible, you can use it with just about any network.

NET The catch-all network command center for Windows computers, for users who prefer working at the command prompt. You can use NET commands with Windows for Workgroups, Windows 95, or Windows NT.

NETBIOS *Network basic input output system,* a high-level networking standard developed by IBM and used by most peer-to-peer networks. It can be used with NetWare as well.

Netscape The company that makes Navigator, the most popular program for browsing the World Wide Web.

NetWare The chief priest of network operating systems, the proud child of Novell, Inc.

NetWare 2.2 NetWare's "Good" version, designed for 80286-based processors and still widely used on smaller networks.

NetWare 3.12 NetWare's "Better" version, designed with 80386 processors in mind. The best choice for most new networks.

NetWare 4.11 NetWare's "Almost the Best" version, filled with all sorts of bells and whistles for larger networks, but a bit much for the novice

to take on. The latest and very best version is called IntranetWare.

NetWare Directory Services The cool new feature of NetWare 4.0 whereby the resources of the servers are pooled together to form a single entity.

NetWare Loadable Module A program that's loaded at the file server. A.k.a. *NLM.* NLMs extend the functionality of NetWare by providing additional services. Btrieve runs as an NLM, as do various backup, antivirus, and other utilities.

network What this book is about. For more information, see Chapters 1 through 31.

network drive A drive that resides somewhere out in the network rather than on your own computer.

network interface card An adapter card that lets the computer attach to a network cable. A.k.a. *NIC.*

network layer One of the layers somewhere near the middle of the OSI reference model. It addresses the interconnection of networks.

network manager Hope that it's someone other than you.

Network Operating System An operating system for networks, such as NetWare or Windows NT Server. A.k.a. *NOS.*

network resource A disk drive, printer, or other device that's located in a server computer and shared with other users, in contrast with a *local resource,* which is located in a user's computer.

Newsgroup Internet discussion groups similar to discussion forums in an online service.

NIC See *network interface card*.

NLM See *NetWare Loadable Module*.

node A device on the network, typically a computer or printer. A router is also a node.

Norton Utilities A big box chock-full of useful utilities, all for one affordable price. Get it.

NOS See *Network Operating System*.

Novell The folks you can thank or blame for NetWare, depending on your mood.

off-line Not available on the network.

on-line Available on the network.

operator A user who has control over operational aspects of the network, but doesn't necessarily have the power to grant or revoke access rights, create user accounts, and so on.

OSI The agency Lee Majors worked for in *The Six Million Dollar Man*. Also, the *Open System Interconnection* reference model, a seven-layer fruitcake framework upon which networking standards are hung.

packets Data is sent over the network in manageable chunks called *packets,* or *frames.* The size and makeup of a packet is determined by the protocol being used.

parallel port A port normally used to connect printers to DOS-based computers, sometimes called a *printer port.* Parallel ports send data over eight "parallel" wires, one byte at a time. See *serial port*.

partition A division of a single disk drive into several smaller units that are treated by the operating system as if they were separate drives.

password The only thing protecting your files from an impostor masquerading as you. Keep your password secret and you'll have a long and happy life.

patch cable A short cable used to connect a computer to a wall outlet, or one running from a patch panel to a hub.

PCI *Peripheral Component Interconnect,* the high-speed bus design found in modern Pentium computers.

PCONSOLE The NetWare command you use from a DOS command prompt to manage network printing.

peer-to-peer network A network in which any computer can be a server if it wants to be. Kind of like the network version of the Great American Dream. Peer-to-peer networks can be easily constructed using Windows 95.

PhoneNET An alternative cabling scheme for Macintosh networks, cheaper than Apple's LocalTalk cables.

physical layer The lowest layer of the OSI reference model (whatever that is). It refers to the parts of the network you can touch: cables, connectors, and so on.

pocket protector A status symbol among computer geeks.

port A connector on the back of your computer that you can use to connect a device such as a printer, modem, mouse, and so on.

PPP The most common way of connecting to the Internet for World Wide Web access. PPP stands for *Point to Point Protocol.*

presentation layer The sixth layer of the OSI reference model, which handles data conversions, compression, decompression, and other menial tasks.

print job A report, letter, memo, or other document that has been sent to a network printer but hasn't printed yet. Print jobs wait patiently in the queue until a printer agrees to print them.

Print Manager In old-style Windows (Windows 3.1 and Windows for Workgroups), the program that handles print spooling.

print queue The line that print jobs wait in until a printer becomes available.

print server A computer that handles network printing or a device such as a JetDirect which enables the printer to attach directly to the network.

PRN The DOS code name for the first parallel port. A.k.a. LPT1.

protocol The rules of the network game. Protocols define standardized formats for data packets, techniques for detecting and correcting errors, and so on.

punch-down block A gadget for quickly connecting a bunch of wires, used in telephone and network wiring closets.

QIC *Quarter-inch cartridge,* the most popular and least-expensive form of tape backup. See **DAT**.

queue A list of items waiting to be processed. The term usually refers to the list of print jobs waiting to be printed, but networks have lots of other types of queues as well.

RAID *Redundant Array of Inexpensive Disks,* a bunch of disk drives strung together and treated as if they were one drive. The data is spread out over several drives, and one of the drives keeps checking information so that if any one of the drives fails, the data can be reconstructed.

RAM *Random access memory,* your computer's memory chips.

redirection One of the basic concepts of networking, in which a device such as a disk drive or printer appears to be a local device but actually resides on the network. The networking software on your computer intercepts I/O requests for the device and redirects them to the network.

repeater A device that strengthens a signal so that it can travel on. Repeaters are used to lengthen the cable distance between two nodes. A *multiport repeater* is the same as a *hub*.

resource A disk drive, disk directory, printer, modem, CD-ROM, or other device that can be shared on the network.

ring A type of network topology in which computers are connected to one another in a way that forms a complete circle. Imagine the Waltons standing around the Thanksgiving table holding hands and you have the idea of a ring topology.

RJ-45 The kind of plug used by 10baseT networks. It looks kind of like a modular phone plug, but it's bigger.

router A device that works kind of like a bridge but can handle different protocols. For example, a router can link Ethernet to LocalTalk or a mainframe.

ScanDisk A DOS 6.2 and Windows 95 command that examines your hard disk for physical defects.

scheduling software Software that schedules meetings of network users. Works only if all network users keep their calendars up-to-date.

SCSI *Small computer systems interface,* a connection used mostly for disk drives but also suitable for CD-ROM, tape drives, and just about anything else. Also winner of the Acronym Computer Geeks Love to Pronounce Most award.

segment A single-run cable, which may connect more than two computers, with a terminator on each end.

serial port A port normally used to connect a modem or mouse to a DOS-based computer, sometimes called a communications port. See *parallel port*.

server A computer that's on the network and shares resources with other network users. The server may be dedicated, which means that its sole purpose in life is to provide service for network users, or it may be used as a client as well. See *client*.

session layer A layer somewhere near the middle of the beloved OSI reference model that deals with sessions between network nodes.

SFT *System Fault Tolerance,* a set of networking features designed to protect the network from faults, such as stepping on the line (known as a "foot fault").

shared resource A resource such as a disk or printer that is made available to other network users.

shielded twisted pair Twisted-pair cable with shielding, used mostly for Token Ring networks. A.k.a. STP. See *twisted pair*.

smiley A face made from various keyboard characters; often used in e-mail messages to convey emotion :)

SNA *Systems Network Architecture,* a networking standard developed by IBM that dates from the mid-Mainframerasic, approximately 65 million years ago. Used by fine IBM mainframe and AS/400 minicomputers everywhere.

sneakernet The cheapest form of network, in which users exchange files by copying them to a disk and walking them between computers.

SNMP *Simple Network Management Protocol,* a standard for exchanging network management information between network devices that is anything but simple.

ST-506 An old type of disk drive interface that's obsolete but still found on far too many computers.

star A type of network topology in which each node is connected to a central wiring hub. This gives the network a star-like appearance.

SUPERVISOR The top-dog account in NetWare. Log in as SUPERVISOR and you can do just about anything.

switch A super-efficient bridge which is able to create connections between any number of ports.

SYS The volume name of the system volume on most NetWare servers.

system fault tolerance See *SFT.*

tape drive The best way to back up a network server. Tape drives have become so inexpensive that even small networks should have one.

task For a technically accurate description, enroll in a computer science graduate course. For a layperson's understanding of what a task is, picture the guy who used to spin plates on the *Ed Sullivan Show.* Each plate is a task. The poor guy had to frantically move from plate to plate to keep them all spinning. Computers work the same way. Each program task is like one of those spinning plates; the computer must service each one periodically to keep it going.

TB *Terrazzo bytes,* imported from Italy. Approximately one trillion bytes (1,024 GB to be precise). (Just kidding about *terrazzo bytes.* Actually, TB stands for terabytes.)

TCP/IP *Transmission Control Protocol/Internet Protocol,* the protocol used by Internet.

terminator The little plug you have to use at each end of a segment of thin coax cable (10baseT).

thinnet See *10base2.*

three-letter acronym See *TLA.*

time sharing A technique used on mainframe computers to enable several users to access the computer at the same time.

time-out How long the print server will wait while receiving print output before deciding that the print job has finished.

TLA A three-letter acronym, such as FAT (File Allocation Table), DUM (Dirty Upper Memory), and HPY (Heuristic Private Yodel).

token The thing that gets passed around the network in a Token Ring topology. See ***Token Ring***.

Token Ring A network that's cabled in a ring topology in which a special packet called a token is passed from computer to computer. A computer must wait until it receives the token before sending data over the network.

topology The shape of the network; how its computers and cables are arranged. See ***bus, star,*** and ***ring***.

transceiver A doohicky that connects a Network Interface Card (NIC) to a network cable. A transceiver is always required to connect a computer to the network, but 10base2 and 10baseT NICs have built-in transceivers. Transceivers were originally used with yellow cable. You can also get transceivers that convert an AUI port to 10baseT.

transport layer One of those layers somewhere near the middle of the OSI reference model that addresses the way data is escorted around the network.

Travan A newer technology for inexpensive tape backup able to record up to 800MB on a single tape cartridge. See ***QIC*** and ***DAT***.

trojan horse A program that looks interesting but turns out to be something nasty, like a hard-disk reformatter.

twisted pair A type of cable that consists of one or more pairs of wires that are twisted in a certain way to improve the cable's electrical characteristics. See ***unshielded twisted pair*** and ***shielded twisted pair***.

uninterruptible power supply See ***UPS***.

unshielded twisted pair Twisted-pair cable that doesn't have a heavy metal shield around it. Used for 10baseT networks. A.k.a. UTP. See ***twisted pair***.

upper memory The portion of memory jammed in between 640K and 1MB. It's set apart for use by device adapters like disk controllers and video cards. Because much of it is unused in most computers, DOS 5 and 6 can reclaim it for other uses. With Windows 95 or Windows NT, you don't have to worry about upper memory.

UPS *Uninterruptible power supply,* a gizmo that switches to battery power whenever the power cuts out. The Enterprise didn't have one of these, which is why the lights always went out until Spock could switch to auxiliary power.

URL *Uniform Resource Locator,* a fancy term for an Internet address. URLs are those familiar "dot" addresses, such as "www-dot-microsoft-dot-com" or "www-dot-idgbooks-dot-com."

user ID The name by which you're known to the network.

users' group A local association of computer users, sometimes with a particular interest, such as networking.

UTP *Unshielded twisted pair.* See *10baseT*.

Value Added Processes See *VAP*.

vampire tap A whirlygig that enables you to tap into a 10base5 cable to attach a transceiver.

VAP Value added processes, Programs that run at the server computer with NetWare 2.2. VAPs were replaced by NLMs in NetWare 3.

VGA *Video Graphics Array,* the current standard in video monitors. Most VGA adapters these days are actually super VGA adapters, which are compatible with VGA adapters, but have extra bells and whistles.

Vines A network operating system made by Banyan, comparable to *NetWare* or *Windows NT Server*.

virus An evil computer program that slips into your computer undetected, tries to spread itself to other computers, and may eventually do something bad like trash your hard disk.

volume name In NetWare, each disk volume has a name. Most NetWare servers have a volume named SYS.

Web browser A program that enables you to display information retrieved from the Internet's World Wide Web.

Windows An "operating environment" that makes DOS computers easier to use, courtesy of Microsoft.

Windows for Workgroups The peer-to-peer version of Windows.

Windows 95 A version of Windows which became available in — you guessed it — 1995. Windows 95 was the first version of Windows that did not require DOS.

Windows NT Client Microsoft's advanced version of Windows, designed to operate as a network client.

Windows NT Server Microsoft's premier server operating system ideal for running dedicated servers in small or large networks.

wiring closet Large networks need a place where cables can congregate. A closet is ideal.

workstation See *client*.

World Wide Web A graphical method of accessing information on the Internet.

WWW See *World Wide Web*.

yellow cable See *10base5*.

Index

(continued)

YOUR ONLINE RESOURCE

WWW.DUMMIES.COM

Discover Dummies Online!

The Dummies Web Site is your fun and friendly online resource for the latest information about ...*For Dummies*® books and your favorite topics. The Web site is the place to communicate with us, exchange ideas with other ...*For Dummies* readers, chat with authors, and have fun!

Ten Fun and Useful Things You Can Do at www.dummies.com

1. Win free ...*For Dummies* books and more!
2. Register your book and be entered in a prize drawing.
3. Meet your favorite authors through the IDG Books Author Chat Series.
4. Exchange helpful information with other ...*For Dummies* readers.
5. Discover other great ...*For Dummies* books you must have!
6. Purchase Dummieswear™ exclusively from our Web site.
7. Buy ...*For Dummies* books online.
8. Talk to us. Make comments, ask questions, get answers!
9. Download free software.
10. Find additional useful resources from authors.

Link directly to these ten fun and useful things at
http://www.dummies.com/10useful

WWW.DUMMIES.COM

For other technology titles from IDG Books Worldwide, go to
www.idgbooks.com

Not on the Web yet? It's easy to get started with *Dummies 101*®: *The Internet For Windows*® *98* or *The Internet For Dummies*,® 5th Edition, at local retailers everywhere.

IDG BOOKS WORLDWIDE

Find other ...*For Dummies* books on these topics:
Business • Career • Databases • Food & Beverage • Games • Gardening • Graphics • Hardware
Health & Fitness • Internet and the World Wide Web • Networking • Office Suites
Operating Systems • Personal Finance • Pets • Programming • Recreation • Sports
Spreadsheets • Teacher Resources • Test Prep • Word Processing

IDG BOOKS WORLDWIDE
BOOK REGISTRATION

Register This Book and Win!

We want to hear from you!

Visit **http://my2cents.dummies.com** to register this book and tell us how you liked it!

✔ Get entered in our monthly prize giveaway.

✔ Give us feedback about this book — tell us what you like best, what you like least, or maybe what you'd like to ask the author and us to change!

✔ Let us know any other *...For Dummies*® topics that interest you.

Your feedback helps us determine what books to publish, tells us what coverage to add as we revise our books, and lets us know whether we're meeting your needs as a *...For Dummies* reader. You're our most valuable resource, and what you have to say is important to us!

Not on the Web yet? It's easy to get started with *Dummies 101*®: *The Internet For Windows*® *98* or *The Internet For Dummies*,® 5th Edition, at local retailers everywhere.

Or let us know what you think by sending us a letter at the following address:

...For Dummies Book Registration
Dummies Press
7260 Shadeland Station, Suite 100
Indianapolis, IN 46256-3945
Fax 317-596-5498

BESTSELLING BOOK SERIES FROM IDG